The
Anglican Shakespeare

The
Anglican Shakespeare

ELIZABETHAN
ORTHODOXY IN THE
GREAT HISTORIES

by

Daniel L. Wright
Associate Professor of English
Concordia College, Portland

VANCOUVER: PACIFIC-COLUMBIA BOOKS

Pacific-Columbia Books
Broadway Station
1701 Broadway, Suite 310
Vancouver, WA 98663

The paper in this book meets the guidelines for performance and durability of the Committee on Production Guidelines for Book Longevity of the Council on Library Resources.

Library of Congress Cataloging-in-Publication Data

Wright, Daniel L. (Daniel Lee), 1954-
    The Anglican Shakespeare : Elizabethan orthodoxy in the great histories / by Daniel L. Wright.
        p.   cm.
    Includes bibliographical references.
    ISBN 1-880365-94-4 (alk. paper)
    1. Shakespeare, William, 1564-1616--Histories. 2. Literature and history--Great Britain--History--16th century. 3. England--Church history--16th century--Historiography. 4. Anglican Communion--England--History--16th century. 5. Historical drama, English--History and criticism. 6. Great Britain--History--1066-1687--Historiography. 7. Christian drama, English--History and criticism. 8. Shakespeare. William, 1564-1616--Religion,
I. Title.
PR2982.W75   1993   94-667
822.3'3--dc20   CIP

Printed in the United States of America
at the Professional Press, Chapel Hill, North Carolina

To Michael

Contents

Note on orthography: This book retains the spelling of texts cited, but printed forms of the language that are not characteristic of modern English have been altered.

Acknowledgments

It is never possible adequately to thank all the persons who, in large and small ways, make possible the accomplishment of any of our efforts, but I trust that those who have contributed to my work, particularly to this project— however indirect the ways or limited those contributions may seem—know of my deep appreciation to them for their assistance. I can only insufficiently acknowledge these individuals by assuring them that they and all they have done for me mean more than perhaps they know. Therefore, to the unnamed many—you know who you are—profound thanks for all that you have been, are and will continue to be. The completion of this work would not have been possible without you.

Particularly, however, I am appreciative of the enthusiastic support of my work that has been provided by the administration and faculty of Concordia College. No professor in America has better colleagues among whom to live and work than I.

Few individuals can hope to enjoy the careful and generous attention of such a consummate scholar, teacher, friend, and guide as I have had in Dr. Frances Rippy, specialist in the works of Matthew Prior and Christopher Fry, Professor of English, and former Director of Graduate Studies in English at Ball State University; for her contribution of the Foreword to this book I am especially appreciative.

Dr. Tetsumaro Hayashi, Director of the International Steinbeck Institute, deserves thanks for the provision of his wisdom, insight and support of my research—not only in this endeavor but in my studies of Meiji and Showa Era Japanese literature as well. For his informed Shakespearean commentary and introduction to me of the genius of Natsume Soseki and Yukio Mishima I shall ever be indebted.

I am grateful to my fraternity brother, Brian Preuss, of Rochester, New York for his provision of the cover design for this book.

Finally, the author and his publisher extend their thanks to the people at Dover Press for their kind permission to use their reproductions of the Albrecht Dürer woodcuts.

M_{en} make their own history, but they do not make it just as they please; they do not make it under circumstances chosen by themselves, but under circumstances directly found, given and transmitted by the past. The tradition of all the dead generations weighs like a nightmare on the brain of the living. And just when they seem engaged in revolutionizing themselves and things, in creating something entirely new, precisely in such epochs of revolutionary crisis they anxiously conjure up the spirit of the past.

Karl Marx
from *The Eighteenth Brumaire of Louis Bonaparte*

Foreword

When Dr. Johnson was praising a sixteen-line section from Gray's *Elegy*, he wrote of it that the lines were to him original: "I have never seen the notions in any other place; yet he that reads them here, persuades himself that he has always felt them."

Daniel Wright's *The Anglican Shakespeare* possesses a like quality. It raises a number of points that have never been made in quite this fashion about Shakespeare's English history plays and interprets them in ways in which they have never before been read, yet the reader familiar with Shakespeare's histories who finishes Wright's study will close it convinced that all its truths are so self-evident that he, too, feels like he always has known them. This is perhaps the mark of the soundest and greatest literary criticism: it is not so much dazzling as it is inevitable. All its chief points seem mere common sense. Who would have thought otherwise? It is with some surprise that we find that no one has previously raised these same apparently unavoidable claims—at least not in quite this manner or context.

Dr. Wright points out the comparative neglect that the history plays have suffered. Neither comedy nor tragedy, they often found themselves ignored when some of Shakespeare's lesser efforts in the two more traditional genres were receiving close attention.

Wright further observes the Elizabethan attitude toward fact in these history plays. Shakespeare and his fellow Elizabethans, he argues, did not write history books or history plays merely or even principally to recapture the events of previous eras. Rather, they saw history as "progressive revelatory sign, a vision enabled by mythography derived from the emblems and rhetoric of the sixteenth-century Anglican Christian tradition." Looking back at monarchs and happenings in the British past, Shakespeare and his fellows saw these as types prefiguring the Elizabethan present and predicting its future, therein revealing the unique destiny of the British nation.

Daniel Wright sees in Shakespeare's history plays "a distinctively Anglican character and conviction. "If Shakespeare was serving as Tudor political propagandist in these plays, he was equally serving as "an apologist for the Protestant Reformation in England," defending not only the realm but the Crown and the Anglican Church as well. Behind these plays, Wright admits, is the full weight of the Middle Ages, so much so that, as he shows, a whole school of critics has maintained that Shakespeare must have been himself a Roman Catholic. But even stronger than the medieval impact upon the plays, Wright contends, was the force of the Renaissance in art and the Reformation in theology. It is the Reformation, Wright asserts, that shaped both Shakespeare's rhetoric and his iconography in his history plays. Like other Tudors, Shakespeare was manipulating medieval myth to accommodate scientific fact—in a fashion taught him by the Reformation. He wrote his histories to instruct his audience and give them illustrations, thus further defining and refining the ancient and medieval mythology surrounding the monarch.

It is this Anglican refining of the myth that Wright finds everywhere in Shakespeare's history plays, taking things a step further than their initial position, making of aesthetic and intellectual devices something more involved and subtle and modern and ancient than they first appear to be, so that Shakespeare gives us not only symbols but emblems, not only history but historiography, not only cosmology but cosmogony as well.

The emblems and historiography and cosmogony have become particularly intricate, Wright argues, because the Renaissance and the Reformation have wrought strange sea-changes upon the medieval sense of order that Shakespeare still in some sense retains. If free will has become more important, then how do we re-judge the behavior of men in power? If the king is now not only head of state but head of church as well, then is his power and authority in the Renaissance not even greater than his purportedly absolute power in the Middle Ages? And if the transcendent purpose of the English nation is to become the New Israel, who is to gainsay her in her pursuit of her role in history? Is there not a "providential destiny of a nation whose very birth and sustenance in adversity form a sign of its election to grace and divine favor"?

The usefulness of Dr. Wright's interpretation of Shakespeare as Anglican is nowhere more apparent than in his detailed explications of those two disturbing figures who open and close the Lancastrian tetralogy: Richard II and Henry V. Audiences have reacted ambivalently to both figures, for opposite reasons. If Shakespeare really favors an absolute monarchy, as he seems to, why does he paint a portrait of Richard II that suggests that he contributes to his own uncrowning and death? And why does young Prince Hal, questionable in both claim to the throne and early behavior, become the apotheosized Henry V? Daniel Wright's Anglican thesis answers both troubling questions. Richard II should not be destroyed or dethroned by any outsider, because absolute power is rightfully his—but he delegitimizes himself by embodying the corrosive vices of late medieval Roman Catholicism: corruption, immorality, luxury, autocracy, indifference. Conversely, Henry V, like the Anglican Church, can soar above questionable origins in becoming an icon of virtues emblematic of a purified English Christianity.

Daniel Wright's *The Anglican Shakespeare* should prove an important and helpful aid to a better reading of Shakespeare's history plays, that most neglected category of Shakespearean drama. It has the inevitability and the persuasiveness of any valuable critical discovery; it is a book difficult to dispute. Its impressive philosophical framework tests out well in the only crucible in which literary theory may be tried—it explains convincingly some of the most puzzling cruxes in Shakespeare's English history plays, most strikingly Shakespeare's shifting ambivalence—and ours— toward two of his most enigmatic historical re-creations: Richard II and Henry V.

Frances Mayhew Rippy
Ball State University
August 1993

Preface

In recent years, critics and scholars have proposed many inconclusive arguments in the attempt to establish Shakespeare's religious (or non-religious) convictions. Much of this argumentation has been speculative and governed by presumption more informed by intuition than reasoned scholarship. Indeed, as Roland Frye has remarked, many conventional Christian critics of Shakespeare have offered too many "theological assertion[s] without theological evidence" (*Shakespeare and Christian Doctrine* 20). Especially when one considers such theses as those promoted by works such as Thomas Carter's *Shakespeare: Puritan and Recusant* (AMS, 1970) and Mutschmann and Wentersdorf's *Shakespeare and Catholicism* (Sheed and Ward, 1952), one is compelled to concede Frye's point. Improbable as it may be definitively to identify Shakespeare's religious faith, we can, however, with some measure of certainty, discern his public theology.

The rhetoric and iconography of the Shakespearean histories—especially that within the Lancaster cycle of plays (the sometimes so-called Great Histories, distinct from the Yorkist cycle of plays [the so-called Lesser Histories])—significantly contribute to our recognition that the theological center of Shakespeare's historical drama is distinctively Anglican. Shakespeare (whether he personally was an Anglican Churchman) invokes in the Lancaster plays the symbols and speech definitive of the Protestant Reformation in order to illustrate dramatically the Crown's convictions of the transcendent purpose of the English nation in history, especially as that purpose had been defined by Tudor historiography. Shakespeare's histories demonstrate a conviction therefore, broadly conceived and illustrated, of faith in the providential destiny of a nation whose very birth and sustenance in adversity form a sign of its election to grace and divine favor.

Furthermore, Shakespeare's Lancaster plays, by continuing the didactic tradition of the medieval stage, embrace the precepts of Tudor monarchy and apply those principles of government and Reformation theology to the Elizabethan stage. Shakespeare's histories therein interpret history; they do not recollect if—except in the spirit of sixteenth-century imagination, harmonized with legend and myth. Consequently, the Lancaster cycle of histories constitutes a unified dramatic quartet in which history as fact is eschewed in favor of history as progressive revelatory sign, a vision enabled by mythography derived from the emblems and rhetoric of the sixteenth-century Anglican tradition.

Introduction

Apologia Pro Propositio Sua

This study of Shakespeare's Lancaster cycle continues several recent generations of Shakespearean criticism,[1] although this particular study suggests that the integration of a Christian hermeneutic and sensibility into the larger critical tradition provides for fuller comprehension of the purposes of Shakespearean drama. Admittedly, such an approach has had its detractors and still has them, especially among the practitioners of New Criticism and their more contemporary methodological heirs such as the structuralists.[2] Adherents of the structuralist school of literary research, such as F. R. Leavis, contend that Christian criticism threatens the purity of scientific inquiry: "There can be no substitute for the scrupulous and disinterested approach of the literary critic. If Christian belief and Christian attitudes have . . . affected the critic's sensibility, then they will play their due part in his perceptions and judgements" ("The Logic" 254).

It is the contention of this study, however, that every critic, Christian or not, is governed by a "sensibility" and no critical approach can be completely disinterested. In any case, the Christian critic, contrary to Leavis's contention, imposes no particular view (Cary 94); he is merely receptive to those features of Christian faith and practice which may be embedded by the author in the work which the critic studies. As G. Wilson Knight observes, the modern critical reliance upon an application of a purportedly scientific method to literary study reveals our contemporary scholarly captivity to "a pseudo-intellectualism which, by claiming a final authority and logical clarity that it in no sense possesses . . . points to one instance, or symptom, of a dangerous disease in the modern mind [wherein] we mask under the veneer of realism, intellectualism and objectivity an unfettered subjectivity leading to intellectual chaos" ("On the Principles of Shakespearean Interpretation" 4-5). Leslie Fiedler also confirms that "[t]here is no 'work itself,' no independent formal unity which is its own sole context; the poem is the sum total of many contexts, all of which must be known to know it and evaluate it" (267); and Jackson Benson agrees: "It is our sense of a writer, a person, behind the text that gives the text its meaning. Even when the identity of the writer is unknown, we respond with the expectation that we can reach out to find some basis of commonality" (109). Every critic therefore creates Shakespeare in his own image (Ralli 4). Who, therefore, can authoritatively argue that the insights derived from a self-conscious Christian sensibility provide us with interpretations which are any less definitive or revelatory than those derived from the supposedly objective and decontextualized mechanics of structuralist inquiry?

The argument for a disinterested approach and objective method is itself, ironically, no disinterested or objective argument. Despite T. S. Eliot's contention to the contrary, no artist, in fact, can produce a work that is "objective" and uninformed by his own personal vision.[3] As Oscar Wilde observes in "The Decay of Lying," "No great artist ever sees things as they really are. If he did, he would cease to be an artist" (65). And as Wilde continues, no critic can produce a purely impersonal work of criticism either, for criticism, as he describes it, is finally "the record of one's own soul" ("*The Critic*" 132).

In fact, even if the impossible objectivity of the New Criticism and its derivative methodologies were possible, the critic who purposely affected Leavis's "disinterested approach" would inexcusably dismiss, ignore, or misapprehend those very signs, rhetorical and symbolic, which the artist may have deliberately (or even accidentally) selected to impart his convictions or generate a desired response. As a consequence, such a dispassionate critic, by utilizing a methodology predicated on the assumptions of New Critical science, could not claim to be thoroughly familiar with or even fully comprehend all the dimensions of the work under study. Therefore, current practitioners of contemporary structuralist and related criticism, in a zeal for an impartiality unknown even in the physical sciences, have coopted a myth—the myth of science—and theologized its rationalistic principles by transforming simple functions—the mechanics of science—into an infallible methodical technology by which Truth (though by definition, only "scientific" Truth) might be discovered.

Indeed, Robert Scholes apocalyptically writes that "structuralism is . . . a methodology which is seeking nothing less than the unification of all the sciences into a new system of belief" [2]). Robert Selden acknowledges, too, that "[a]t the heart of structuralism is a *scientific* ambition" (69). Martin Lings notes, however, that by Truth, the Elizabethan audience did not mean modern scientific truth:

> [F]or modern man the supreme distinction is between "fiction and truth," [or] as we say, between art on the one hand and "reality" on the other. [But for the Shakespearean audiences, the distinction] was not so sharp. They were not in the habit of speaking and thinking of life as "truth." By truth, by reality, they meant something different; for them the supreme distinction was not between life and art, but between the next world, that is, Truth, and this world which is the shadow of Truth. (Lings 126)

Christian scholarship, therefore, acknowledges the need to subject any literary work to the tests first established by Dante, who, in *Il Convivio* [*The Banquet* (1308)], became but the first among many Christian scholars and critics to assert that all literature is subject to literal, allegorical, moral, and anagogical interpretation (42-44). Christian scholars in our own age such as Martha Fleischer (*The Iconography of the English History Play*, 1974) have extended this interpretive effort to include study of the influence of Christian myth, ritual, and sacred tradition in the work of the literary artist and have striven to define and analyze the scope of that influence, chiefly by their examinations of the rhetorical and iconographic character of the work in question. J. Dover Wilson also emphasizes our need to affirm extratextual considerations in our criticism of Shakespeare, for he argues persuasively that responsible critics must recognize that Shakespeare lived in a world defined by Plato and explained by Saint Augustine, whereas we, at least since the French Revolution, have lived in a world largely shaped by Rousseau and his philosophical kindred; to ignore or overlook such important features, writes Wilson, "lays many traps of misunderstanding for unsuspecting readers [of Shakespeare]" (*Shakespearian Dimensions* 7).

It is equally important for the thoroughgoing critic of Shakespeare who acknowledges the mandates of critical inquiry and who sufficiently apprehends the distinctions between our age and Shakespeare's to recognize the limitations imposed by positivistic methods upon modern criticism's scholarly task.

Modern New Critical methods such as structuralism challenge the breadth of traditional literary inquiry by deifying the rational hermeneutic and by discrediting those approaches which endeavor to understand and impart to an untutored audience the medieval/Renaissance perspective of humanity and events that inform Shakespearean drama. A more intuitive perspective affirms man's need to look beyond and rely upon more than his own ahistorical reason. Such important cautions against intellectual (or perhaps more correctly, rationalist) presumption have been articulated not only through the Shakespearean theatre itself (e.g., recall Lear's admonition to Regan and Goneril that they, in questioning his desire for companionship in his dotage, should "reason not the need" [II.iv.264])[4] but have been advanced by such distinguished representatives of the medieval/Renaissance synthesis as Luther, Milton, Erasmus, and Saint Bernard.

The fundamental divergence between contemporary rationalist criticism and Christian criticism of Shakespeare resides principally in the insistence by the modern New Critic that we must read Shakespeare autotelically (as though to read Shakespeare with an attentive eye upon the larger cultural context within which he worked would somehow threaten our ability to appreciate him or disable our capacity to understand him) and the Christian critic's assertion that the attempt to achieve an objective posture in criticism is to invent a posture in itself and impose rationalistic assumptions upon a text which came into being within a decidedly historical context that was informed by many presumptions, theological and otherwise.[5] As Eugene Tucker instructs us, "Texts from the past must be interpreted in terms of their historical meaning—what they said in and to their own times—[as] at least one step essential to their understanding" (Tucker vi).

In the face of such methodological claims and aspirations as those characteristic of the structuralist school of criticism, one must emphasize that the achievement of total objectivity and impersonality is an artistic as well as critical impossibility. "Writing and reading are reciprocal social acts," notes Jerry Beasley, "whose reciprocity must be taken into account before any fully meaningful experience of a given literary work can occur" (335). It is the artist's particular ability to participate in and impart profound human truths and experience which defines him as an artist. Similarly, therefore, it must be the critic's duty to disclose the mystery of that art—not that art might thereby be demystified and made rationally intelligible, but rather that art's mystery might be appreciated and apprehended by those who otherwise may see the work imperfectly, because they lack the capacity, without the informed critic's assistance, to comprehend the artist's inner, original vision. The critic's purpose, therefore, is to give sight where no sight exists, though he is but the procurer of that sight: the sight he bestows is the artist's own, mediated through the person of the critic. The critic sees, not so much that we may see what he sees, but that we may see what the artist has seen. Such is the revelatory dimension and higher purpose of informed critical review—one which cannot be exercised in obedience to the doctrines of Barthes and Saussure but only in response to the aforementioned imperatives of Dante.

Shakespeare's purpose within the Lancastrian cycle is not just the dramatic adaptation of early fifteenth-century monarchy" to the exigencies of Tudor political thought (Traversi, *Shakespeare* 1-2), nor is it the simple attempt "to educate the magistrate by showing him how to avoid error" (Reese, "Origins of the History Play" 43), though these purposes, among many others, are evident in the plays. To the critic attuned to the theological content of the plays, the Lancaster plays reveal a distinctively Anglican character and conviction, and establish Shakespeare not as a mere propagandist for the Tudor dynasty but an apologist for the Protestant Reformation in England. As Ernest Howse remarks, Shakespeare, through his historical drama, "was speaking in a voice that could sound only at the period of the Renaissance and the Reformation when . . . Greece rose from the dead with the New Testament in her hand" (10).

Whether or not Shakespeare himself shared a personal Reformation conviction apart from his dramatic posture in the tetralogy is debatable. For our purposes, such a debate is largely irrelevant however. Knowing the identity of an author, though often helpful in deciphering his work, is not altogether essential for thorough inquiry. Such biographical information may, in fact, even work against good critical study, especially if assumptions about the author's life are too casually and indiscriminately applied to the author's work; hence, the critic's struggle to avoid the intentional fallacy.[6] When an author reveals a face for study, he does not necessarily present his own profile for scrutiny. As Oscar Wilde notes, when Hamlet asserts that art holds the mirror up to nature, he "no more represents Shakespeare's real views upon art than the speeches of Iago represent his real view upon morals" ("The Decay of Lying" 67). To proceed from such extrapolative logic and flawed assumptions, Wilde continues, one might just as well conclude that Shakespeare was mad because he wrote *King Lear* ("The Soul of Man Under Socialism" 38).

Consequently, though we may assume Shakespeare to have been an Anglican (and there surely is reason so to conclude), whether or not he personally was sympathetic to the Reformation is less important to us than the fact that the theological center of his composition in the Great Histories is Anglican; his plays assume an apologetic stance on behalf of the Church of England—a stance disclosed to us not in the histrionics of noisy propaganda and the open devices of medieval allegory but in the subtleties of a deliberate rhetoric and the artful evocation of familiar iconography. A knowledge of the fields of rhetoric and theology which informed Shakespeare's composition, therefore, will lead to the fuller apprehension of the Lancaster cycle's proper place within Elizabethan historiography and apologetic which more limited examinations of the plays insufficiently reveal. As Edgar Krentz warns biblical exegetes, "Restrict yourself to the canon and you will not understand the canon" (48).

Familiarity with a variety of disciplines will also prevent the critic's separation of himself from the theological, psychological, philosophical, biographical, and other important revelatory dimensions of the work he is examining, and it will also much enhance his general evaluative abilities by providing him with a more informed intelligence—wherewith he may more knowledgeably discern the effect of the artist and the artist's age upon his craft. Lacking this informed understanding, the critic who attempts to investigate and fully explicate the content of an artistic work will find himself solely reliant upon the altogether insufficient (because decontextualized) mechanics of rational inquiry and subsequently be displaced from both familiarity with and understanding of the larger cultural context within which the artist worked. Joel Hurstfield, for example, forcefully rejects the conclusion that such decontextualization can profitably serve the critical task; indeed, he insists that "the conditions of the twenty years which precede a man's birth set the pattern of his early thinking and leave a permanent mark upon him" (27); and Ernest Jones, a Freudian critic, substantially agrees:

> A work of art is too often regarded as a finished thing-in-itself, something almost independent of the creator's personality . . . . Informed criticism, however, shows that a correlated study of the two sheds light in both directions, on the inner nature of the composition and on the creative impulse of the author. The two can be separated only at the expense of diminished appreciation, whereas to increase our knowledge of either automatically deepens our understanding of the other. (12)

In defense, too, of the critic's responsibility to acknowledge rather than reject considerations regarding the significance and possible influence upon a work by those features of culture which are contemporary with the artist's life and work, G. Wilson Knight observes that many scholars of the late twentieth century have divorced themselves from serious attention to or scrutiny of the symbolic in Shakespeare. Knight reminds us that

> [t]he Elizabethan period was poetical and symbolical whereas we live in a peculiarly unimaginative age. We have not seen the symbolisms in Shakespeare, and when they are pointed out we say . . . that they are incompatible with the period of their creation. What we mean is that they are incompatible with the period of our criticism. ("On the Principles of Shakespearian Interpretation" 5)

Knight's affirmation of the importance of studying the historical context of a literary work will enhance the investigation of the critical scholar who embraces it, for the acceptance and application of this helpful recommendation will improve both one's comprehension and subsequent articulation of the significance of the play before him, just as ignorance of such distinctions will inhibit . . . any thorough investigation of the ritualistic sources and mythic analogues of drama . . ." —an unfortunate but inevitable consequence of the ahistorical perspective of New Criticism" (Weimann xx).

The writers of history at the time of Shakespeare were not diarists or mere chroniclers of indifferent history; the writing of history at the time of Shakespeare and before was, in fact, an interpretive as well as documentary task (Elton 32; Wheeldon 34). Tudor historians, much influenced by the historiography of the Italian Renaissance, were especially determined to explain events of the past—notably the errors of princes—in order to provide instruction and guidance to princes for their better conduct in the future (Campbell, *Shakespeare's Histories* 106-16; Downer 43). For example, when Polydore Vergil published his *Anglica Historica* in 1534, he presented the world with a history of England which not only chronicled the events of the past but argued for the right of the Tudors to occupy the throne. When Edward Hall published *The Union of the Two Noble and Illustrious Families of Lancaster and York* in 1548 (also known as Hall's *Chronicle* since republished in 1809), he suggested that the resolution of the civil conflict of the previous century, accomplished by the accession of Henry Tudor, was part of the providential design of a benevolent God who, having punished the realm for its crimes against his anointed deputy in Richard II, had redeemed the realm by the bestowal of the Tudor dynasty as a new incarnation of the divine purpose for the nation. Furthermore, the judgments and historical perspective of Vergil and Hall were shared by other influential Tudor and Stuart historians such as Raphael Holinshed (*Chronicles of England, Scotland, and Ireland* [1577]), Samuel Daniel (*Archi-Episcopal Priority Jnstjtuted [sic] By Christ* [1642]), and William Baldwin, et al. (*The Mirror for Magistrates* [1559]), who, through their works, lent support to the Christian and nationalistic premises of Tudor historiography.[7]

According to medieval cosmogony, all beings and objects occupied an assigned place in a created order, the maintenance of which was to be shared by God and man; and on earth, God's principal agent for the preservation of order was the person of God's anointed representative, the king. As God was believed to reign over the angels, so the sun was believed to govern among the stars; the lion was thought to

rule over the beasts, and the eagle, the birds. In such a
universe, monarchy naturally best emblemized God's own
rule, and the king's government was conceived to have been
modeled after God's sovereignty and established among
men to reflect the divine order and serve God's temporal
purpose (Tillyard, *The Elizabethan World Picture* 29-30).
Given the hierarchical principles upon which this intricate
human social order was constructed, in seeming obedience
to a divine and harmonious scheme of preciously delicate
balance, any violation of this meticulously crafted handi-
work was generally believed to invite—and indeed precipi-
tate—the fragmentation of the realm, the release of the
forces of chaos, and the sundering of the social fabric. So
Ulysses speaks of the world and its relationship to the
cosmos (*Troilus and Cressida* I.iii.94-101), and so Calpurnia
warns her husband of the foreboding signs of evil (*Julius
Caesar* II.ii.17-24). In *King Lear,* the Earl Of Gloucester
prophesies disaster for the realm and bases his interpretation
of such disaster on signs in the heavens—many of which were
thought to warn men of worldly ruin, for the heavenly bodies'
correspondence with the earth was believed to signify graver
conditions for mankind than the uninformed judgment of
men might otherwise derive from untutored observation
(I.ii.103-14). In *Richard II,* the Welsh captain similarly prophesies—his prophecies predicated upon the revelatory power of
Nature to disclose that which is otherwise concealed:

> The bay-trees in our country are all wither'd,
> And meteors fright the fixed stars of heaven,
> The pale-fac'd moon looks bloody on the earth,
> And lean-look'd prophets whisper fearful change,
> Rich men look sad, and ruffians dance and leap,

These signs forerun the death or fall of kings.

(II.iv.8-12,15)

observations which Salisbury, addressing Richard, confirms:

> The sun sets weeping in the lowly west,
> Witnessing storms to come, woe, and unrest.
> Thy friends are fled to wait upon thy foes,
> And crossly to thy good all fortune goes.
>
> (II.iv.21-24)[8]

Pythagorean and Platonic, this medieval sense of order
in which the events of heaven and earth were presumably
related continued to be affirmed in such non-medieval
works as Thomas Elyot's *The Governour* (1531)—see especially his description of the hierarchy of nature (8-9)—and
in the first book of Hooker's *Laws of Ecclesiastical Polity*
(1593). As one readily observes in the Elizabethan *Exhortation concerning good Ordre and Obedience to Rulers and
Magistrates* (1547), reflected within that Renaissance ser-
mon is the proclamation of the very essence of the stratified
universe of medieval theology, a universe compassionately
conceived by God for the benefit of man:

> [W]here there is no right ordre, there reigneth all
> abuse, carnall libertie, enormitie, synne, and
> Babylonical confusion. Take awaie Kynges, Princes,
> Rulers, Magistrates, Judges, and suche states of
> God's ordre, [and] no man shall ride or go by the
> high way unrobbed, no man shal slepe in his owne
> house or bed unkilled, no man shall kepe his wife,
> children, and possessions in quietnesse, all things
> shall be common, and there muste nedes folowe all
> mischief and utter destruction . . . . (142-43)

J. H. Walter, too, endorses the conclusion that English Renaissance historiography was close to the medieval temperament and perception of a structured universe in which all beings had, and should rightly discern, their proper states. He, in fact, concludes that "the medieval habit of mind did not disappear with the Renaissance and Copernicus . . . .[Rather] the Renaissance was the most medieval thing the Middle Ages produced" (163).[9] As Milton and Shakespeare amply demonstrate, even the Renaissance revolution in scientific apprehension and evaluation of phenomena did not instantly displace the sixteenth century's acceptance of medieval principle; rather, medieval myth was manipulated to accommodate scientific fact. Lear, for example, is one character who, without apparent contradiction, can simultaneously embrace the medieval belief in a flat earth's enclosure within a heavenly vault (V.iii.259-60) and, in an apostrophe to the heavens, still summon the thunder to "strike flat the thick rotundity o' th' world" (III.ii.7).

However, unlike the medieval annalists such as Matthew Paris, Thomas Walsingham, Randolph Higden, and Geoffrey of Monmouth, Tudor historiographers were disinclined to see the hand of God directly involved in all of the affairs of men, ordering in an intricate and individual way, all the varied events of history. Unlike their more uniformly theistically-conscious predecessors, the Renaissance historians did not discount the involvement of God in the affairs of men—especially in issues of state—but their more expansive and rather more humanistically-influenced accounts suggested to their contemporaries that providence governed men's lives more by indirection than by deliberate and obvious intrusion. This divine governance, they concluded, could be most clearly observed in the ordered processes and intrinsic harmony of natural law. Men's actions were considered by these Renaissance historians to be essentially free (see Cassius's "Men at some time are masters of their fates" [*Julius Caesar* I.ii.139-41] and Edmund's soliloquy, "This is the excellent foppery of the world" [*King Lear* I.ii.118-33] for Shakespearean statements of the principle), although such acts were believed to be performed within an ordered cosmos, a conviction principally derived from Italian historiography and Reformation precepts attending the definition of free will.[10] That man's free will and acts could not supplant the rule of God or abort his intent for man, for example, is affirmed in Ralegh's *History of the World* (1614), in which the author declares that God's will manifests itself through "the medium of men's affections and appetites" (201), for "the corrupted affections of men, impugning the revealed will of God, accomplish, nevertheless, his hidden purpose and without miraculous means confound themselves in the seeming wise devices of their folly" (203). Paul Siegel also assumes this posture, affirming that Shakespeare, like Ralegh, endorses the position that one can acknowledge the simultaneous existence of personal freedom within a providentially governed universe. Shakespearean drama, declares Siegel, "conveys an impression of an omnipotent power that is in command of the universe while somehow allowing man's will to be free to choose good or evil" (*Shakespeare in His Times* 84). Such an ability to accommodate two apparently contradictory realities and work with them in a unified context also complements S. K. Heninger Jr.'s observation that "unlike the medieval poet, Shakespeare did not see the world *sub specie aeternitatis;* but neither, like the romantic, did he circumscribe the meaning of personal experience. The power of Shakespeare . . . derives from an ability to look simultaneously at both the common and the minute" (326).

Not only does Shakespeare share the more general theological/philosophical presumptions of other Renaissance historiographers, however (Tillyard, "The Elizabethan World Order" 33); in his literature, he also nurtures the ancient Anglo-Saxon myth of England as the progeny of a chosen people, a new Israel which has been directed to a promised land across a great sea and to which material blessing and spiritual salvation has been assured (Howe 33-71).

Historians of England, long before Shakespeare, supported such a national mythology based upon the example of Scripture. Among the more notable of these historians is the Venerable Bede, who fosters the idea of England as a providentially nurtured kingdom in his *Historica Ecclesiastica* of 731.[11] Indeed, Rogert Ray proposes that Bede's five-book structure in the *Historica Ecclesiastica* is so thoroughly indebted to sacred tradition that it may be deliberately modeled after a similar chronology of Israelite history in the Pentateuch (134-35). Judith McClure agrees and asserts, as well, that Bede's interpretation of the proper role of the English sovereign is directly informed by the understanding of monarchy that is expounded in the books of the Hebrew prophet Samuel (76-98). Nicholas Howe also sees the ancient warrior epic, *Beowulf*, as another embodiment of a pagan/Christian myth of a chosen people in Britain. He writes:

> *Beowulf* may be read as a model to apprehend and
> interpret the historical process by which Anglo-

Saxon culture was transformed from its origin in pagan Germania to its converted state in Christian England . . . . [T]he correspondences between the cultures lie in . . . an exodus from a place of spiritual bondage across the water to a land of spiritual salvation. (176, 179)

Shakespeare, therefore, does not venture into any new literary territory by crafting an extensive dramatic history of England that corresponds to popular associations of England with Israel, a land of special grace and fair regard (for particular confirmation, listen especially to John of Gaunt's epideictic oratory in praise of England in *Richard II* (II.i.40-66), an oratorical style similar to other plays in which the theme of England's providence is sung, e.g., *3 Henry VI* (IV.i.39-46), *King John* (II.i.l9-31), and *Cymbeline* (III.i.78-82). Shakespeare's unique contribution to the tradition of England as a providentially-graced and protected land is not his mere repetition of these old cultural verities but his shaping of that older Biblical tradition into a less generically Christian and more specifically Anglican outline of the role of God in the affairs of Britain, especially as the role is assumed by the person of the king, "God's substitute" (*Richard II* II.i.37), his "deputy anointed in his sight" (II.i.38), a ruler who, for Shakespeare, becomes, because of the Reformation, not only a secular head of state but the temporal head of the Church of England, deferential to the authority of Canterbury ("the noble sinew of our power" [*Henry V* I.ii.223]), the supreme embodiment of the Anglican type.

Shakespeare's purposes, therefore, especially in his histories, are to illustrate and instruct by expanding upon and further defining an ancient mythology. Jane Chance suggests that he "reinterpret[s] . . . myth . . . to invest his own characters, or images, with an original signification" (28), and Joseph B. Collins argues that religious instruction is one of the special purposes of Shakespeare in the Lancastrian Tetralogy; he observes, too, that Shakespeare's convictions would hardly be singular among Elizabethans (vii). When one considers the violently anti-papal dramaturgy of Marlowe's *Doctor Faustus* and John Bale's *King Johan*, one can readily see muted examples of the Anglican principle demonstrated elsewhere in dramatic literature. But in the Lancastrian plays, in particular, Shakespeare more thoroughly exploits his audience's familiarity with the faith and practice of the Church of England than is done in these other plays in order to (1) consolidate the gains of the Reformation, (2) demonstrate that the ends of the English Church and State are inseparable, and (3) dramatically confirm the tenets of the Tudor Myth (especially the assertion that the accession of the Tudors was providentially ordered). He compresses an entire nation's story into four plays which, governed by the orthodox canons of Tudor political and theological truth, creatively and imaginatively interpret and apply the events of less than a quarter century's duration to an entire nation's history. Therefore, though not fulfilling the generally accepted conditions of epic, by mythologizing an otherwise tumultuous period of national decline and revival, Shakespeare nevertheless creates a history which possesses an "epic sweep" of mythic proportions that imparts no limited or narrowly personal vision but offers, instead, a panorama of national redemption emblemized in the rhetoric and iconography of the Anglican faith.[12]

As noted earlier, it is impossible to determine whether Shakespeare personally accepted all the political and religious premises of this elaborate Tudor mythology, but it is evident that he aggressively incorporated into his plays (especially the histories) much of the political and religious content of the historical works he consulted.[13] Shakespearean drama, as broadly representative of the Elizabethan era, speaks therefore not only as an advocate theatre for Tudor absolutism but also apologizes for the Reformation in England. It thus is useful to examine the principal figures of this Shakespearean theatre, especially in the Lancaster cycle, who represent not only their historical selves but who embody within their persons the emblems of Roman Catholic, Puritan, and Anglican Christianity. Accordingly, Richard II, in Shakespeare, emblemizes decadent luxuriousness, autocracy, and indifference, as well as foreign affectation—the very qualities imputed by Anglican Christianity to the Roman Catholicism which the Elizabethan audience found so offensive. In contrast, Henry V, through his personal transformation and the attainment of the apotheosis of monarchy (accompanied by surrounding praise which echoes the *Book of Common Prayer*) embodies the very image of reformed English Christianity: pure, unaffected, simple righteousness; for Henry, like the Church of which he is an icon, though born in the turmoil of national schism, is destined for greatness and the achievement of national unity.

The present study does not suggest that Shakespeare's histories are mere allegories of the Reformation, but that as a propagandist for the realm (thereby, also, for the Crown and Church), Shakespeare fashions his characters in such a way that they project not only their individual identities but also internalize and reflect their incorporation of those identities of things greater than themselves[14]—and in whom better to embody the identities of both Church and State, for example, than he who, according to Anglican confessional theology, is head of both Church and State? In studiously applying a familiar sacramental iconography and rhetoric of Anglican character to the persons and events of his plays, Shakespeare imparts the Reformation tenets of the Anglican faith to his audience and establishes himself as an apologist for both the Tudor monarchy and the Church of England, setting himself (at least through his drama) firmly against the detractors, critics, and opponents of absolute monarchy and Anglican theology.

Notes

[1]In the several decades since 1944 when E. M. W. Tillyard's study of the Shakespearean histories (*Shakespeare's History Plays*) was published, twenty-seven major, diverse studies in the histories have been published. These books include Lily B. Campbell's *Shakespeare's Histories: Mirrors of Elizabethan Policy* (1947), Derek Traversi's *Shakespeare from Richard II to Henry V* (1957), G. Wilson Knight's *The Sovereian Flower: On Shakespeare as the Poet of Royalism. Together with Related Essays and Indexes to Earlier Volumes* (1958), M. M. Reese's *The Cease of Majesty: A Study of Shakespeare's History Plays* (1961), S. C. Sen Gupta's *Shakespeare's Historical Plays* (1964), H. M. Richmond's *Shakespeare's Political Plays* (1967), James Winney's *The Player King: A Theme of Shakespeare's Histories* (1968), Henry A. Kelly's *Divine Providence in the England of Shakespeare's Histories* (1970), David Riggs's *Shakespeare's Heroical Histories: "Henry VI" and Its Literary Tradition* (1971), Robert Pierce's *Shakespeare's History Plays: The Family and the State* (1971), John Bromley's *The Shakespearean Kings* (1971), Robert Ornstein's *A Kingdom for a Stage* (1972), Moody E. Prior's *The Drama of Power: Studies in Shakespeare's History Plays* (1973), Edward I. Berry's *Patterns of Decay: Shakespeare's Early Histories* (1975), Larry S. Champion's *Perspective in Shakespeare's English Histories* (1976), David L. Frey's *The First Tetralogy: Shakespeare's Scrutiny of the Tudor Myth* (1976), George Joseph Becker's *Shakespeare's Histories* (1977), James T. Henke's *The Ego-King: An Archetype Approach to Elizabethan Political Thought and Shakespeare's Henry IV Plays*

(1977), Peter Saccio's *Shakespeare's English Kings* (1977), Edna Zwick Boris's *Shakespeare's English Kings. the People. and the Law* (1978), John Wilders's *The Lost Garden: A View of Shakespeare's English and Roman History Plays (1978)*, James L. Calderwood's *Metadrama in Shakespeare's Henriad: Richard II to Henry V* (1979), H. R. Coursen's *The Leasing Out of England: Shakespeare's Second* Henriad (1982), C. G. Thayer's Shakespearean Politics: *Government and Misgovernment in the Great Histories* (1983), Graham Holderness's *Shakespeare's History* (1985), Paul N. Siegel's *Shakespeare's English and Roman History Plays: A Marxist Approach* (1986), and Alexander Leggatt's *Shakespeare's Political Drama: The History Plays and the Roman Plays* (1988).

[2]Of Christian criticism, most of those critical scholars who have expressed reservations at least and dismissal at worst include the New Critics and their derivative methodologists. In the past half century, the New Critics and their scholarly progeny—most notably the structuralists—have argued that contrary to the premises of Christian criticism, a work is best understood when studied apart from those literary, historical, theological, philosophical, psychological, and other diachronic considerations which informed its composition; contemporary structuralist criticism, for example, invites us to concentrate, instead, upon a work's synchronics, i.e., those singularly linguistic characteristics which allow a work to generate the meaning which the structuralists suggest that a work possesses in itself as a text—a paradigm and approach to literary study first developed and defined by John Crowe Ransom (*The New Criticism*, 1941) and F. R. Leavis (*The Great Tradition*, 1948) that were, in turn, developed by more contemporary

exponents of the structuralist method such as Ferdinand de Saussure (most noted for his posthumously published *Course in General Linguistics* [1966], Roland Barthes (*Writing Degree Zero and Elements of Semiology*, 1970), and Robert Scholes (*Structuralism in Literature*, 1974). Art Berman defines the close relationship between New Critical and structuralist methodological presumptions:

> The New Critical methodology is designed to yield...an interpretation of a meaning that is *in* the text, not an imposition upon it. If multiple interpretations are possible, it is because the text itself contains them in the ambiguities that are characteristic of poetic language.... The structuralists seek the mechanisms through which meaning is generated [e.g.,] those linguistic elements that do not themselves have meaning (phonemes, grammatical structure. . . .) (142)

[3]T. S. Eliot, in "Tradition and the Individual Talent," declares that "the progress of the artist [involves] . . . the continual extinction of personality [and] it is in this depersonalization that art may be said to approach the condition of science" (7).

[4]All citations and quotations are taken from *The Riverside Shakespeare*. Eds. G. Blakemore Evans et al. (Boston: Houghton Mifflin, 1974). All citations and quotations hereafter will be included in the text.

[5]Consider, for example, James Calderwood's several points:

> For the sixteenth-century Christian, religious faith and verbal faith coalesce, most notably in prayer and ritual . . . . The written word, too, especially in biblical form, exercised an influence on Elizabethan

> conceptions of language that can hardly be overrated
> . . . . The reverence accorded the Holy Book [and
> Shakespeare's Bible of authority would seem to be
> the Protestant Geneva edition (Cumberland 276-
> 84; Dickens 288; Neill 130; Noble 43)] inevitably
> rubbed off on ordinary books and words as well, so
> that verbal expression in general would seem a
> natural vehicle of truth . . . . (198-200)

[6]For example, given the difficulty in attempting definitively to establish the personal faith of a dramatist such as Shakespeare, one therefore must be especially careful—even when one is reasonably confident of the accuracy of one's suppositions—not inordinately to conclude too much from those suppositions, regardless of (or perhaps in spite of) their authority. As Robert Fitch notes, "proof that the playwright has a certain faith does not [mean that he] automatically insert[s] that faith into [his] plays" (72).

[7]The extensive influence of the many English chronicles on the formation of Shakespearean drama, historical and otherwise, is universally acknowledged. A brief synopsis of those principal sources of the English history play may be reviewed in Appendix C of Irving Ribner's *The English History Play in the Age of Shakespeare* (New York, 1979). Ribner's study is also a rich bibliographical resource for those interested in pursuing more specialized research with reproductions or microfilms of the original historical texts. The work supplements, in its breadth of detail, Ribner and Clifford Hoffman's subsequent *Tudor and Stuart Drama* (Arlington Heights, 1978), a bibliography of studies of non-Shakespearean Tudor and Stuart dramatic works.

[8]The significance of the divergence in presumptions about the operations of history from the time of the Renaissance to our own ought not be underestimated. The differences in perception are nothing less than enormous and points of correspondence few. Even nearly a century-and-a-quarter ago, historian Henry Thomas Buckle bitterly derided what he considered the gross inadequacies of Renaissance historiography:

> It is difficult for an ordinary reader, living in the midst of the nineteenth century, to understand, that only three hundred years before he was born, the public mind was in [such a] benighted state. . . . It is still more difficult for him to understand that the darkness was shared not merely by men of an average education, but by men of considerable ability, men in every respect among the foremost of their age . . . . [H]e will find it hard to conceive that there ever was a state of society in which such miserable absurdities were welcomed as . . . sober truths . . . . Not only in historical literature, but in all kinds of literature . . . the presiding principle was a blind and unhesitating credulity. (241)

[9]In dramatic composition, too, this intimate bond between the medieval and Renaissance temperaments is secured in patterns of continuity. As O. B. Hardison observes, for example, "The parallel between the Corpus Christi cycle [of medieval mystery plays] and Shakespeare's histories is evidence of the persistence of the medieval tradition in the Renaissance" (290).

[10]An insight perhaps disguised under such possibly misleading treatises as Martin Luther's *De servo arbitrio*

[*Bondage of the Will* (1525)] and the seventh chapter in Book One of Hooker's *Laws of Ecclesiastical Polity* (1593) ("There is in the Will of man naturally that freedom, whereby it is apt to take or refuse any particular object whatsoever being presented unto it" [124]), wherein man's freedom is affirmed, although this freedom is regarded as a capacity for thought and action inextricably linked to the uniformly sinful condition of a fallen humanity.

[11]Other ancient but perhaps less influential works which also propagate the belief in England as a nation of providential destiny and character include the anonymous *Anglo-Saxon Chronicle* (c. 890) and Gildas's *De Excidio et Conquesta Britanniae* (c. 550).

[12]Writers who examine the rhetoric and high art of the Renaissance that may have inspired some of Shakespeare's dramatic iconography include Andre Grabar (*Christian Iconography : A Study of Its Origins* [Princeton: Princeton UP, 1968]), Arthur M. Hind (*Engraving in England in the Sixteenth and Seventeenth Centuries.* 3 vols. [Cambridge: Cambridge UP, 1953-64]), Ernst Kantorowicz (*Laudes Regiae: A Study in Liturgical Acclamations and Mediaeval Ruler Worship.* University of California Publications in History, vol. 33. 2nd ed. [Berkeley: U of California P, 1958]), Erwin Panofsky (*Studies in Iconology: Humanistic Themes in the Art of the Renaissance* [Oxford: Oxford UP, 1939]), Gertrud Schiller (*Iconography of Christian Art.* Trans. Janet Seligman. 2 vols. [Greenwich, CT: New York Graphic Society, 1971-72]), and Roy Strong (*The English Icon: Elizabethan and Jacobean Portraiture* [New Haven: Yale UP, 1969]). Peter Daly, Leslie T. Duer, and Anthony Raspa have also recently edited the first volume of what

promises to become a fine collection: *The English Emblem Tradition* (Toronto: U of Toronto P, 1988).

[13]Apart from the conventional sources of information from which he drew the materials for his individual interpretation of the events leading to the Wars of the Roses, Shakespeare was probably also familiar with and reliant upon Boethius's *Consolation of Philosophy* and Saint Augustine's *City of God*. Both works express the ancient Christian belief that God's beneficent purposes are cloaked in mystery or disguised under their apparent opposites (the death of Christ serving as the principal paradigm of this conviction). For example, as Saint Augustine writes, in the experiences of life, not only does evil sometimes overtake good, but evil sometimes overtakes evil as well; therefore, no discernment of justice in the universe can be accomplished by the mere observation of isolated events alone; the disadvantage of lacking privileged knowledge about the divine purpose prevents this discernment (347-48), as such examples as Job's suffering and Christ's passion demonstrate. Given this assumption, individual events which otherwise might appear to be irreconcilable with a scheme of divine justice form a more comprehensible pattern as they fold themselves into one another, achieving a sense of ordered progression toward a point of historical consummation; in effect, the events, patterned into dramatic form, eventually assume a discernible teleology and anticipate a kind of eschaton. Consequently, apart from the typological features within the Lancaster cycle, the very structure of the cycle articulates the secular, national messianism of the tetralogy, the prototype of which is the anticipatory character of the Old Testament itself. The unity of Shakespeare's

tetralogies, then, is achieved in the application of the messianic character of sacred history to the events of secular history in order that England might identify with and incorporate into its own national mythology a belief in the essentially providential quality of her history and the messianic nature of her Tudor monarchy.

[14]Jean Seznec suggests that such emblematic types are less a consequence of Shakespeare's commitment to the repristination of a conventional device of character inflation and, instead, are the natural result of his neo-Platonic assumptions and figurative view of the world (103-04).

Chapter One

The Shakespearean Histories:
The Assessment of the Twentieth Century

"Noble philosopher, your company"—*King Lear*

Shakespearean criticism in our century diverges from the critical traditions of earlier eras not only in the volume of criticism produced in this century relative to former times, but in the many perspectives which twentieth-century commentators have generated and brought to the task of critical review. Although no age has ever produced unanimity of opinion with respect to the works of Shakespeare, some eras have more approximated consensus than ours. Among Neo-Classical critics such as Dryden, Pope, and Johnson, praise of Shakespeare's poetic genius is considerable, though not unqualified,[1] although relatively little of their criticism focuses extensively upon specific Shakespearean works. Neo-Classical criticism, therein, while not unspecific in content, is more generalized in focus than twentieth-century critical schools of thought such as Marxism and Freudianism—although Neo-Classical commentary is not less observant or valuable than contemporary criticism for its relative absence of these narrow, limited, and sometimes perhaps too-carefully-defined perspectives.

Romantic critics of Shakespeare are likewise similar to one another in their perspectives and approaches to Shakespeare.[2] Generally united in their celebratory praise of

Shakespeare's talent, the Romantics also share a nearly boundless, congratulatory enthusiasm for what they perceive as Shakespeare's embodiment of the Romantic ideal, and they invite their readers to join their effusive praise of the Shakespearean ability to "create peoples and societies from complete worlds, much as nature himself does"—illustrating therein the demonstration of a perfected imagination which, among the Romantics, according to Northrop Frye, "raised Shakespeare almost to divinity" (*A Study of English Romanticism* 23). Coleridge also acknowledges, however, that Shakespeare had practical as well as ideal purposes to accomplish in his histories; he suggests, for example, that "one great object of [Shakespeare in his] history plays . . . was to make his countrymen more patriotic; to make Englishmen proud of being Englishmen" (238).

If the Romantics enthusiastically responded to Shakespeare and applauded him as a man whose imagination transcended culturally-imposed limitations upon an elevated universal human sensibility, many Victorians essentially regarded the poet of Stratford as a Tory, a defender of bourgeois morality and empire.[3] Thomas Sauer maintains, however, that "the Victorians [took] for granted the Romantics' contention that Shakespeare was a great artist. They chose not to investigate further . . . . They accepted the advocacy of their predecessors" (145); but Aron Stavisky, in contrast, argues that, in fact, "[t]he Victorians did not develop their ideas about Shakespeare from within the romantic tradition. Instead, drawing from the eighteenth century, they brought to full flower...the moral criteria of Johnson" (vii). Indeed, consistent with Stavisky's interpretation, many Victorians appear to have perceived Shakespeare as something of a moral exemplum in his histories; to many, he was a sixteenth-century Kipling, a poet-patriot who, especially in *Henry V*, created a play of such "fervent nationalism" (Manvell 38) that its tone suggested to such later, postwar readers as William Butler Yeats that the play had to be a dramatic exercise in irony (133). S. L. Bethell has remarked, too, that many "Victorian critics . . . displayed bitter resentment . . . against Shakespeare . . . for [his] refus[al] to sentimentalize" (22). Other representative Victorians such as Charles Kingsley indignantly denounced Shakespeare's historical, comic, tragic, and romantic art as uniformly "effeminate" (331), while Edward Dowden, in his essay "The Mood of Shakespeare's Last Plays," laments that in such later works of Shakespeare as *Henry VIII*, "ethical unity is sacrificed to the vulgar demand for . . . spectacle" (378).[4]

If previous ages devoted more time to describing the character of Shakespeare's art and to providing generalized commentary focusing on the tragedies, comedies, romances, and sonnets rather than scrutinizing the Shakespearean histories, the twentieth century substantially changed precedent. New schools of thought developed, matured, and were applied to various art forms, and the earlier scholarly neglect of the histories, accompanied by the dismissal of these plays to the lower regions of Shakespearean criticism, gradually diminished. The histories of both the York and Lancaster cycles invited twentieth-century exploration of this previously "undiscovered country," and the Shakespearean histories began to receive new attention, if not actual prominence, in criticism and commentary.

Harold Jenkins has assembled a detailed review of the scholarship on the Shakespearean histories, criticism composed between 1900-51,[5] and Dennis Burden has supplemented this work by Jenkins with his own continuation of the survey in "Shakespeare's History Plays: 1952-83."[6] As these studies note, there exists among the moderns a far greater variety of opinion in Shakespearean criticism than that which appears among the representatives of previous eras. Indeed, even among those modern scholars who agree with one another, consensus exists only within broadly defined categories of opinion. For example, J. Dover Wilson suggests that the history plays are essentially moralities; in fact, he declares *Henry IV* to be "Shakespeare's greatest morality play" (*The Fortunes of Falstaff* 14), but Lily B. Campbell sees the histories as elaborate allegorical dramas based on actual persons and events which surrounded and were familiar to the Elizabethan court; she suggests that the plays' primary purpose is provision of propaganda for the Crown and that through these plays, Shakespeare is principally interested in repeating the propositions of Tudor doctrine derived from dynastic myth (*Shakespeare's Histories* 125). A. P. Rossiter also perceives the plays primarily as political vehicles and writes that in the histories "[the] old allegory of man's duty toward God, within his Catholic and universal church was narrowed toward the allegory of men's duties as subjects under a God-representing king" (*English Drama* 124). O. B. Hardison, Jr. shares some of these sentiments in his work, *Christian Rite and Christian Drama in the Middle Ages,* although he insists that

> in the cycle of plays from *Richard II* to *Richard III* it is evident that we have a secular equivalent to the sacred cycle of the Middle Ages. The protagonist of the cycle is *respublica* rather than Holy Church, and its rationale is the religio-political synthesis of the Tudor apologists rather than Catholic theology. (209)

E. M. W. Tillyard also proposes that the Henriad is a repository of political dogma, especially of those doctrines which support the divine election of the Tudors and the morality idea of *respublica* (*Shakespeare's History Plays* 242). Likewise, according to Irving Ribner, these plays "comprise a unified tetralogy devoted to the triumph of the House of Lancaster" (*The English History Play* 151), while James Leverett maintains that "the story within the story of the [Lancaster cycle] seems to be one of human frailty and inadequacy in the face of the onerous demands of government" (96). G. Wilson Knight, however, believes that Shakespeare's histories anachronistically depict an England that is more reflective of Tudor and Anglican England than the actual England of the early fifteenth century: as Knight writes of the England of the histories, "England functions as England, with a new sense of sovereignty, a new church, a new national allegiance. That is how the Renaissance and the Reformation affect, or rather create, the England we know. The voice of the new nation is Shakespeare" (*The Olive and the Sword* 4). Alfred Harbage shares Knight's evaluation of the primacy of this nationalistic character in the plays in his declaration that "Shakespeare's plays are not pro-absolutist, pro-aristocratic, or pro-democratic, but [they] certainly are pro-English" (155). Harbage notes, too, that these nationalistic elements did not escape the attention of such non-Englishmen as Victor Hugo, who suggested that the tetralogy was less proudly nationalistic than arrogantly jingoistic and complained, therefore, that Shakespeare "is very English—too English" (155). John Blanpied, however, sees less of this glorification of the State in the histories than does Hugo and suggests that "if there is a fundamental motive in the histories, it is the need to make a future" (15), while John Wilders reverses that interpretation and suggests that Shakespeare's histories portray their age as a time when many thought that with the death of Richard II, a golden age, an "ideal past," had vanished: in *Richard II*, writes Wilders, "the sense of a lost paradise and of a country falling into ruin . . . is conveyed most powerfully" (135). Of *Richard II*, J. A. Bryant, Jr. writes that

> what really sets this remarkable play apart from Shakespeare's own earlier work and the work of all his contemporaries is an approach . . . which reveals Shakespeare clearly as a poet with a metaphysical turn of mind, capable of seeing the particular event both as something unique and as something participating in a universal web of analogy. ("The Linked Analogies" 421)

Bryant discovers features of metaphysical significance, for example, in *Richard II,* when he compares the causes, dimensions, and consequences of Richard's fall with those falls from lofty heights of such legendary figures as Oedipus, Creon, Agamemnon, and Clytaemnestra:

> What Shakespeare was giving [his audience] in this presentation of Richard . . . was nothing less than a typological interpretation of history . . . . Whether he realized it or not at the time, Shakespeare, in laying the outlines of such a complex and richly suggestive symbol against the surface of his chronicle material, had given to secular fable a significance that it had achieved only rarely in drama since the days of Aeschylus and Sophocles.

To paraphrase Dryden, he had affected the meta-physical in his treatment of it. ("The Linked Analogies" 426)

Bryant also declares that in Shakespeare there is such an intimate correspondence between the historical material and the poet's natural genius that he is able to fashion and transform history and its characters by creating a ritual world in which "a great metaphysical framework of allusion" (432) allows for the redefinition of history in sacramental terms. G. Wilson Knight substantially agrees with Bryant. Echoing much of Bryant's interpretation, he writes that

> the source of [Shakespeare's] poetry is rooted in the otherness of mental or spiritual realities: these, how-ever, are a "nothing" until mated with earthly shapes. Creation is thus born of a union between "earth" and "heaven," the material and the spiritual. ("On the Principles of Shakespearean Interpretation" 7)

Shakespeare, as Harold Toliver notes, was assuredly not original in his analysis of history; he borrowed heavily from other dramatists, mythographers, and historians of his day ("Falstaff" 64), although other critics disagree; indeed, Rene Girard sees Shakespeare as the Renaissance's "most daringly perspicacious interpreter of the monarchic principle" (304). However, in Shakespeare's dramatiza-tion of the events of the fifteenth century, he was guided, in the opinion of A. R. Humphreys, not only by national-istic enthusiasm ("Shakespeare and the Tudor Perception" 52) but by precepts that were even more particularly Anglican and Tudor. In effect, through his drama, Humphreys seems to imply, he became an apologist for an England that was heir to a providential destiny, of which the advent of the Tudors and the Reformation Church were pre-eminent signs.

Much like Lily B. Campbell, Sigurd Burckhardt writes that Shakespeare's histories are deliberately and creatively anachronistic, in order that the Elizabethan audience might apply wisdom from the past to present experience; as such, the social realism of the histories is contemporary—not historical (76)—a condition which Burckhardt identifies as the "dramatic present" (175). Henry Wells and H. H. Anniah Gouda similarly propose that the histories provide "a historical exemplum of general principles" (32). Patricia Barry, however, thinks Shakespeare's purposes rather more specific. She argues that Shakespeare nurtured his dramaturgy in an age which made the display of royal magnificence and the manipulation of verbal artifice the tools of an official propaganda to promote the supremacy of the English monarchy over papal princes and continental sovereigns (258). With respect to these observations, Paul Korshin notes the nature of the historical composition of Shakespeare's predecessors from which the Stratford poet drew his inspiration and fashioned his likeness: "The historians of antiquity generally conceived of history as a progression from shadowy beginnings to a glorious fulfillment, for historians, then as now, were often apologists for an established government or certain accepted ideas, and they conceived it useful to describe the present as an antitype held forth by the past" (79).

More specifically, Alfred Hart asserts that especially from the Tudor historiographers and homilists, Shakespeare borrowed the doctrine of the king's divine right, the duty of the subject to be passively obedient, and a belief in the monstrous gravity of offense committed by the sin of rebellion (74);[7] such ideas, linked to the nationalistic and providential assumptions of history which supported the Tudor dynasty, were shared not only by spokesmen for Crown and Church but by those of the theatre as well (Dollimore 87), as one might well observe by a cursory review of other historical dramas of the period, e.g., John Bale's *King Johan* (c. 1530-36) and Thomas Legge's *Richardus Tertius* (1579).

The premises of the so-called "Tudor Myth" — first defined by Tillyard in 1944[8] and extensively discussed in many works since that time[9]—although not original with Shakespeare, were given scope and dramatic substance by Shakespeare before a larger audience than the Crown could have anticipated. Though universal acceptance of the Tudor doctrine of history clearly was desired by the English government's patronage of official histories in which the Tudor version of history was articulated, in John Gillingham's opinion, it was not through these official histories but rather through Shakespeare's dramatizations of the events which these histories recorded that a "view of the past which happened to suit the government of Tudor England was indelibly forged in the mind of the Elizabethan public" (10). Otis Stuart also agrees that this manipulative historical drama of Shakespeare was instrumental in popularizing the Tudor version of English history; the Yorkist Richard, depicted as a demonic conspirator and murderer, was, he proposes, "the offspring of one of the Tudor dynasty's contributions to modern society, the propaganda machine, [of which] its most blissful servant [was] William Shakespeare" (97).

Henry Ansgar Kelly, in *Divine Providence in the England of Shakespeare's Histories*, has recently produced the most comprehensive examination of the role or Providence in the lives of the English monarchs—as that role was interpreted by the chroniclers of the late medieval and early Renaissance eras (inclusive of such historical dramatists as Marlowe and Shakespeare). Of the histories, Kelly maintains that "each play creates its own moral ethos and mythos" (306); but each play also demonstrates that all of the Shakespearean histories are unambiguously characterized by a general sense of providential design in their portraitures of England's kings as the recipients of divine wrath or reward, administered or bestowed according to the canons of a divine and inscrutable justice—a justice which, though perhaps not immediately evident, is revealed when joined with a larger view of the divine will as it works itself out through the events of history. In other words, in Kelly's interpretation, Shakespeare seems to say that though God's ways may be unfathomable in the particular, they are readily apparent when seen with an expanded perspective—a perspective much in conformity with the view articulated by Judaic wisdom literature, especially the book of Job. Such extensive reliance on Scriptural typology suggests that Shakespeare invites his audience to witness the unfolding of England's history with the aid of such an informed perspective, for such typological constructions, according to G. R. Hibbard, would have no signal value whatsoever if the premises of sacred historical progress were not accepted as orthodox Christian truths by those who are spectators of his drama ("George Chapman" 27).

"The 'Tudor myth,'" writes M. C. Bradbrook, "reflected the national anxiety . . ." (qtd. in Manheim 71)—and as

Northrop Frye has astutely argued, "the anxiety of [a] society, when it urges the authority of a myth and the necessity of believing it, seems…less to proclaim its truth than to prevent anyone from questioning it. It aims at consent . . . rather than conviction" (*The Secular Scripture* 16). As a result, Tillyard argues, in the vigorous attempt to obtain such consent to the Tudor government, this dynastic myth was intrusively asserted in the drama of Tudor England. Its provision of an interpretive context for recent English history allowed Tudor England to account for the otherwise almost unintelligible events of the late fourteenth and early fifteenth centuries by endowing those chaotic years with meaning and significant purpose (Tillyard, *Shakespeare's History Plays* 29-32)—much as the perhaps otherwise unaccountable sufferings of Job and Christ are clarified when placed within the larger context of salvation history. After all, as Irving Ribner has written of Renaissance historiography, "The purpose of a history was not to present truth about the past for its own sake; it was to use the past for didactic purposes . . . " (*The English History Play* 8)—an attitude alien to our existential apprehension of the seemingly meaningless events of our own era: "The philosophy of the modern world," Hardin Craig observes, "lacks the unity, the integration, the intelligible practicality of the philosophy of the Renaissance" (264) and therein invites us to conclude that this loss may be due to the modern world's failure to frame the inexplicable within mythological structures which offer or suggest explanation.

Shakespeare, then, in his emphasis upon the pedagogical capacity of historical drama, diverged only slightly and almost imperceptibly from the humanistic tradition of Italian historiography (which, unlike the work of the historians of

Renaissance England, was somewhat less concerned with a raw didacticism and more concerned with clearly distinguishing fact from legend [Ribner, *The English History Play* 14], though D. R. Woolf has declared that the distinction of history as truth [fact] from history as fable [fiction] was, in fact, an Elizabethan commonplace [19]). In his drama, however, Shakespeare appealed to an already largely-established, if perhaps imperfectly understood or but marginally-accepted body of belief. Accordingly, of these plays, Marion Trousdale confirms that "the teaching done by the literature with which we are concerned is fundamentally a *modus legendi*. One must participate emotionally and intellectually in the process of the play if one is to be instructed in the ways in which one is meant to be instructed by the events of the stage" (144).

As a result of the non-representational quality of the Elizabethan history (a characteristic also reflected in the staging of the Shakespearean theatre), the perception of history as a documentary record of verifiable incidents and persons was subordinated to the conception of dramatic history as a ritual affirmation of established values (Jackson) which "proceed from an interest . . . [in] the primacy of eternal things" (Cormican, "Medieval Idiom in Shakespeare [1]" 200). Cormican also suggests that those who deem Shakespeare's histories to be impoverished or defective because of their lack of attention to historical accuracy fail to understand that Shakespeare's histories are not meant to chronicle history; they are meant, instead, to apply (at least in part) the lessons of the past to the present through the medium of a drama committed to the confirmation of an historical vision rather than the mere re-enactment of historical event ("Medieval Idiom in

Shakespeare [II]" 311)—a distinction, earlier noted by Craig, which is not easily comprehended by the rationalist biases of the twentieth century. As Northrop Frye defines the purpose of historical drama, "The poet's job is not to tell you what happened, but what happens: not what did take place, but . . . [what] always . . . take[s] place. He gives you the typical, recurring, or what Aristotle calls the universal event" (*The Educated Imagination* 63-64). Martha Fleischer agrees: "Elizabethan [history] plays . . . mirror [not a specific but] the general human history" (32). Such is the reason that, in *Richard II*, we, in part, sympathize and grieve for Richard, for he is cast less as the actual monarch and often more as a kind of medieval Adam, so that his fall becomes mankind's fall, and hence ours. Shakespeare's historical characters, therefore, in their very conception, do not so much reveal the past as they anachronistically invoke and apply to themselves those qualities of the Tudor future—which, of course, is Shakespeare's audience's present (Rackin, "Shakespeare's Use"). An historical dramatist, accordingly, may remain faithful to historical truth while distancing himself from historical fact (Barnaby). As Oscar Wilde reminds us in "The Truth of Masks," "the aesthetic value of Shakespeare's plays does not, in the slightest degree, depend on their facts, but on Truth, and Truth is independent of facts always, inventing or selecting them at pleasure" (220).[10]

The Marxist critic Graham Holderness fully agrees that Shakespeare has no interest in attempting to reproduce a "true"—which is to say factually accurate—version of English history in his plays; according to Holderness, as the "great poet of bourgeois society," Shakespeare's dramatic efforts are essentially calculated, reactionary, anachronistic attempts to apply to events of the fifteenth century a dogma conceived to support the interest of the Tudor dynasty in its attempt to acquire hegemony over the British people by establishing as the premise for the exercise of its tyranny an historical legitimacy which it never, in fact, possessed (158-60; 223-25). Irving Ribner disputes little of Holderness's analysis. "Medieval kings were not considered to be responsible to God alone," Ribner emphasizes, for such a relationship of king to deity "was a Renaissance political doctrine which was not asserted until the coming of the Tudors. Historically, the deposition of Richard occurred in a medieval, feudal context, and not in the later Tudor absolutist terms of Shakespeare's play" ("The Historical Richard" 13). Peter Saccio further reminds us that "[Richard's absolutist concept of monarchy] is couched . . . in language and concepts developed by Elizabethan political theorists rather than in medieval terms" (23). The Shakespearean histories, therefore, unambiguously and unmistakably reveal the imposition of assumptions derived from the prose chronicles of English history which Shakespeare consulted prior to drafting his own historical drama. Such a suggestion, then, as A. C. Bradley's, which argues that "Elizabethan drama was almost wholly secular and . . . Shakespeare [as a representative Elizabethan] confined his view to the world of non-theological observation and thought" (25) is unconvincing to critics who recognize that Shakespeare composed dramatic works which consist of far more than the mere re-enactment of unrelated events arranged in chronological succession (Orgel 108).

Many modern critics contend that Shakespeare's histories were conceived in fidelity to the age's conviction that the study of history is more authentically pursued by the acquisition of lessons conveyed by the exposition of "historical truths rather than [by] historical facts" (Campbell, *Tudor Conceptions of History* 27).

Among the values which the Renaissance made attendant upon the study of history— apart from the rather limited and dynastically selfish interests of the Tudors—was the average Elizabethan citizen's belief that "the reading of history was an exercise second only to a study of Holy Writ in its power to induce good morality and shape the individual into a worthy member of society" (Wright, "Middle-Class Culture" 297), an opinion reinforced by the early example of John Bale, who both wrote and "recommended histories to Christian governors as mirrors wherein the cause and reformation of abuses might be seen . . . link[ing] Biblical and secular history together . . ." (Campbell, "English History" 20). Professor Campbell points out that the great Anglican systematician Richard Hooker also recognized and affirmed the value of the study of histories; as Hooker wrote to Walter Ralegh in 1587,

> Among all the infinite good blessings, . . . I think none more expedient and necessarie, than the use and knowledge of histories and chronicles: which are the most assured registers of the innumerable benefits and commodities, which have and dailie doo grow to the church of God, and to the civill government throughout all nations. (27)

Scholars sometimes have seen less of a general advocacy of Crown and Church and more of a composite allegory of Elizabethan court history in Shakespeare's history plays (see Ribner's somewhat qualified though essentially sympathetic evaluation of this theory [first offered by Lily B. Campbell in 1947], which recurs throughout his study of *The English History Play in the Age of Shakespeare)*. Lily B. Campbell, indeed, offers the rather sweeping assumption that "each of the Shakespeare histories serves a special purpose in elucidating a political problem of Elizabeth's day ..." *(Shakespeare's Histories* 125). More plausible, perhaps, however, is Marjorie Garber's suggestion that more than a crude analogue of the Shakespearean present, "the [Shakespearean] history play . . . is . . . lodged in the paradoxical temporality of what the French call the *futur anterieur*, the prior future, the tense of what 'will have occurred'" (306-07), an analysis which recognizes the character of a dramatic genre that, with some difficulty, merges the sensibilities of one age with the actions of another.

Elizabethans may have discovered analogies in all things (Siegel, *Shakespeare in His Times* 47), but Arthur Humphreys, for example, argues that it does not therefore follow that to them all things were necessarily analogues; as a result, even the occasional analogical presentation of the truisms of English history, whether delivered through the prose histories of the age, the homilies of the Reformation pulpit, or the historical dramas of the stage, served to fortify the repetitive and familiar patterns of thought which reinforced conventional habits of mind that Elizabethan society had been conditioned to accept as valid. Such convictions of the Tudor historian as those found, for example, in Hall's *Chronicle* of 1548 declared that, in response to rebellion, the kindling of God's wrath against rebels is certain— though the evidence of that wrath either may not be immediately evident or may be delivered under signs which might be apprehended only within a more expansive context that magnifies and clarifies the original crime ("Shakes-peare and the Tudor Perception" 51-67); such convictions are echoed, Humphreys notes, in the scaffold speech of Sir Thomas Wyatt (a speech first recorded in Grafton's *Chronicle* of 1563 and delivered by Wyatt at the time of his execution in 1554 for having participated in the Northumberland Rebellion against Queen Mary):

> Peruse the Chronicles through, and you shall see that neuer rebellion attempted subjects against their prince and countrye from the begynning did euer prosper or had better successe, except the case of king Henry the fourth, who although he became a Prince; yet in his act was but a Rebell, for so I must call him. And though he prevayled for a time, yet it was not long, but that his heires were depriued and those that had right againe restored to the kingdome and crowne, and the vsurpation so sharpley revenged afterward in his bloud, as it well appeared that the long delaye of Gods vengeance was supplyed with more grieuous plague in the third and fourth generation. For the loue of God and all you Gentlemen that be here present, remember and be taught as well by examples past as also by this my present infelicity and most wretched case. (67)

Such accounts as this, recorded by Hall, Grafton, and others, confirm that English Renaissance historiographers "did not abandon the premises of . . . Christian historiog-raphy" (Ribner, *The English History Play* 20) but interpreted history, even in its individual details, as illustrative of the inseparability of the purposes of God and the Tudors. Furthermore, as Thomas Parrott and Robert Ball illustrate,

this interpretive framework and didactic method, as qualities of Renaissance historiography, were not limited to the
strictly historical works of the age. These were characteristics that were inherited from the medieval mystery, morality,
and miracle play traditions (10-23)—dramatic influences
upon Shakespeare so pronounced that, as noted earlier,
some critics have seen in such a play as *Henry IV* the
reflection, if not the actual substance, of the English morality play. Such a conclusion, moreover, is not incompatible
with Rossiter's contention that the designation of "moral
history" could be applied to Shakespeare's historical tetralogies, for within them is contained a "shadow show of a
greater drama [which] plays continually behind the
characters" (*Woodstock* 9).

The relationship of the mystery, morality, and miracle
play traditions to that of the history play has been extensively
documented, especially by A. P. Rossiter's *English Drama
from Early Times to the Elizabethans* (New York, 1950), M.
M. Reese's *The Cease of Majesty: A Study of Shakespeare's
History Plays* (New York, 1961), and Parrott and Ball's *A
Short View of Elizabethan Drama* (New York, 1943). Mary
Marshall has also identified the principal influence exerted
by the mystery plays upon the later histories as the mysteries'
ability—given their greater reliance upon the Old and New
Testaments rather than any other narrative source—to
"dramatiz[e] . . . the materials of sacred history" (991), and
Robert Weimann has acknowledged the more than coinciden-
tal characterization which links the qualities of the earlier
mysteries' Herod to the later histories' Richard III (69, 114).

Of the didactic element which figures so prominently in
the medieval drama, especially in the morality, Parrott and

Ball have written of its fusion with the other characteristics in the emerging genre of historical drama: "With the dawn of the Renaissance in England in the early years of the sixteenth century new types of the Moral begin to appear. The didactic purpose still remains, but the theme changes and the old ethical exhortation gives place to . . . political and theological propaganda" (19). Of the miracle tradition, they declare that "[though] the spirit of nationalsim that sprang up under the Tudors demanded historic and patriotic rather than sacred plays...even such masterpieces...as... Shakespeare's Histories show plainly remaining traces of the old miracle plays" (14)—including such presumably trace qualities of the miracle, broadly and perhaps too generally defined by Parrott and Ball as "strong and simple realism," "[no] attempt at historical accuracy," "some...fine poetry," "a great deal of lively dialogue," "a real sense of dramatic values," and "a genuine sincerity" (14). The miracle play, furthermore, could have reminded Shakespeare of the influence of the Church's liturgy in the shaping of his dramatic works in a manner that the folk play could not, for due to the more primitive character of the folk play and its inability to attain "the didactic, philosophical and political scope [of] the mature historical drama," the miracle play found itself to be the more accommodating genre model for the increasingly sophisticated demands of a mature theatre, a theatre which already had begun, through the emergence of the miracle tradition, to dramatize and humanize those articles of the Christian faith already well-known to the people through the Church's liturgical celebrations of the events of salvation history (Ribner, *The English History Play* 31).

A.P. Rossiter comments upon the dramatic evolution of

focus, technique, and quality of characterization within the
morality which gradually perfected the quality of the Renaissance history play (*English Drama* 115), and Ribner
likewise proposes that the York and Lancaster tetralogies
reflect a developed Christian philosophy of history patterned after the less specific and more general Christian
assumptions of the moralities (*The English History Play* 98).
In each tetralogy, for example, England labors under the
burden of her oppressive condition until first redeemed by
a "Henry." In the case of the Lancaster cycle, it is, of course,
Henry V, "the mirror of all Christian kings" [II Chorus 6],
who prefigures the fuller salvation of England by another
Henry—Henry Tudor; and it is Henry Tudor's destiny to
triumph over Richard III, the Evil One who, more fully than
any other Shakespearean despot, reflects the traditional
iconography associated with the Prince of Darkness ("one
that hath ever been God's enemy" [*Richard III* V.iii.252]).
Of the histories' indebtedness to their dramatic predecessors, Eugene Waith comments that "several scholars [have
seen] that the forms of the histories could be traced back to
medieval mystery plays, which presented Old and New
Testament history, and to morality plays, in which the moral
encounters of mankind were represented allegorically . . .
[and] the morality plays," he continues, "provided examples
of a new kind of drama where theme rather than story
determined the organization" (Introduction 7). Thematic
integrity rather than sequential continuity, therefore, offers
itself as the more important structural lens through which to
view the histories and evaluate their purpose.

Substantiating many of these observations is Campbell's
own examination of English Renaissance histories in which

she attests to the prominence of the polemical content and selective point of view utilized in the writing of histories— not only Shakespeare's, but those of other historians as well. In demonstration of this point, she directs us to the example of Thomas More's *History of Richard the Third* and its subsequent redaction by Richard Grafton, observing that while More's history is clearly the work of a Christian humanist, Grafton's edition of the play in Hardyng's *Chronicle* of 1543 reveals the authorial hand of a distinctively Reformation humanist ("English History" 21-23). Though as a devout Roman Catholic and eventual martyr for the cause of the Roman Church in England, More, suggests Henry Kelly, would have eschewed any Anglican interpretation of the events of Richard's reign, but he nonetheless probably would have agreed substantially with most of Grafton's interpretation of Richard's monarchy and likely would have had little quarrel with the substance of John Rous's *Historia regum Angliae*, a work which compares Richard's tyranny to that of Antichrist to come, a theme substantially reflected in Shakespeare's own work (71).

Henry Wells and H. H. Anniah Gouda warn that, when reading these histories, we need to be especially attentive to the infusion of this theological dimension from the moralities into the histories and acknowledge that religious ideas derived therefrom controlled much of the chroniclers' evaluation of the lives and reigns of former monarchs (87). Katherine Bates agrees, too, that the history play descends in large part, both in content and form, from the English morality tradition, as the morality play eventually became "less and less dramatic and more and more controversial, usually in support of the Reformed faith" (203). Shakespeare, therefore, like his contemporaries, wrote as a man of public religious conviction; as Cornelius van der Spek contends, "The advent of the Reformation and the struggle between the old Church and the new gave rise to the polemical play. Just as in the fifteenth century the stage had been made an instrument for teaching biblical history, it was now made to serve the purpose of religious and political controversy" (173). Fredson Bowers also maintains that a transcendent purpose attends these histories and that all of Shakespeare's sophistication of plot and design is meaningless "unless the action . . . form[s] something larger than itself in total effect . . . ." To contend otherwise, he proposes, is akin to suggesting that "Milton [wrote] *Paradise Lost* and then put in the theology" ("Theme and Structure" 43). Robert Fitch has more specifically suggested, however, that that which disappointed Roman Catholic readers of Shakespeare have called Shakespeare's theological "triomphe de l'équivoque" (Looten 60) is actually nothing less than Anglicanism (19), and Paul Stapfer has confirmed that "Shakespeare était *plus que protestant* . . . Il est aussi loin d'eux que du pape; à la distance où il voit et le pape et Luther et Calvin, Shakespeare est effrayé de leur petitesse" (231), a conclusion with which Fitch also finds himself in substantial agreement, declaring, in *Shakespeare: The Perspective of Value*, that "the religion that runs through the histories . . . that is the matrix out of which all else comes, must be called Catholic Anglicanism" (81).

Tolstoy is reputed to have said, "The theatre is man's strongest pulpit" (Hall)—and given that the English Renaissance stage and Anglican pulpit sometimes were, quite literally, in close proximity to each other—plays often were performed in the naves and chancels of churches as well as on the public stage, even in the seventeenth century (Bucknell 67)—the continuity of symbolic content and pedagogical intent between the explicitly religious drama and the marginally secular public theatre demonstrates the secular stage's assimilation of many of the conventions bequeathed it by the religious dramatic tradition (Weimann 104). The Elizabethan stage therefore sought not only to enlighten and tutor its audiences in political ideology but also to instruct in the religious convictions of the day, an aim evident not only in the theological supports upon which foundation the intricacies of the Tudor Myth were constructed but discernible in the rhetoric and iconography of the theatre as well. G. R. Owst's analysis of the histories sees the Yorkist and Lancaster plays as representative of a universal religious theme that pervades all Shakespearean drama: the terrifying consequence of sin in human affairs (592), and Tibor Rlaniczay even more broadly considers the effects of the Protestant Reformation, in particular, to be singularly significant in the development of whole national literatures—among which works the Shakespearean English histories are representative: "Die Reformation . . . wurde in so viele Ländern zur Geburtsstunde der Literatur . . . die auf Errungenschaften der Renaissance und des Humanismus aufbauten" (144).

These same histories, which Professor Lindley Hubbell calls "England's greatest spiritual possession" (224) and which Martin Lings suggests belong to the "treasury of Christian civilization" (121) are not universally perceived to be such readily apparent repositories of the medieval or Renaissance religious traditions, however. One who divorces Shakespeare's drama from its otherwise almost universally

acknowledged didactic presumptions in religion is Roland
Frye; he contends that "[Shakespeare's] references to the
commonplace topics of theology are never introduced into
the drama for doctrinaire reasons, and the action of the play
is never subservient to the presentation of any systematic
theology" (*Shakespeare* 9).[11] David Gwilymn Jones suggests
that Elizabethan dramatists in general, and Shakespeare in
particular, "did not think as Christians" (91), and of
Shakespeare's commitment to any specific expression of the
Christian faith, Jones, like his predecessor, George Santayana,
contends that "Shakespeare set himself to divest his play of
any framework of Christian belief and deliberately denied
himself any occasion for its expression" (120-21).[12] Representative of the liberal criticism of the 1920s, John Masefield
similarly declares that "religion meant almost nothing to
[Shakespeare] . . . superstition very much indeed" (10).
Somewhat more temperately, Sylvan Barnet, in "Some
Limitations of a Christian Approach to Shakespeare"—
though reluctant to acknowledge any identifiably Christian character to Shakespearean drama—nonetheless
concedes that "Christian sentiments abound in
Shakespeare's dramas, especially the history plays" (204),
and he acknowledges, too, that a study of Anglican
liturgy will disclose at least a choreographic relationship
between the drama of the Elizabethan stage and the
ritual of the Church (201).

In his use of religious rhetoric and iconography, others,
according to Jonathon Crawford, have seen in Shakespeare
something less of the Anglican theologian and more of the
Tudor politician, and these critics (unnamed by Crawford
but represented by such scholars as Graham Holderness and

John Dollimore) contend that to the extent that any religious qualities can be discerned in the histories, their function is intended to be purely utilitarian and their capacity entirely political; Shakespeare's introduction of theological ideas, Crawford implies, was pursued solely to consolidate the authority of a regime, the legitimacy of which was not beyond serious question. Given the propositions of the Tudor Myth, these critics, according to Professor Crawford, contend that Shakespeare pragmatically recognized the ability of religion, skillfully applied, to elicit (if not command) a needed obedience and fidelity to the persons and institutions of Elizabethan society, and these critics, he alleges, suggest that Shakespeare thereby hoped to advance a common identity among the people by urging and affirming the successful establishment and maintenance of a government whose authority should be regarded as possessive of no less mandate than that of heaven itself ("The Importance of the Supernatural"). Similarly affirmative of the role of the supernatural in the achievement of Shakespeare's purposes in the histories (especially within the Lancaster cycle) are Derek Traversi's remarks that "the political thought expressed in [the Lancaster plays] combines the fervent nationalism of the day, fostered for practical ends by the ruling dynasty, with sacramental notions of monarchy more venerable than itself" (*Shakespeare* 2). And Roy Battenhouse, too, has argued that Shakespeare was perhaps less exclusively a cold and indifferent propagandist for the Tudors than a conventional interpreter of historical process under the guidance of Providence, as this guidance was thought to operate according to the traditional canons of Christian thought ("Revising Tillyard").

Such a critical position as Battenhouse's does not destroy, negate, or ignore the essential indivisibility of theological and political thought in Tudor doctrine; rather, it allows for Shakespeare's affirmation of the political character of the doctrine without disallowing, in an excess of secularist zeal, the existence of the specifically Anglican theology which suffuses so much of the Tudor mythology that theologically legitimates that dynasty's adoption of the Royal Supremacy, i.e., the doctrine which affirms the sovereignty of the English monarch over Church as well as State—a position anathematized by Roman Catholicism at the Council of Trent as nothing less than the coarse, political usurpation of sovereign pontifical authority which properly belongs to Rome (*Canons and Decrees* 168-69). However, in response to Roman claims to the contrary, the Royal Supremacy was affirmed by the Anglican Church in the Thirty-nine Articles as not only politic but catholic—and its definition and promulgation a "prerogative which," as Thomas quotes from the Thirty-Nine Articles, "we see to have been given always to all godly Princes . . . [who] should rule all states and degrees committed to their charge by God, whether they be Ecclesiastical or Temporal . . . [for] the Bishop of Rome hath no jurisdiction in this realm of *England*" [461]).

Other approaches to the histories contend for the fundamentally Christian character of these plays. Michael Quinn sees the unfolding of a providential will in both tetralogies, though he acknowledges that it is more evident in the Lancaster cycle than in the Yorkist plays (45-52). J. A. Bryant writes that Shakespeare's philosophical temperament is "derived from a catholic and Christian view of life . . ." *(Hippolyta's View* vii); Roy Battenhouse agrees and urges that Shakespeare's plays are "Christian" because they are "profoundly revelatory of human experience[s] . . . as only a Christian can portray these" ("Shakespearean Tragedy" 98). Francis Fergusson declares that Shakespeare, like his contemporaries, "read history . . . in the faith that God spoke through it" (*Trope and Allegory* 77-78). Harold S. Wilson maintains that "[Shakespeare's] Christian point of view *does* materially influence his representation of life . . ." (7) and declares that "the quality of Shakespeare's Christian faith, as it is reflected in the plays, is the quality of Edmund Spenser's faith as it is reflected in *The Fairie Queene,* or that of Richard Hooker's faith as it is reflected in "The *Laws of Ecclesiastical Polity* . . ." (217).

Such scholars see the world of Shakespeare's histories not as the "moral order" of A.C. Bradley (26)—a world guided by a seemingly indifferent obedience to some nameless, ultimate compulsion—but rather a world wherein the Elizabethan playgoer witnesses the extension of a providential hand—which is to say God—the work of whom does not coerce but rather invites belief. They contend that Shakespeare's world, especially as it is drawn in the histories, is not the world of those less artful Christian polemics which attempt to articulate a philosophy of life that trumpets Christian propositions and bludgeons the reader into adopting the author's sectarian sensibilities, for to say that Shakespeare's plays impart a distinctive Christian vision is not to say that they give object lessons in Christian doctrine. It is to say, with Paul Siegel, that Shakespeare's drama "is an expression of the dominant Christian humanist ideology of his time in its representation of human life as part of a divinely appointed cosmological, social and psychological order . . ." (*Shakespeare in His Times* 56), for the lingering medieval conviction of Shakespeare's age "was that Religion was co-terminous with life and conduct . . . [and] there was nothing which could rightly be excluded intentionally from Religion" (Cormican, "Medieval Idiom in Shakespeare [I]" 189-90).

No artistic work, Siegel suggests, lacks vision, conviction, purpose, and design, for all art, *as* art, imposes an interpretive order upon life that shapes our experience of life and invites us to see our world in new ways (*Shakespeare in His Times* 3)—a view which opposes Martin Esslin's contention that "it is one of the roots of Shakespeare's universality that his work seems totally free of any ideological position" (xviii). Siegel's posture therefore agrees with R. W. Chambers's testimony that "the great poets speak to all time only through the language, conventions, and beliefs of their own age" (279) and affirms Northrop Frye's observation that "any given literature is rooted in a specific culture and is contained by the mythological structure of that culture" (*A Study of English Romanticism* 46).

Of Shakespeare's theology, in particular, W. Moelwyn Merchant finds it curious that so many elect not to consider it, "as though the existence of credal assumptions in a dramatist's work implied a crippling limitation of his creative power" ("Shakespeare's Theology" 72)[13]—a reluctance which many critics find all the more difficult to understand given the cultic origins of the classical theatrical tradition in Dionysian ritual (Brockett 17). In fact, the Shakespearean histories significantly demonstrate their continuity with ancient Hellenic theatre not only in their preservation of a theological context for the work but also in their presentation of the monarch as a unifying symbol, "the visible center of the traditional world order," a monarch whose function in Shakespeare is not unlike the role assumed by the king in Sophoclean drama: "ruler, high priest, and father of the community" (Fergusson, *The Idea of the Theatre* 117). Indeed, as Fergusson continues to note in a later work, in Shakespearean drama, "the monarch is a figure of God whose character reveals 'the form and pressure' of his time . . . . Faith in the ruler and his right government is therefore a religious faith . . ." (*Trope and Allegory* 71-72).

This sacred character of the king, contends Martha Fleischer, was emblemized on the Shakespearean stage, among other devices, not only by his robes of state but with "regal badges which suggest[ed] an association with Christ, communal head of the mystical body the church . . ." (277), a not insignificant association to nourish for a monarchy which Parliament had declared to be the appointed temporal seat of authority for the Church as well as the State. Indeed, as John Shaw reminds us in his essay on *1 Henry IV,* that the Shakespearean stage was an emblematic one in general is widely conceded (61). The Shakespearean stage, too, writes Fergusson, symbolically restructured the conventional scheme of the universe and thus became a means in miniature by which the events of human experience, physical and metaphysical alike, could be effectively dramatized (*The Idea of a Theatre* 116) with much the same mingling of secular and sacred realities as was produced in the ancient dithyramb, wherein dramatic performance closely approximated the sacred, ritual action of Dionysiac worship (Brockett 17-18). And, as we have learned from the discovery of contemporary drawings and archeological evidence, the physical character of the Elizabethan playhouse possessed an architecturally stately quality, a feature which not only accommodated the creation of a regal atmosphere so necessary for the staging of the histories, but which also allowed for the theatrical replication of the patterned and hierarchically-ordered structure of the universe;[14] as Robert Weimann puts it, "[W]hile the Elizabethan theatre did not strive to create a visual illusion of actuality, it did attempt to imitate nature, albeit in poetically heightened terms" (216). Just as the essential harmony of the universe—the musical score of the cosmic dance—was thought to be reflected (or intended to be reflected) in the institutions and offices of the temporal order, the conventions of the Elizabethan stage and its appointments would therefore reasonably be expected by Shakespeare's audience to demonstrate the theatre's participation in a delicately balanced universal order which, if it could not be perceived, at least could be believed (Tillyard, *The Elizabethan World Picture* 88-89).

Bernard Beckerman has written that in their drama, "Elizabethans did not expect particular realism but [the exposition of] universal truths" (28). Figural types and representative characters were familiar to the Elizabethan audience, principally because of the tradition of the morality play; non-Shakespearean drama that yet would be watched by Shakespearean audiences were crafted with little concern for satisfying such forthcoming Neo-classical theatrical requirements as rigorous dramatic conformity to Aristotelian doctrine; the cultivation of realism in the presentation of psychology, situation, plot, and character; attention to verisimilitude in staging; and an extensive use of properties.

Rather, most Elizabethan plays, in their repetition of the verities of the age and in their allusive capacity as works derived from familiar lessons of the Elizabethan Homilies and Holy Writ, fulfilled their fundamentally didactic function within an essentially emblematic theatrical universe. Confirming the Renaissance stage's retention of its medieval purpose, J. L. Styan writes: "The symmetry of the stage, the ceremonial of its theatrical tradition, . . . and its norm of poetic speech all encouraged the allusive qualities in Elizabethan drama" (*Shakespeare's Stagecraft* 211), for the power to "suffuse a scene with . . . emblematic meaning" required but modest manipulation of the drama: the introduction of a special prop, the formation of a familiar tableau, or the considered placement of a particular speech (Smith, "Perspectives" 57).

Knight argues that the Shakespearean stage was more than ceremonial; it was a ritual universe, to which, especially with the history plays, "we must bring a sense of the sacramental" (*Shakespearean Production* 150). These plays sought to reincarnate the past and give it not only heightened but transcendent significance. As Noel Purdon tells us, "Shakespeare insists on his right to . . . tell tales that are demonstrably 'untrue' but which possess higher value than 'truth'" (204). In the Lancaster cycle, Shakespeare's purpose is more than historical; it is mythical, and as Northrop Frye recognizes, "the real interest of myth is to draw a circumference around a human community and look inward toward that community" (*The Great Code* 37). Shakespeare draws that circle around the reigns of Richard II, Henry IV, and Henry V, shaping them into a history of England that evokes correspondence with the sacred history of Israel which awaits the coming of a Messiah in the lineage of

David, and he invites his audience to see a reflection of David's rise and glorious reign in the ascent and reign of Henry V—types each of even greater kings and kingdoms to come (Evett 139-61).

Such characterization was not uncommon on the Elizabethan stage. Huston Diehl points out that characterization in Elizabethan drama, though less symbolic and more realistic than its medieval counterpart, nevertheless retained a largely symbolic function, for the purposes of Renaissance drama were neither purely modern and naturalistic nor entirely medieval and allegorical, despite the contentions of psychological critics of the former view and symbolist critics of the latter ("Iconography and Characterization" 20). As Robert Weimann contends, "On the basis of popular stage practice and experience the leading English dramatists of the early sixteenth century . . . began to adapt the medieval heritage to the themes of the Reformation . . ." (104). English Renaissance drama endeavored to combine the individual definition of personality which characterizes realistic theatre with the less realistic and more symbolic dimensions of character conveyed by the medieval stage. Consequently, notes Weimann, the characters of the English Renaissance stage, though singular in their identities, are never *just* their given identities (11). Irving Ribner likewise argues that "[Elizabethan] dramatists are always more interested in mankind than in individual men . . . . They rarely hesitate to sacrifice the consistency of character portraiture to the needs of larger symbolic statement" ("Elizabethan Action" 154).

In Shakespeare's history plays, for example, Richard is Richard, but he is also more than Richard; and Hal is Hal, although he is sometimes more than Hal. Objection to this inherence of simultaneous identities within a particular dramatic character reflects not only a representative modern insistence upon the establishment of sharply-defined distinctions that admit of few ambiguities or uncomfortable complexities, but such objections also inaccuratsly suggest that the characters of the Renaissance stage were less emblematic and less suited to multiple dramatic purpose than their medieval theatrical forbearers; indeed, Huston Diehl sees this "modern tendency to divide what the Renaissance saw as indivisible" as a limited and limiting perspective which disallows the possibility of affirming that "a character can simultaneously be a realistic individual *and* a symbolic abstraction" ("Iconography and Characterization" 12).

Furthermore, the refusal to recognize that Renaissance characters were fashioned to variable purpose negates the possibility of considering that Shakespeare could have had any goal in his composition other than the intent to create either a simplistic narrative drama or a vast, arcane allegorical enterprise of the type described by Lily Campbell's *Shakespeare's Histories: Mirrors of Elizabethan Policy*. However, Ribner has written that "to conceive of the [history] play as an elaborate allegory makes little sense" (*English History Play* 186), and Phyllis Rackin reminds us that the complex, multi-faceted English Renaissance theatre was the "theatre of a world of transition [and] the English Renaissance stage offered a field of contention for competing ideologies" ("Androgyny" 32).

Clearly, Shakespeare was open to many dramatic possibilities, especially in character creation. As Christopher

Baker emphasizes, "the Tudor and Stuart playwrights . . . routinely fuse individual character with Platonic essence, thereby satisfying both the tendency to individualize and particularize and the tendency to personify and typify" (68-69). John Steadman notes that by treating characters which could emblemize more than their literal selves and still not be rigid allegorical constructs, Shakespeare was able to open his drama to almost unlimited polemical possibilities, creating "vehicles for moral and political persuasion, alchemical and Platonic doctrine, religious instruction and devotion" (51), a point also affirmed by those who acknowledge that religious instruction is assuredly one of the principal purposes of the Lancastrian Tetralogy and that, in this respect, Shakespeare would hardly be unique among Elizabethan authors (Collins vii).[15]

In the history plays then, Shakespeare's intent is of infinitely less importance to us than the plays' content. Though we could speculate about Shakespeare's intentions, we ought not be persuaded by that which is too much reliant on conjecture. We cannot presume to know Shakespeare's mind. We can demonstrate, however, that Shakespeare's achievements are coincident with those of writers of similar works of the age; and we can illustrate the interrelatedness of textual and sacred traditions which, in turn, can suggest to us that in the Lancastrian Tetralogy, a new salvation history does unfold—an epic in miniature of a nation's peril and rescue.

In 1993, criticism of Shakespeare's histories promises to be revitalized by this renewed appreciation for the relationship between a text and its context, as well as by a growing conviction among scholars for approaches to Shakespearean studies which embrace the convictions of historical-critical method. Alan Hager's newest work (*Shakespeare's Political Animal: Schema and Schemata in the Canon* [Newark, 1990]) is only the latest study to confirm what Edward Pechter announced through *PMLA* in 1987: we are now entering a post-structuralist age in Renaissance literary criticism which is distinguished from its predecessor eras by a regenerate interest in the diachronics of literature and the "rehistoricization" of texts (Hager 12; Pechter 292). To this newly reinvigorated sensibility and critical commitment in literary inquiry, this book offers its insights in the exploration of Shakespeare's Reformation apologetic on behalf of the Crown in the cause of the Church.

Notes

[1]For example, of the Bolingbroke plays, Dr. Johnson writes:

> Perhaps no author has ever in two plays [*1 Henry IV* and *2 Henry IV*] afforded so much delight. The great events are interesting, for the fate of kingdoms depends upon them; the slighter occurrences are diverting, and except for one or two, sufficiently probable; the incidents are multiplied with wonderful fertility of invention, and the characters diversified with the utmost nicety of discernment, and the profoundest skill in the nature of man. (*Selections* 187)

He says, too, of *Henry V*:

> This play has many scenes of high dignity, and many of easy merriment . . . . The lines given to the chorus have many admirers; but the truth is, that in them little may be praised, and much must be forgiven [although] the great defect of the play is the emptiness and narrowness of the last act, which a very little diligence might have easily avoided. (*Selections* 206)

Pope is somewhat less effusive about Shakespeare's Lancastrian histories, but he attributes Shakespeare's weaknesses to his "wrong judgments" as an actor rather than as a playwright, and he does concede that *Henry V*, especially, is very fine, "much improved" over those chronicle plays of Henry V which preceded Shakespeare's composition (165).

John Dryden, however, compliments Shakespeare rather less than either Dr. Johnson or Pope, and he especially chastises Shakespeare's creation of the character of Falstaff, for he sees in the fat knight little redeeming merit or moral weight; and while Dryden acknowledges the comic hilarity of Sir John, yet he disclaims any enduring measure of worth in Falstaff, for the Ancients, he contends, eschewed such vulgar, low comedy as Falstaff personifies (*Essays* 84-85). Indeed, even of the general structure of his plays, Pope advises his contemporaries to qualify their praise of Shakespeare by recognizing the more primitive character of his drama; he writes that "one may look upon his works, in comparison of those that are more finished and regular, as upon an ancient majestic piece of Gothic architecture, compared with a neat modern building . . ." (175).

A review of some of the representative criticism of the Augustan era can be surveyed in Johnson's famous "Preface to Shakespeare" in *Samuel Johnson: Rasselas, Poems, and Selected Prose*. 3rd ed. Ed. Bertrand H. Bronson. (New York: Holt, Rinehart and Winston, 1958: 261-307); W. K. Wimsatt, Jr.'s edition of *Samuel Johnson on Shakespeare* (New York: Hill and Wang, 1960); Pope's "Preface to the Works of Shakespeare" in *Literary Criticism of Alexander Pope*. Ed. Bernard A. Goldgar. (Lincoln: U of Nebraska P, 1965. 161-75); and Dryden's *An Essay of Dramatic Poesy* (Oxford, 1899). James Blickenderfer also prints a useful survey of Augustan criticism in *The Eighteenth Century* (New York: Scribner's, 1929) as does Paul Siegel in the essay "Change and Continuity in Shakespearean Criticism" published in the critical anthology, *His Infinite Variety: Major Shakespearean Criticism Since Johnson*. Ed. Paul N. Siegel. (Philadelphia: J. B. Lippincott, 1964: 1-5).

[2]Coleridge, for example, observes that *Richard II* is a rare example of the "purely historical play," although this quality is not attributable to the

> quantity of historical events [in *Richard*] compared
> with the fictions, for there is as much history in
> *Macbeth* as in *Richard* . . . . In [*Richard*, however]
> the history *informs* the plot; in the mixt [tragicom-
> edies] it *directs* it; in the rest, as *Macbeth, Hamlet,
> Cymbeline, Lear*, it subserves it. (221)

Coleridge notes, too, that in his opinion, the whole of the
Lancaster cycle, though vast in scope, constitutes no epic,
because Shakespeare's history does not conform to the
conventions of epic, a chief characteristic of which is man
humbled under the power of Destiny (a conclusion by
Coleridge which assuredly is defensible, especially given the
unqualified triumphalism of *Henry V*):

> In the epic a pre-announced fate gradually adjusts
> and employs the will and the incidents as its instru-
> ments (επομαι, *sequor*), while the drama places fate
> and will in opposition and is then most perfect when
> the victory of fate is obtained in consequence of
> imperfections in the opposing will, so as to leave the
> final impression that the fate itself is but a higher and
> more intelligent Will . . . . In epic, the prominent
> character is ever under [the direction of fate] . . . . When
> accidents are introduced, they are the results of causes
> over which . . . will has no power. (221, 238)

William Hazlitt, another Romantic critic, is more particular and less congratulatory in his focus, however: he
dislikes Henry V as a man and *Henry V* as a play, for Henry's
ethics, Hazlitt suggests, are guided by "brute force, glossed
over with a little religious hypocrisy and archiepiscopal [sic]
advice" (157). Though Hazlitt in 1817 offered this rebuttal
in opposition to the general praise of his fellow Romantic

critics, his tone and focus upon moral considerations in evaluating a work of art are rather more characteristically Victorian. Still, John Crawford considers "the most denunciatory of Romantics critics [to be] John Masefield [who] accuses Henry [V] of . . . emotional and intellectual insensitivity, and in general of possessing a personality unlike that of Hamlet" (131); but Crawford's evaluation of Masefield as a legitimate representative of the Romantic critics is highly arguable, for Masefield did not live or write during the Romantic Era, even though his work, in many respects, demonstrates fidelity to the spirit of the Romantic critical tradition. For a fuller investigation of Romantic criticism of Shakespeare, consult John Crawford's *Romantic Criticism of Shakespearean Drama* (Salzburg: Institute fur Englische Sprache and Literatur, 1978).

[3]Aron Stavisky's *Shakespeare and the Victorians* (Norman: U of Oklahoma P, 1969) is an extensive and fairly comprehensive study of major Victorian criticism of Shakespeare. Thomas Carlyle's noteworthy Victorian essay, "The Poet and the Prophet" (not included in the Stavisky collection) is also worth reading and can be found in Robert Peter's edition of *Victorians on Literature and Art* (New York: Appleton-Century-Crofts, 1961)17-24.

[4]Oscar Wilde, a contemporary of Kingsley and Dowden (though less the representative Victorian and more the Aesthete), chides such critical perspectives as those of Kingsley and Dowden in his reminder to the editor of *The Scots Observer* that

> an artist, sir, has no ethical sympathies at all. Virtue and wickedness are to him simply what the colors on his palette are to the painter. They are no more, and

they are no less. He sees that by their means a certain artistic effect can be produced and he produces it. Iago may be morally horrible and Imogen stainlessly pure. Shakespeare, as Keats said, had as much delight in creating the one as he had in creating the other. (qtd. in Hyde, *Oscar Wilde* 118)

[5]See Harold Jenkins, "Shakespeare's History Plays: 1900-51," in *Shakespeare Survey* 6 (1953) 1-15.

[6]Consult Dennis H. Burden, "Shakespeare's History Plays: 1952-83," in *Shakespeare Survey* 38 (1985) 1-18.

[7]As the Elizabethan homily, *Against Disobedience and Willful Rebellion,* proclaims, "A rebel is worse than the worst prince, and rebellion worse than the worst government of the worst prince" (114).

[8]Tillyard defines the myth cultivated by the Tudors as "a scheme fundamentally religious, by which events [were believed to] evolve under a law of justice and under the ruling of God's Providence, and of which Elizabeth's England was the acknowledged outcome" (*Shakespeare's History Plays* 320-21). See also note 9 (below).

[9]The Tudor myth (more fully discussed in its doctrinal intricacies in Tillyard's *Shakespeare's History Plays* [London: Chatto and Windus, 1944] in Ribner's *The English History Play in the Age of Shakespeare* [New York: Octagon, 1979] 104-06; in Leonard Dean's "Tudor Theories of History Writing" in *University of Michigan Contributions in Modern Philology* 1 [1941] 24; in Henry Ansgar Kelly's *Divine Providence in the England of Shakespeare's Histories* [Cambridge: Harvard UP, 1970]; and elsewhere) has been accepted by most Shakespearean scholars as evident, not only in Shakespeare's York and Lancaster plays, but also

within those "intensely nationalistic" and "deliberately propagandistic" prose histories of Shakespeare's day (Ribner, *The English History Play* 2). However, reservations about the Tudor myth's prevalence in Shakespeare and other Renaissance literatures have been raised by John Wilders (*The Lost Garden: A View of Shakespeare's English and Roman History Plays* [Totowa, NJ: Rowman and Littlefield, 1978] and M. M. Reese *The Cease of Majesty: A Study of Shakespeare's History Plays* [New York: St. Martin's, 1961]). Wilders, however, though rejecting the concept of providential design in the plays and contending instead that Shakespeare writes as an agnostic and ironist, concedes that "the history plays, especially *Richard II* onwards, do communicate . . . the sense of destiny, however incomprehensible, which frustrates [Shakespeare's] characters of their hopes and even, at times, assists them in hastening their own dooms" (75). M. M. Reese offers troublesome (because conflicting) assessments of Shakespeare's work: he argues, for example, that Shakespeare's plays invite no search for profound meaning, for they were written merely to "turn human actions into poetry" and were intended to impart no "moralizing dogmas and system of thought" (*The Cease of Majesty* 91); yet Reese contradictorily offers the proposition that the "feeling for order and stability everywhere evident in Shakespeare's plays was an expression of his deepest moral convictions" (91), and he furthermore declares that "it is surely a grave misunderstanding of his purpose to suppose that the great cycle of English historical drama was written just as a poetic exercise" (111). Reese also acknowledges Shakespeare's debts to Edward Hall ("the laureate of the Reformation aristocracy" [51]), the Elizabethan homilists, and *The Mirror for Magistrates,* asserting that with these writers and works, "he [Shakespeare] took his stand" (91). Thus, even the few skeptics of Shakespeare's commitment to the Tudor myth do not maintain their position with consistency.

[10]Wilde also supported these observations on literary aesthetics in a letter to the *St. James Gazette,* published on 26 June 1890, wherein he declared: "The function of the artist is to invent, not to chronicle . . . . Life by its realism is always spoiling the subject-matter of art. The supreme pleasure in literature is to realize the nonexistent" (222). It is difficult to imagine a statement about the role of the artist to which the Tudors could have been more receptive—presuming, of course, that the imaginative mythology conceived by the artist harmonized with the political purposes and vision of the sovereign.

[11]Frye may reach his conclusion because more aggressively doctrinaire dramas were not wanting in Elizabethan England. Quasi-dramatic popular celebrations rooted in specific doctrinal beliefs were so frequent in Reformation England that even the less refined spectacles (such as the cult of the "boy bishop" which dramatized the doctrine of the *communicatio idiomatum*) were tolerated and tacitly approved by the Church (Luxton 61), despite the Church's apprehensions of the capacity of such plays to trivialize or distort doctrine.

[12]Santayana inaugurated a minor school of Shakespearean criticism (which culminated in the rise of the largely secularist school of criticism of the 20s) by writing in 1900 that "Shakespeare [was] remarkable

among the greater poets for being without a philosophy and without a religion" (163). Few critics today, of course, share Santayana's presumptions about Shakespeare's dramatic work. Indeed, any contention offered in the late twentieth century that would propose a similar thesis would be received with no inconsiderable measure of surprise.

[13]Even Roland Frye, no sympathizer with Christian readings of Shakespeare, considers Shakespeare "an intelligent and maturely informed layman, whose citation of theological doctrines . . . shows an easy and intimate familiarity with Christian theology" (*Shakespeare* 13).

[14]Perhaps the most authoritative—yet dated and not unquestioned—study of the physical character of the Elizabethan playhouse is John Cranford Adams's *The Globe Playhouse: Its Design and Equipment.* (2nd ed. 1942. New York: Barnes and Noble, 1961). Though yet the definitive study is its field, some of Adams's assumptions, especially those respecting his contention that the Globe and like theatres possessed inner and third level stages, have been occasionally challenged in recent years, however.

[15]Herbert Coursen, for example, has written that "Shakespeare's use of ritual within his plays emanates from his belief in the validity of the Prayer Book's version of Communion, Marriage, and Baptism. Shakespeare knew that many of his spectators were conditioned to respond—perhaps even subliminally—to certain configurations within his scenes and plays, basic rituals imitated or refracted, whose service only hints at the archetype beneath" ("Sacramental Elements" 8); and he

stresses elsewhere that "Elizabethan drama, particularly Shakespeare's . . . , explor[es] the sacramental possibilities of characters within worlds predicated on the Christian dynamic and represented most profoundly by the Communion Service" (*Christian Ritual* 22).

Chapter Two

Richard the Second:

Descent into the Abyss

"See how belief may suffer by foul show!"—*Pericles*

Of all the plays in the Lancastrian Tetralogy, none is more deeply inlaid with the iconography of the sacramental and decorated with the rhetoric of sacred tradition than is *Richard the Second*. The first of four plays devoted to the triumph of the Anglican ideal, *Richard the Second* "employ[s] a highly emblematic style and depend[s] heavily on religious iconography and stage spectacle" (Fleischer, 269-70).[1] But it is not Richard who emblemizes the Anglican ideal; rather, he is sculpted, among other things, into a figure of pretentious Roman tyranny—a personification of medieval Catholic imperiousness and affectation. Richard, therefore, in this play, is only occasionally emblematic of Christ, whose person as temporal head of the Church of England he would anachronistically represent to Elizabethan audiences; instead, during much of the play, he is a figure of disorder and willful rebellion against the very state that he has been commissioned by sacred rite to serve. In effect, at such times, he is a reflection of Satan—one who would subvert divinely established authority[2] for the satisfaction of power; in short, he becomes a tyrant, and in this regard Paul Siegel comments:

> The antithesis of the Christian prince is the tyrant. The tyrant is unable to rule others, for he is unable to rule himself. Swayed by his emotions rather than governed by his reason, he rules not in accordance with the natural law . . . but in accordance with his arbitrary will. In doing so, he [like Satan] revolts against God, whose deputy he is, and disrupts the moral order of the universe. (*Shakespearean Tragedy* 50)

As Honor Matthews continues, "Shakespeare accepted the myth of Lucifer's rebellion as the archetype of sin and . . . found an acceptable reflection of it in the history of his own country" (14). Richard's deposition, then, is accomplished by Shakespeare against the familiar background of sacred tradition ("[H]eaven hath a hand in these events," as the Duke as York attests [V.ii.37]). Richard's fall from the throne in Shakespeare's play is couched in imagery and rhetoric as fully resplendent as Satan's meteoric fall from heaven is bright ("headlong flaming from th' ethereal sky," as Milton imagines it [*Paradise Lost* I.45]). Both Richard and Satan, though much to be pitied, receive, however, according to Anglican moral calculus, the only just consequence of rebellion. Richard's fall, therefore, is "a second fall of cursed man" (III.iv.76); and, as William Armstrong indicates, "[t]he terrible fate of tyrants is a pre-eminent example of the computative justice which so many Protestant moralists of the Renascence believed to operate in human affairs" (176).[3]

Richard II, however, does not altogether despair of the titular king's qualities. Shakespeare does strive to provide us with a limited iconography of Richard as Christ,[4] especially during the time of the king's trial, passion and death (see esp. IV.i.239-42 and cf. with St. Matthew 27:24); to this end, the sumptuous regal verse and stately ceremonial scenes of the play also contribute much. Indeed, Gordon Ripling contends that "the pageantry does not merely compare Richard to Christ, rather, it stages Richard's epiphany as a type of Christ" (90). We also sometimes see Richard as Adam—one to whom a kingdom not unlike Eden (II.i.42) is entrusted but who loses it because of his weakness. In these respects, J. A. Bryant concludes that "[w]hat Shakespeare [gives us] in this presentation of Richard [is] a sort of Adam-Christ [through whom we see developed] nothing less than a typological interpretation of history"' ("The Linked Analogies" 426).

A typological interpretation of history attempts to adduce correspondences between events of past and present significance in order to illustrate the continuity within time of those qualities which, once established as significant or normative in human experience, endure in the signs, symbols, and rhetoric of later generations. Typology, writes Northrop Erye, is "a form of rhetoric, . . . a mode of thought [that] both assumes and leads to . . . a theory of . . . historical process: an assumption that there is some meaning and point to history tin which] some event or events will occur which will indicate what that meaning or point is . . . " (*The Great Code* 80-81). As such, in typological drama, historical persons and events are fashioned so as to "link the present moment to the past [and] typological[ly] fulfill the figures of the past" (Bergeron 97).

Richard, for one, serves such a purpose in this particular historical drama ("Thus play I in one person many people" [V.v.31]), as do other characters of the Lancaster cycle

whom Shakespeare either invents or endows with significance that transcends actual circumstances or historical
experience. Richard, in Richard II, is therefore frequently
more than Richard; he is, as Nicholas Howe suggests, a
character held in apposition (175); he is by turns a type of
Adam, type of Christ, type of Satan; he is sometimes even
the personified type of medieval Catholicism itself—a
nefarious foreign deceit of nothing less than demonic
quality in Reformation appraisal—an appraisal of sixteenth-
century Catholicism which Shakespeare demonstrably shares,
or at least conveys, through his drama. A. L. Rowse, for
example, writes that the convictions of Shakespeare were
"deeply Christian, Anglican, normally Protestant [perhaps
with more precision, Edward Wilson refers to these convictions as 'orthodox Protestant' (86)] . . . just like the
Queen . . . . In truth, he stood precisely where the Queen
stood: no trouble from him" (7-8, 74).[5]

A typological rendering of history in his historical plays
would hardly in itself distinguish Shakespeare as singular
among Elizabethan playwrights, however. The medieval
drama had long utilized typological interpretations of
history to shape the religious focus of its audiences in
accord with royal preference. As Alice-Lyle Scoufos attests,
"the typological method of biblical exegesis had a profound effect upon characterization and structure in medieval English drama" (309), an observation with which Paul
Korshin's study in typological composition concurs: "Typology is [that] system of exegesis . . . [which] the
Protestant reformers found . . . an effective method [in]
using the facts of salvific history to emphasize the rectitude
of their cause and their independence from Rome" (20, 25).

Indeed, Harvey Harnack notes that from about 1590 to 1660—precisely the period when Shakespeare was composing the Lancaster and Yorkist histories—"the employment of monarchial typology in English Renaissance literature . . . reaches its fullest expression;" and just as Shakespeare typologically endows his Lancaster kings with emblems of Anglican character and Reformation virtue, so Edmund Spenser concurrently suffuses Queen Elizabeth I (in *The Fairie Queene* [1589]) with such typological significance that, according to Harnack, "in her terrestrial majesty she becomes nothing less than the great penultimate sign of the Church's eschatological glory in Christ" (5851-A). In fact, Korshin notes many such typological renderings of historical figures during this era: "In seventeenth-century England," he argues, "the urge to typologize the monarchy seems to have been greater than at any other time in English history since the Reformation" (117).

Shakespeare, therefore, in his typological use of history, was no innovator. His purposes were consistent with those of his predecessors and contemporaries. The typological contents of his histories—the substance and purposes of which supplant careful attention to psychological accuracy of character (Paul 23)—are utilized by Shakespeare in order to elicit that perception of the world which he, the playwright, believes to be abiding and true, irrespective of what another account—perhaps a non-typological analysis—might propose as more historically authentic or psychologically accurate. In acknowledging this syncretistic purpose and method which allowed Shakespeare to enlarge his drama by fusing it with ahistorical myth, L. A. Cormican declares that Shakespeare's "Platonic mind . . . enabled him to treat the facts of history with considerable freedom, seeing in the historical sources not so much a mere account of things that were once done, but rather a parable or paradigm of what human beings continue to do ("Medieval Idiom in Shakespeare [I]" 199-200). Shakespeare's English histories are therefore fully "imagined universe[s]" which are no less iconologically complete than those worlds which are "presupposed in medieval literature" (Lewis 13).

To imaginatively connect his own world and its past with the world of sacred Christian tradition, Shakespeare invokes a familiar iconography in his Lancaster histories; in so doing, he introduces nothing in method which is essentially new to English dramatic composition. Christian iconography permeates many other non-Shakespearean histories of the Elizabethan Renaissance. Martha Fleischer establishes, for example, that "in a number of [Renaissance history plays] murder is committed in an atmosphere of ritual sacrifice created by symbolism recalling the archetypal death of Christ," and "[i]n most, the murder of a king is celebrated in a liturgical scene" (226). Richard's "atoning" death in Act V of Shakespeare's history is therefore as iconographically "Christlike" as is Sejanus's in Jonson's play about the tragic fall of Tiberius Caesar's consul and prefect of the praetorian guard (*Sejanus, His Fall* [1603]). For example, in a scene iconographically reminiscent of Christ's abandonment by his followers during his lonely march to Golgotha, Jonson tells us, through the character of Arruntius (and in verse as only Ben Jonson can torture it), of the similar desertion of Sejanus by his loyalists as the fallen prefect is led away to execution:

> They that before, like gnats, played in his beams,
> And thronged to circumscribe him, now not seen,
> Nor deign to hold a common seat with him!
> Others . . .
> Now inhumanely ravish him to prison,
> Whom but this morn they followed as their Lord!
> Guard through the streets, bound like a fugitive,
> Instead of wreaths give fetters, strokes for stoops:
> Blind shame for honours, and black taunts for titles!
>   (V.x.236-44)

The use of such Christian iconography, i.e., the magnified representation, within a distinctive rhetoric and imagery, of persons and/or events known to sacred tradition, reflects the Renaissance interpretation of *ut pictura poesis* (Mitchell 42-43), i.e., the conviction that most of the iconographic art of drama must finally be mediated through words. While the natural vehicle of myth is the drama (Bruner 176), purely visual means by which the icons of myth can be presented are decidedly limited, irregular, and, of course, not even accessible to those who must read a play instead of seeing it performed. Eric LaGuardia, like Noel Purdon (see endnote 1), concurs: "[I]t is primarily through verbal behavior that the possibilities of symbolic forms . . . are illuminated for us" (70).[6]

Richard II is suffused in this iconography of the sacred, especially as that tradition is mediated through Anglican experience. Just as *Henry V* embraces and promotes much Anglican doctrine,[7] so *Richard II* affords us the opportunity to see Catholicism discredited in Richard's fall and Anglicanism nurtured and celebrated in Henry's rise, especially through our witness of the collapse of what Tillyard calls "the essential medievalism of *Richard II*" and the ascent of "art of the high Renaissance" in the Henry plays (*Shakespeare's History Plays* 257). *Richard II*, however, is not just reflective of limited Reformation sentiment; the rhetoric of *Richard II* is the rhetoric of messianic faith: prophetic, proleptic, revelatory, and eschatological, the language of this tragedy and indeed of the whole Lancaster cycle is the language of the Scriptures. That this is so ought hardly be surprising though, for Shakespeare "knew the Bible so well that, in hundreds, indeed in thousands, of his passages we can trace its phraseology, and beyond its phraseology we can trace its thought" (Howse 10). His inspiration, asserts Martin Lings, is rooted in the tradition of ages past when, "before its final secularization in the XVIth century, [English] drama was concerned with . . . one topic only: human salvation" (18).

The messianism of the Lancaster plays is largely confined to the final play of the tetralogy, however, for it is King Henry V who most completely bears the messianic destiny of England upon his shoulders, although Richard, from time to time, as previously noted, is occasionally typed as Christ as well. Shakespeare's treatment of Richard as a type of Christ is decidedly different from his treatment of Hal, however, for Richard, unlike Hal, never functions in Christ's capacity as savior and redeemer; indeed, he cannot; these sacred and messianic roles are reserved for the apotheosis of Anglican sovereignty, Henry V. Yet, to heighten Richard's pathos and to magnify the solemnity and gravity of Richard's fall, he sometimes is typed by Shakespeare as the betrayed Christ, the sacrificial Christ, the suffering Christ; his deposition, as I.B. Cauthen writes, suggests a "symbolic

crucifixion" (46). Furthermore, such typological constructions enhance Shakespeare's tragic purpose in *Richard II*;
and indeed, other Renaissance dramatists are known to have
done much the same thing in other plays of the era in order
to achieve the amplified sense of a world's demise which is
so essential to tragedy. Virgil Whitaker notes, for example,
that "Elizabethan dramatic tragedies . . . though centered in
this world, are . . . played against the background of eternity,
and sometimes that background emerges into the foreground
of explicit statement" (*The Mirror* 21). Such a tragic drama, G.
Wilson Knight continues, is "a ceremony in which actors and
audience share in the formal unfurling of some deeply significant pattern . . . . We are held by a metaphysical rather than a
moral recognition" (*Shakesperian Production* 148, 153).

Some critics argue that Shakespeare's typological purpose within such a tragic framework cannot succeed and has
not succeeded, however; Christian tragedy, they vigorously
contend, is an oxymoronic construct. O. B. Hardison, for
example, declares that "the archetypal form of Christian
drama is not tragic . . . but comic. The uplift is neither
accidental nor cathartic . . . but the first hint of rebirth—of
a movement toward theophany" (291). With some qualifi-
cation, Thomas McFarland of Princeton University concurs: "Christianity and tragedy . . . can . . . never meet . . .[;]
yet in its rising, out of the recognition of disharmony,
defeat, and nothingness, to a transcendent affirmation,
tragedy parallels the movement of Christianity" (10,11).
Alex Aronson curtly suggests that "since death is the end [in
tragedy], tragedy must dispense with the total Christian
vision" (80), but J. A. Bryant contradicts such appraisals and
observes that a Christian definition of tragedy is indeed

possible, because the prototype of all Christian tragedy is contained in the events surrounding the Fall, a tragedy to which all men and all their circumstances are heir (*Hippolyta's View* 113).[8] In fact, inasmuch as we recognize that the story of the fall of Adam was not written by the authors of Genesis to chronicle an historical event but was rather conceived as a mythic narrative in order to account for the collapse of all humanity into self-centered egoism, we can affirm that this tragic fall in Eden can be retold through any story which illustrates man's vain desire to surmount the constraints of his mortality in the effort to become more than he is. Every tragedy, therefore, whatever its culture and time, is only a repetition of Genesis 3.

Richard's attempts in *Richard II* to overcome the insurmountable (asserting his individual greatness against the "Greatness of the National Destiny," as A. P. Rossiter expresses it ["Ambivalence" 3]) conform to this pattern of tragic character development; yet in striving to be that which he is not, Richard assumes a dimension of character that not only consolidates his tragic persona but emblazons him with qualities which invite us to see him as significantly different from other tragic figures who may not so completely accommodate our dramatic expectations of self-transformation of the tragic character. Examples might include characters such as Tamora (*Titus Andronicus*), Macbeth, and Othello in Shakespeare's more straightforward tragedies of revenge, failed ambition, or ungoverned hubris.

George Becker suggests, for example, that in *Richard II* "[t]he Richard whom we see at the beginning of the play is only an animated icon, a resplendent figure frozen in ritual and formality" (19). Viewed in this or similar ways, Richard may be said not only to be *other* than Richard but even *less* than Richard—particularly inasmuch as the king repeatedly assumes himself to be someone other than who he truly is. Richard's vain conceits isolate him from any real understanding of himself, and he subsequently divorces himself from a right understanding of both himself and his world: he rules over a kingdom that exists only in the grandiose hallucinations of his mind (Knight, *The Imperial Theme* 363). "He scatters himself into a multitude of images," writes Coleridge, "and . . . endeavors to shelter himself from that which is around him by a cloud of his own thoughts" (234). In the fragmentation and disintegration of his person, Richard fearfully considers that forsaking his role as king may result in the complete collapse of identity (Foreman 58; Thompson 162). As Donald Stauffer confirms, *Richard II* offers "a succession of situations . . . that show Richard's inability to square circumstances with his own emotional distortion of them" (93).[9]

Richard, for example, captive to a world of grief and tears (Clemen 58), purposefully approximates a rhetoric evocative of the betrayed Christ on several occasions, e.g., as he cries out in Act III against the presumed treason of his courtiers, "O villains, vipers, damn'd without redemption! / Three Judases, each one thrice worse than Judas!" (ii.129,132). But Shakespeare sometimes less flatteringly depicts Richard, instead, as a type of Adam, a royal example of original failed humanity. The King's fall, for instance, occurs within a world suffused in garden imagery (Spurgeon 213), an Edenic world, a "demi-paradise" (II.i.42) where, tempted to imagine himself more than he is (III.ii.10-26), he succumbs to the coarse realities of power which ravage his

fanciful hallucinations of what he believes himself to be
("The breath of worldly men cannot depose / The deputy
elected by the Lord" [III.ii.56-57]).[10] Like Adam, Richard
also neglects his "blessed plot" ("O, what a pity is it / That
he had not trimm'd and dress'd his land / As we this
garden!" [III.iv.55-57]); and, tempted to devour the "ripest
fruit" (Shakespeare's Edenic garden metaphor for the seat
of the House of Lancaster in II.i.153), Richard, like Adam,
assures his own destruction by capitulating to its allure: in
swallowing the Lancaster estate, Richard unknowingly consumes that which in unsavory digestion will result in his
expulsion from the throne upon which God had placed him.
Indeed, Brents Stirling argues that Richard's deposition
"was viewed by Elizabethan historians as a kind of secular
fall of man which tainted generations unborn until England
was redeemed from consequent civil war by the Tudor
messiah, Henry, Earl of Richmond" (26-27). Additionally,
in the murder of one of his royal brethren, Thomas of
Woodstock (for which he is generally reputed to be responsible [Palmer, *Kings* 59]), Richard also presents himself as
a type of Cain, and just as Cain's sentence for fratricide is that
he forever be "a fugitive and a wanderer on the earth" (Gen.
4:12),[11] Richard's deposition from his royal seat can be
interpreted as yet another kind of exile from the garden
which is England, so edenically defined by Shakespeare in
this play by generous allusions to Scripture.

England's plunge into ruin from its majestic height is
further illustrated by Shakespeare's frequent use of negatives in the play. Such signs of disintegration, incompletion,
and reversal in the kingdom are conveyed by words like
"unstooped" (I.i.121), "undeaf" (II.i.18), "unsay" (IV.i.9)

and "unkiss" (V.i.78); offices are "unpeopled" (I.ii.69), youthful recklessness is "unstayed" (II.i.2), the state is "uncivil" (III.iii.102), domestic bliss is "unhappied" (III.i.10), and death comes "untimely (V.vi.52); music is "untun'd" (I.iii.134), justice is "unfeeling" (I.iii.168), subordinates are "unreverent" (II.i.123), tongues are "ungracious" (II.iii.89); and Richard himself is finally "undeck[ed]" (IV.i.253) and "unking'd" (IV.i.222; V.iv.38) by "unrightful" (V.i.63) authority. Thomistic philosophy would posit that the divorce signaled by these negatives is effected by a division of *signum* from *res*, i.e., the separation of the sign from that which it signifies: specifically, the loss of king's Dignity from the king's person and the retention of an outward form no longer united to inward substance. The ruined king, in the division of his person, therein serves to illustrate, as J. L. Barroll observes, the "disparity between the king role as societal function and the king role as attestation of some quasi-transcendental personal validity" (210). Richard's appearance, therefore, is ultimately but a "show" (III.iii.71); only "looks he like a king" (as York anastrophically expresses it [III.iii.68]). If the king, as Eric Laguardia tells us, is indeed the "single *imago* of the sacred idea of the state" (73), then Richard, even in the protestation of his royalty, is not throughout this play that sacred image which suggests the unity of the immanent and transcendent which the royal person is supposed to signify.

The division of Richard's person from his Dignity also underscores Shakespeare's confidence in the doctrine of the king's two natures and the divisibility of these natures by breach of the covenant which brings them together (Shakespeare invokes this doctrine elsewhere, as in Hamlet's rejoinder to

Rosenkrantz: "The body is with the King, but the King is not with the body" [III.ii.27-28]).[12] Such a distinction of the breach which divides the king's public self from his private person also demonstrates how Richard, the man, could evince real pity from Elizabethan audiences while those audiences could yet remain steadfast in their abiding contempt for a king who, in affecting foreign airs, betraying his sacred trust, plundering the realm for personal gain, and exercising a despotic—indeed, an "almost insanely tyrannical" authority (Seward 142)—would remind England more of imperious Roman pontiffs than an English monarch and steward of high majesty. Governed by their perception of the king's possession of two natures, Shakespearean audiences could thereby forge an easy distinction between their personal grief for Richard and their satisfaction in beholding justice exercised by a God who would rightly wish deposed one who had become—as Kent says of Oswald in *King Lear*—"a bawd in way of good service" (II.ii.20).

Richard's association with imagery, rhetoric, and conduct which is imitative of Roman Catholicism in general and the medieval papacy in particular is deliberately contrived by Shakespeare to foster empathetic distance between Richard and the Elizabethan audience. Given Richard's appeals to the sanctity of his government, were Shakespeare not careful to craft the king as one who, like the Roman Church, has betrayed a divine commission, a British and patriotic audience might not be sufficiently persuaded of Richard's lack of legitimacy to accept his deposition as a work of divine providence and Henry Bolingbroke's accession as the secular complement of the Reformation (Warner 89-90). Richard's fraudulence—and its intimate connection to an ecclesiastical order of Tudor disrepute—is asserted by Eric La Guardia: "[i]n the figure of the king we recognize a priestly manner which is not quite authentic" (72).

Indeed, like Richard's fourteenth-century monarchy, the Roman Church of the medieval era, according to Anglican prejudice, thought itself "not born to sue but to command" (I.i.196): yet like Richard, frustrated with an inability to exact compliance with its demands, the Roman Church, under the Tudors, discovered that its power, influence—and ultimately its legitimacy—was called into unprecedented question. The Roman Catholic Church in England, like the splendid but effete king who is its iconographic representative in *Richard II*, is enfeebled—an ironic contrast to its apparent strength. As the Duke of Lancaster, John of Gaunt, a Shakespearean voice for England, attests:

> Richard. Thou, now a-dying, say'st thou flatterest me.
> Gaunt. O, no! thou diest, though I the sicker be.
>
> (II.i.90-91)

Furthermore, as Richard acquires or displays airs of frosty, regal detachment (as opposed to Bolingbroke's [and Bolingbroke's son's] more earthy sensitivities), the king's quality as an alien in a land which is not his spiritual home underscores Richard's resemblance to the Roman Church in England. For example, apart from his imperial arrogance and bomphiological rhetoric, Richard exudes a haughty indifference to the troubles of the land that is his sacred care ("Vex not yourself, nor strive with your breath / For all in vain comes counsel to his ear" mourns the Duke of York in Act II [i.3-4]). Richard is avaricious, luxurious, willful, and treacherous (I.ii.4-5; II.i.160-62), in marked contrast to Henry V, the unambiguously Anglican king of the final play of the tetralogy who, unlike Richard, is a dispenser of free grace (*Henry V* I.ii.39-57), humble before God (III.vi.169), theologically astute ("Hear him but reason in divinity" [I.i.38]), abjuring ceremony for its own sake (IV.i.240-80).

Indeed, though once a sacramental sign of the unity of purpose between God and man in the person of his steward, Richard's monarchy declines from the sacramental to the merely ceremonial. Richard's monarchy, as he himself ironically and periergeically defines it (especially during his deposition), is one which embraces only the external tokens of legitimacy—crown, scepter, robes of state—but not that which they signify. Richard appropriates the form of monarchy but not its content; he lacks the incarnate dignity which he has forfeited by his participation in sacrilegious murder; he projects the illusion of sanctity without, in fact, possessing it. As a result, he and his kingdom become diseased: the garden, this "other Eden . . . built . . . against infection" (II.i.42-44) erupts with sickness and threatens the very life of the realm.

To develop this association of Richard's decaying rule and apply its diseased associations to the Roman Church in England, Shakespeare cultivates a decadent medievalism in his presentation of the Plantagenet court which he severely contrasts with the studied pragmatism and asceticism of the Lancasters. Richard's inoperant and contemplative medievalism, in contrast to Henry's lean Renaissance practice, is decidedly artificial, misplaced, and unrealistic; it almost is less anachronistic than simply irrelevant: in such a context of impotence, Bolingbroke's capture of the throne appears an all too easy accomplishment. Richard tumbles from the throne "like glist'ring Phaëton" (III.iii.178), not so much because his weapons of resistance are antique but because they are fanciful; as one who is "more concerned with how he behaves than with the fitness of his conduct to the occasion" (Tillyard) *Shakespeare's History Plays* 247), Richard calls for stones to rise up as soldiers (III.ii.24-26) and summons angels to fight for a cause that more properly requires the Welsh army which has "dispers'd and fled" (III.ii.60-62,74). Tillyard concurs: "[M]indful of propriety and . . . unmindful of nature," Richard, unlike his more capable opposite, reflects a futile commitment to "ceremony, not . . . passion" (251-52). T. McAlindon similarly agrees; as he observes in *Shakespeare and Decorum*, "Although Richard's performance . . . might well seem creative and imaginative to minds imbued with *fin de siècle* aestheticism, it can only have seemed perverse and destructive to Shakespeare's audience" (38).

"Critical of disorder [Richard is] disorderly himself" (McAlindon 37); he mocks and profanes that which he says he reverences (III.ii.171-73). Such princely debasement of office would not be unfamiliar, however, to an Elizabethan audience, although they likely would not associate it with their own Reformation monarchy. They rather would be aware of their own century's ironic denunciation of Martin Luther by Pope Leo X, who had precipitously excommunicated the Augustinian priest and declared the great reformer to be "a boar in the vineyard" of the Church as well as "a child of Satan" (Erikson 228); Elizabethans, however, heirs as Anglicans to much of that Lutheran Reformation, would less likely think the boar to be loose in their own vineyard than squatting on the throne of Saint Peter in Rome—and Richard's resemblance, in Shakespeare's caricature of the corrupted prince, is assuredly more correspondent to the latter than to the former. Richard's subjective perception of himself as a persecuted innocent (III.iii.153-59) would therefore solicit little sympathetic response from an English audience that would consider Richard to be less like Christ than he thinks and far more like Judas than he knows: more betrayer than betrayed, Richard is more degenerately con-spiratorial than wrongly conspired against. Both John of Gaunt and his Duchess, for example, mournfully acknowl-edge Richard's complicity in the Duke of Gloucester's death (I.ii.16-41; Evans, et al. 808n.), although Richard's role in the death of his uncle is uncertain (Griffiths 193), and he may have been more the efficient rather than the material cause of Woodstock's murder (Ross 98). Little apprecia-tion, in any case, could be presumed to exist among many Elizabethans for such a Judas-king whose deeds, if not his resplendent words, dripped with the blood of innocents, helpless victims of wild, unchecked ambition and a crazed lust for power.[13]

Much of the ability of Richard figuratively to embody the Roman Catholic tradition is also accomplished by his incorporation of Roman, as opposed to Anglican, consecratorial sacramental iconography in his rhetoric and person. Shakespeare, for example, imaginatively invokes parallels to Roman and Anglican sacramental doctrine and practice in his presentation, through *Richard II,* of the controversy surrounding questions of legitimate reception and bestowal of the Crown. Shakespeare knew that Roman doctrine, defined in 1551 by the Council of Trent, had asserted, for example, that the Eucharistic Sacrifice was accomplished by the priestly incantation of a consecratory formula over the species of bread and wine which thereby were transformed into the Body and Blood of Christ.[14] Communion, i.e., the oral reception of the Sacrament, according to this sacramental system, was incidental and unnecessary for the full benefit of the Sacrament to be effected; consecration was all that was necessary. But Anglican theologians disagreed. Thomas Cranmer, for one, writes that "[t]hey [the Catholic party] say that Christ is corporally under or in the forms of bread and wine: we [the Anglicans] say that Christ is not there, neither corporally, nor spiritually; but in them that worthily eat and drink the bread and wine, he is spiritually, and corporally in heaven" ("Of the Pressence of Christ" 54).

The distinction is important. For the Anglican, the Sacrament of the Eucharist is nothing if it is not received, and to receive it is to put the Eucharist to its dominically commanded use by which the reception of the promises connected with the Sacrament is assured: as Martin Parsons emphatically declares in his exposition of the Prayer Book liturgy, "Without the *giving* of the bread to the communicants, it cannot be said to be really consecrated" (102).

Significantly, and absolutely consistent with the Aristotelian mechanics of Roman sacramental doctrine, Richard's appeal to authority as a king is predicated upon the putative power of a sacramental anointing which confers, he maintains, an inviolable and sacred character upon the recipient, irrespective of the use to which that character is put. Richard therefore sees the rite which elevates him to sovereignty as an unction which confers upon him a sacramental grace that is effective in itself (*ex opere operato*) apart from right use, and in so formulating the foundation of his royal authority, he therefore establishes himself firmly and unambiguously within the context of the Roman sacramental tradition. Furthermore, as Percy Schramm points out, in Richard's day, "the consecration of the monarch belonged to the number of the sacraments which had not [yet] been narrowed down to seven" (7); Richard therefore became king not by investiture of the crown, but by the act of sacramental inoiling (Figgis 79).[15] Fritz Kern confirms that anointing was "the tangible rite of consecration . . . that led to the sanctification of the king in the estimation of the people" (52); he quotes from the liturgy used in the sixth-century consecration of Gregory the Great to illustrate the community's regard for the sacramental character of this anointing which transfigures its recipient:

> The grace of God hath this day changed thee into another man, and by the holy rite of unction hath made thee a partaker of its divinity. (37)

Additionally, Gregory himself proclaimed that not only he but all secular authority consecrated to office was so established by the conferral of sacramental grace and the concomitant bestowal of the charism of government by that sacrament, an argument which continued to be reaffirmed half a millennia later even by such a representative of dissident and would-be reformers of ecclesiastical excesses as Peter Damien (A.D. 1007-72). Damien, among others, steadfastly defended royal consecration as a true sacrament of the Church (Kern 36, 40), and this theological conviction, widely affirmed in the medieval Church, was not overruled until the convention, five centuries later, of the Council of Trent (Schramm 119-20); hence, the Richard of history almost certainly would be expected to have embraced this formulation of royal government. As Charles the Bald articulated the doctrine in 859,

> He who is consecrated, anointed, and raised to the throne in accordance with the usages of the Church, can never be deprived of either his sacerdotal character or of his throne, except by the formal judgment of the bishops at whose hands he was consecrated king . . . . (qtd. in Kern 44)

Indeed, reflecting this opinion, ancient Christian art frequently depicted the medieval monarch garbed not only in the robes of state but in priestly vestments as well. This symbolic representation of the sovereign as both king and priest, *rex et sacerdos*, also appears in the later medieval custom of arraying the monarch in sacerdotal vestiture at his coronation (Kern 53).

This spiritual character which was thought to be imparted by inoiling (God's imprimatur upon his elect) was one which the anointed could not surrender to any mortal, as no mortal had bestowed it (Taylor 194);[16] this is why Richard surrenders his power and resigns his sovereignty to God rather than to Henry ("Must we lose / The name of king? a' God's name let it go" [III.iii.145-46]) and explains why Richard and his defenders so insistently and often appeal to his status as one who has been "anointed" in defense of the king's right to retain the crown (I.ii.38; II.iii.96; III.ii.54-55; IV.i.l27).[17] Even Henry's allies defer to the authority of the idea (*1 Henry IV* IV.iii.40), though they do not rely upon it for their vindication with the passionate urgency characteristic of Richard and the Bishop of Carlisle. Gaunt, too, acknowledges the divine imprint, and though he resents Richard's possession of it, he, too, respects it and bows to its authority ("Let heaven revenge, for I may never lift / An angry arm against his minister" [I.ii.40-41]).

Anglican sacramentology could not suffer such a mechanistic concept of grace, however, and looked to its own pervasive emphasis upon the quality of *faithful reception* rather than the doctrine of *sacerdotal infusion* to guide it in its theological deliberations on the question of grace's acquisition. Hence, in its doctrinal teaching on the Eucharist, the Anglican magisterium embraced Richard Hooker's insistence that "[t]he real presence of Christ's most blessed body and blood is not therefore to be sought for in the sacrament, but in the worthy receiver of the sacrament" (291). The sacraments, therefore, are not efficacious if they are indifferently received. As Hooker elsewhere contends, "because [the sacraments] contain *in themselves* no vital force or efficacy, they are not physical but moral instruments of salvation . . . which unless we *perform* as the author of grace requireth, they are unprofitable" (286). Hence, with perfect consistency in doctrine, despairing of the sign but not of what it signifies, Archbishop Cranmer remarks of the "sacrament" of royal consecration in his homily at the coronation of Edward VI:

> For [kings] be God's anointed, not in respect of the oil which the bishop useth, but in consideration of their power . . . . The oil, if added, is but a ceremony; if it be wanting, that king is yet a perfect monarch notwithstanding, and God's anointed, as well as if he was inoiled. ("A Speech at the Coronation" 21)

Richard, therefore, contrary to his claim, does not remain a king in perpetuity according to Anglican criteria, for that which constitutes authentic monarchy, that which signifies divine election in Anglican appraisal, is determined by the *function* of royal power; monarchy is not simply and indifferently conferred by a rite of inoiling anymore than the Eucharist is confected by formulaic incantation alone.

In their defense—and in order to establish a longstanding basis for their refusal to acquiesce to a Roman sacramental system which they regarded as innovative rather than apostolic—Anglicans also appealed to ancient precedent, for in 751, Pope Zecharias had decreed, much like Cranmer, that capacity rather than inoiling confirms the legitimate authority of a sovereign ("It is better that he who possesses power be called king, than he who has none" [qtd. in Kern 29]). Therefore, in Anglican opinion, the more ancient justification for monarchy and its perpetuity in the one to whom it was committed was embodied in the rediscovered principle of governing authority that is confirmed by use—not mere possession. The doctrine, contended Anglicans, had been obscured and corrupted by centuries of malignant practice and theorizing which had separated form from function and elevated the significance of the former to the diminution of the latter.

Richard's delusions of authenticity are based upon more than just his intimate correspondence with and embodiment of a pattern of sacramental thought about monarchy that is unambiguously Catholic and un-Anglican, however. Richard also clings to a discredited notion of legitimacy which is the secular equivalent of the Roman doctrine of apostolicity. Richard, for example, believes that he rules by a uniquely divine right which is not mediated through or directed by human authority; as the Bishop of Carlisle, filled with high fury, cries out in Richard's defense,

What subject can give sentence on his king?
And who sits here that is not Richard's subject?
....
And shall the figure of God's majesty,
His captain, steward, deputy, elect,
Anointed, crowned, planted many years,
Be judg'd by subject and inferior breath,
And he himself not present?
O, forfend it God . . . .

(IV.i.121-22,125-29)

And Richard himself likewise reproaches his captors,

We are amaz'd, and thus long have we stood
To watch the fearful bending of thy knee,
Because we thought ourself thy lawful king;
And if we be, how dare thy joints forget
To pay their awful duty to our presence?
If we be not, show us the hand of God
That hath dismiss'd us from our stewardship . . . .

(III.iii.72-78)

Richard's appeal is the secular correspondent of yet another non-Anglican theological sentiment based upon the speculative conclusions of Roman Catholic theology: specifically, the belief that apostolic faith is secured by the indifferent conferral of sacramental consecration upon a succession of bishops whose ordinators have themselves been infused with the charism of apostolic authority by bishops in an ordered succession, the effect of which is to bestow by "hereditary transmission" (Javierre 17) a kind of ecclesiastical pedigree upon the successors to the apostles who, "to prove the antiquity and legitimacy of their authority . . . often tried to trace their ancestry . . . back to the apostles to Christ himself . . . (Martos 486). [I]t was a supernatural power [that was thought to be conferred], Martos continues in explanation, and neither its reception nor its exercise depended on [the bishops'] natural talents or personal holiness" (498). Therefore, although Anglicanism affirmed the conferral of the historic succession as a valid rite for the consecration of episcopal authority, the authority of the episcopacy in the Church of England never was regarded as absolutely dependent upon the right of succession narrowly defined. As Anglican theologian Reginald Fuller writes,

> The historic episcopate has therefore [only] a relative historical justification . . . . The historic episcopate is the historic way of signalizing the present church's continuity with the church of the apostles. But it is no more than a sign. The *substance* of apostolicity lies in the scriptures, the creed and the sacraments, with their liturgical celebration, as these are . . . rekindled into *viva vox evangelli.* (89-90)[18]

The Anglican Church, consequent to the Reformation, also formally transferred the responsibility for the Church's governance from Rome to the Crown, and during this transition (at least in Roman Catholic opinion) the continuity of the apostolic office was broken in England.[19] At the time of the Reformation, however, the possible interruption of the ritual form of consecration commonly known as "the chain of imposition of hands" (Villain 88) was less crucial to the redefinition of episcopal authority in England than was the need to assert and formulate an apostolicity of validity independent of a mechanistic, juridical rite that would be

authoritative, instead, because of its right exercise and use—
principles coincident with the Anglican redefinition of
rightful monarchy. H. F. Woodhouse summarizes the attitude of sixteenth-century Anglicanism referent to the issue
of the apostolicity of bishops by noting that "[a]postolicity
included [the maintenance and proclamation of] right
doctrine . . . [;] apostolic *faith* had to be retained, heresy
repudiated, schism overcome . . . . Thus stress was laid on
doctrine" (419). Consequently, Woodhouse continues,
Anglican scholars "asserted . . . a constitutional type of
episcopacy, expressing a fatherly and pastoral authority. It
was not prelacy" (421-22).

Accordingly, to the medieval Roman Catholic, apostolicity was principally determined by adherence to an ancient
practice that was intended to assure a linear continuity of order
and submission of the national churches to Rome (Pelikan
110-26), whereas, for the Anglican, apostolicity could not be
guaranteed by a "'pipe-line' theory of episcopal power and
authority," but by the bishops' safeguarding "the fidelity of
teaching . . . of the apostles as recorded in the New Testament"
(Davies 31). Therefore, Richard's assertion that his office was
inviolable because it was canonically obtained and secured—
as opposed to having been faithfully administered—would be
readily perceived by Shakespeare's audience to be an argument
predicated upon a discredited Roman Catholic theory of
authority rather than emblematic of the principles inherent in
the Anglican model of elective episcopacy.[20]

Not only was the investiture of Anglican bishops divorced
from Roman precedent during the Reformation, however;
the monarchy, as noted earlier, also emphasized the
importance of its elective rather than divine character at this

time—although in fact, election, in addition to hereditary right, had comprised a basis for authenticating claims to the English crown since the time of the Norman Conquest (Schramm 152). As Percy Schramm observes, even at the time of Richard's deposition, many counselors declared both the king's deposition and Henry Bolingbroke's elevation to be just and good—a ruling determined by the ancient (though little emphasized) precept that monarchy was to be based "not only on hereditary right, but on the consent of the magnates, or even on the unanimous votes of individual persons" (172-73); it was an argument to which Henry and his successors naturally enough deferred, for Henry IV, in so acquiescing to a new authority for monarchial government, "made the validity of a parliamentary title indispensable to royalty" (173). Indeed, with the establishment of the Tudor dynasty in 1485, Parliament formally invested Henry Tudor as King, which investiture Henry accepted and acknowledged in terms very different from those attending Richard II's claim; as Schramm records, Henry received the royal mantle of England not by the single virtue of heredity but because, in his words, he had been "elected, chosen and required by all three estates of this same land" (175).[21]

The gradual erosion of the monarch's conventional basis for claiming authority preceded the Reformation but was hastened by it, and Anglican divines, anxious to consolidate the new theoretical bases for the exercise of authority in the kingdom, were eager to produce Scriptural precedent of others who had been garlanded with divine responsibility only to have that favor later withdrawn; in such wise, they might theologically justify what, in appearance if not in effect, otherwise appeared to many to be the negation or compromise of sacramental grace. As Robert R. Reed points out in a recent monograph, one precedent from Scripture to which Anglican theologians could point was that of the prophet Samuel, who, for instance, had declared to Saul, "The Lord has torn the kingdom out of your hand, and given it to your brother, David, because you did not obey the voice of the Lord" (1 Samuel 28:17-18); Reed notes, too, that the Scriptures also provided examples of kings other than Saul who similarly had been deprived of their kingdoms for breaches of their divine covenant—kings such as Nebuchadnezzar and Manasseh. Furthermore, in the New Testament, the writer of the Acts of the Apostles had declared, too, that for arrogating to himself an authority which alone belonged to God, Herod Agrippa had been struck down by God's wrath and devoured by worms (Acts 12:21-23) (9-10).

Against the background of this sacred history, Shakespeare placed Richard's deposition in order to illustrate that no charism was indelible; even the repositor of a special charism of grace could be deprived of that sacramental benefit if the dispensation were to be revoked by breach of the covenant through which he had received it. As Fritz Kern attests, "The monarch who violates his own objective law at the same time destroys his own subjective right to dominion . . . *Rex eris si recte regis or recte faciendo regis nomen tenetur, peccando amittur*" (195); or as the Duke of York puts the issue to Richard: "Take Hereford's rights away, and take from Time / His charters and his customary rights; /. . . for how art thou a king / But by fair sequence and succession?" (II.i.195-96, 198-99).

Richard, therefore, whatever the basis of his authority—divine or parliamentary—offends against *both* in the abrogation of his sacred responsibilities and by defiling his land and person ("Landlord of England art thou now, not king" [II.i.113]).

Perhaps to argue for his disfigurement of the sacramental bond of marriage, or merely further to diminish sympathy for Richard's plight in a vigorous effort to discredit and impugn the king's personal authority or merit, Shakespeare also invokes Thomas Walsingham's charge that Richard was promiscuously homosexual, a charge which, though limited to Walsingham in English historical literature (Kelly 11), confirmed or at least compounded the notoriety of Richard's unflattering reputation imputed to him by Holinshed. As Holinshed declares of Richard,

> He was prodigall, ambitious, and much given to the
> pleasure of the bodie . . . . Furthermore, there
> reigned abundantlie the filthe sinne of lecherie and
> fornication, with abhominable adulterie, speciallie in
> the king. (*Holinshed's Chronicle* 51)

Coleridge, however, would probably not think Walsingham's accusation offered without cause, although Coleridge's own critique of the king is derived solely from Shakespeare's characterization of Richard and not from prose histories of the era. In his essay on *Richard II*, Coleridge, for instance, argues that Richard is "a man with a wantoness in feminine shew, feminine friendism, [and possessed of an] intensely woman-like love of those immediately about him . . . . [H]e is weak, variable, and womanish, and possesses feelings which, though amiable in a female, are misplaced in a man and altogether unfit for a king" (228-

233). In a more contemporary account, McAlindon similarly suggests that in *Richard II*, "Richard['s] . . . inconstancy of attitude . . . reveals itself in a perpetual wavering between a high and manly style and a base and effeminate one" (42). However, in his own undisguised indictment of Richard as more than merely wanton or effeminate, Shakespeare confirms Walsingham's judgment in Bolingbroke's astonishing accusations against Bushy and Green (III.i.11-15), accusations in which more than just the king's mannerisms are challenged.[22]

Of course, whether Shakespeare really believed that of which he has Bolinqbroke accuse Richard is probably unknowable, but the fact that he introduces it with such startling abruptness into the play suggests that he may indeed have been attempting to indict Richard according to a popular prejudice of the day (for demonstration of which attitude, see especially Michael Goodich's *The Unmentionable Vice: Homosexuality in the Later Medieval Period* [N.p., Dorset Press, 1979] and/or Alan Bray's *Homosexualitv in Renaissance England* [London: Gay Men's Press, 1982]). Richard's infidelity may be introduced by Shakespeare, however, simply to signify, by yet another example, more sacramental defilement in the person of the king; for irrespective of the sex of the participant or participants in the king's alleged infidelity, it is Richard's faithlessness—not the object of his desire—which fractures the sacramental bond of matrimony.

As Richard shatters the bond of husband and wife, so he likewise destroys the unity of king and land, a symbolic unity which had been nurtured in the British consciousness since the emergence of the legends of Arthur and his predecessors. Indeed, John of Gaunt's sinathrismic speeches at the beginning of the play (II.i.40-68) would seem to confirm this interpretation: he evokes what Herbert Coursen has called "a priestly view of England" ("Theories of History")— a view which can be metaphorically extended to demonstrate Shakespeare's Anglican apologetic, for having divorced himself from England by breaking the sacramental bond which united God's providential grace to the kingdom, Richard, *rex et sacerdos,* forfeits his person as the means through which God's gracious presence can be mediated to the community over which he presides. As Coursen says, "God's deputy has committed acts which prevent God from acting through him. Richard can only preside over ceremonies deprived of their significance" ("Theories of History"). Once again, in the division of the king from the kingdom which is his sacred care, the resemblance of Richard to the Church, of which he, as king, is in part an icon, would likely not have remained unnoticed by perceptive Anglican audiences of Shakespeare's day who were persuaded that God had withdrawn his sacred commission to the Church of Rome in England because of *its* own excesses and abuses in order to establish a purified and truly English Church in its place.

Shakespeare depicts, by other images as well, Richard's movement from this position of majestic grandeur, which he flourishes at the play's commencement, to his position of utter ruin and destruction in captivity at the play's close. The emblem of the sun, which sometimes typified monarchy on the medieval and Renaissance English stage (Fleischer 277), is a particularly striking and recurrent symbol which reinforces our perception of Richard's passage from glory to ruin.

Indeed, the sun imagery applicable to Richard moves us from dawn ("So when this thief, this traitor Bolingbroke, /

Shall see us rising in our throne, the east" [III.iii.47,50]), to early morn ("See, see, King Richard doth himself appear, / As does the blushing discontented sun / From out the fiery portal of the east" [III.iii.62-64]), to sunset ("Thy sun sets weeping in the lowly west, / Witnessing storms to come, woe, and unrest" [II.iv.21-22]), and finally to eclipse ("Discharge my followers, let them hence away, / From Richard's night to Bolingbroke's fair day" [III.ii.217-18]).

The rhetoric of rise and fall suffuses *Richard II* to like purpose. As Richard remarks, "Down court! down king! / For night-owls shriek where mounting larks should sing" (III.iii.182-83); "Up, cousin, up, your heart is up, I know, / Thus high at least, although your knee be low" (III.iii.194-95); "Your cares set up do not pluck my cares down" (IV.i.195); "O, good! convey! Conveyors are you all, / That rise thus nimbly by a true king's fall" (IV.i.317-18). Additionally, this imagery of ascent and descent is complemented by pictures of ladders, measures, and buckets either "dancing in the air" (IV.i.186) or plunging into a well (IV.i.187-88). Henry is "jauning Bolingbroke" (V.v.94) and "high Hereford" (I.iv.2), but the king is "plume-pluck'd Richard" (IV.i.108); Henry will, "in God's name . . . ascend the regal throne" (IV.i.113), while Richard "sit[s] upon the ground / And tell[s] sad stories of the death of kings" (III.ii.155-56) before finally "sink[ing] downward here to die" (V.v.112).

The play's imagery of blood contributes, too, to the nurture of a perception of England as a land injured and dying. Images of blood, for example, appear more often in *Richard II* than in any other Shakespearean history (with the single exception of *King John*). The words "blood," "bloody," and "bleeding" appear fifty-three times in the play and serve to confirm the sense of a general bloodletting, the antisacramental spilling of the realm's life essence (II.i.126-27).[23]

The blood imagery of *Richard II* is anti-eucharistic: it neither gives nor sustains life; it stains the ground (IV.i.137), soils the earth (I.iii.125-26), and infects the state: "Lords, I protest my soul is full of woe / That blood should sprinkle me to make me grow" (V.v.45-46). Its properties are altogether different from those which it possesses in *Henry V*; in *Henry V*, blood invigorates; it is a substance of vitality and power, and most importantly, it is fully eucharistic, for it embraces and unifies in a sacramental context of redemptive sharing; it incorporates the body of the kingdom into that of the king: as Henry promises his fearful company, "he to-day that sheds his blood with me / Shall be my brother" (*Henry V* IV.iii.61-62).

The studied presence of sacramental iconography in *Richard II* and the other Lancastrian histories suggests the concomitant incorporation into the tetralogy of the liturgical structure from which that iconography is substantially derived. And indeed, the Anglican liturgy of the Eucharist, a modest reconfiguration of the traditional form of the Roman Mass, has been acclaimed as the center of much Shakespearean drama. Elizabethan Anglicanism's chief exponent and doctrinal systematician, Richard Hooker, is credited by Eileen Cohen with informing Dr. Johnson's recognition of Shakespeare's reliance on Catholic Anglicanism in formulating Ulysses's statement on order in *Troilus and Cressida* (181). Other authorities who also acknowledge Shakespeare's considerable reliance on Hooker include Virgil Whitaker (see especially pp. 203-08 in *Shakespeare's Use of Learning* [San Marino, CA: The Huntington Library, 1953]), John Danby (review pp. 18-53 in *Shakespeare's Doctrine of Nature* [London: Faber and Faber, 1949]), and Geoffrey Bush (*Shakespeare and the Natural Condition* [Cambridge: Harvard UP, 1956]). In fact, Whitaker declares that "Hooker was to a considerable extent responsible not only for the thought but also for the very structure of some of Shakespeare's greatest plays" (*Shakespeare's Use* 206).[24]

The liturgy, in fact, shaped much of the literary work in Britain prior to Shakespeare and the Reformation. Paul Kretzmann affirms that "the liturgy . . . underlies a great portion of medieval religious tradition" (iii), and John Huizinga argues that "eventually all [medieval] symbols group themselves around the central mystery of the Eucharist" (206). *The Golden Legend* of Jacobus de Voragine also confirms that the ritual of the Mass and the liturgical gestures associated with it are reflected in the literature of the medieval world; the *Legend*, for instance, records that Saint George, in order to spare himself from assassination during a mock Eucharist prepared by Dacien's wicked enchanter, "made the sign of the cross on it [the poisoned cup]"—recalling the manner of the celebrant's consecratory gesture over the chalice during the epiclesis of the Christian Eucharist— "and drank it without grieving him any thing" (130).

In a general sense, though his observation is rather limited to the Western cultural experience, Colin Still sees that "enshrined in all great art, myth and ritual [lies] the Mystery of the Redemption" (qtd. in Hapgood, "Shakespeare and the Ritualists" 116), a point with which the late Robert Graves, in a survey of more broadly religious and less specifically Christian themes, agrees: "The single grand theme of poetry," he writes, [is] the life, death and resurrection of the Spirit of the Year, the Goddess's son . . ." (422). Indeed, Bert States asks, in placing the proposition once again within the Western Christian tradition,

> Is there any model . . . for myth itself, more central to human experience than one based on birth, struggle, death, and revival? What other course could Western myth possibly have taken than one which depicted the Divine King's combat with "an opposing power," his suffering, death, and resurrection? (340)

G. Wilson Knight opines that inasmuch as the ritual of the Mass had, prior to the Elizabethan Age, commanded "the imaginations of Western man for fifteen centuries, it was inevitable that such similarities should appear [in Shakespearean drama]" (*Shakespeare and Religion* 298); indeed, Knight sees the Mass as the "central trunk" of all Shakespearean tragedy and "[e]ach of Shakespeare's tragic heroes," he contends, "is a miniature Christ" (*Principles of Shakespearian Production* 231). Accordingly, J. Dover Wilson proposes that "*Richard II* ought to be played throughout as ritual. As a work of art it stands far closer to the Catholic service of the Mass than to Ibsen's *Brand* or Bernard Shaw's *Saint Joan*" ([Introduction to *Richard II*] xiii); similarly, "'eyed awry,'" contends Bryant, Shakespeare, in Richard II, "presents a ritualistic analogy with the sacrifice of the cross" (*Hippolyta's View* 25-26), the ἀνάμνησις as it were, of the Mass.

In the incorporation of the ritual attributes of the Mass, *Richard II* assumes the character of ritual drama, and as Irving Ribner reminds us, "ritual drama is not concerned with depicting events; it comments upon events, and in order to do so it uses devices allied to religious ritual" (*The English History Play* 97). As Bryant comments,

> It is much more sensible to explain whatever ritual movement we find in *Richard II* as something Shakespeare himself achieved—partly by analogy with existing ritual . . . . [He] shap[ed] a particular event into a living poetic symbol [and] the presence in England of a powerful Christian ritual . . . certainly had something to do with it. ("The Linked Analogies" 423)

However, as Bryant points out elsewhere in the same article, such a recognition need not (indeed, ought not) mandate that ritual drama be identified as ritual itself or suggest that such a drama ought to be played ritualistically (427).

Richard II, then, though not a dramatic reconfiguration of the Mass, is clearly a dramatic exposition of the Mass; both play and rite are mythic dramas which celebrate rebirth, although each requires death as the price for achieving the new birth. In each, the experience of the participants features a movement from guilt to innocence and from separation and brokenness to restoration and communion. As William McCollum proposes, "The character of the Christ-like King Richard is especially well adapted to a ritualistic dramatic form, and the actor who plays the King may be regarded as a priest commemorating the fall of the sacrificial victim" (447-48); J. Dover Wilson also notices that in *Richard II* "a sacramental quality [is revealed] in the agony and death of the sacrificial victim, as it were of the god slain upon the altar" ([Introduction to *Richard II*] xvi).

This iconography of the Christ of Calvary, the Christ offered up in the Sacrifice of the Mass, is developed by Shakespeare's endowment of Richard with attributes associated almost exclusively with the Passion. As Maynard Mack attests, "[Richard's] frequent comparisons of himself to Christ in the hands of Pilate and Judas further enlarge the web of divine connections that in this play surround the idea of the king" (23).

In each instance of betrayal, for example, the king is betrayed into the power of his enemies by a *kiss*. Judas betrays Christ with a kiss (St. Luke 22:47), and Bolingbroke inaugurates his rebellion against Richard by defying Mowbray and, in so doing, offers Richard a kiss of supposed fealty which, in fact, is a token of betrayal (I.iii.46-47). Furthermore, as Jesus is betrayed by one of his intimates, so is Richard, for Henry Bolingbroke is his nearest cousin by birth; following each king's betrayal, each betrayed king finds himself desolate and alone; as Richard, in Act IV, bewails his abject and deserted state,

> Yet I well remember
> The favors of these men. Were they not mine?
> Did they not [sometimes] cry "All hail!" to me?
> So Judas did to Christ; but He, in twelve,
> Found truth in all but one; I, in, twelve thousand, none.
> God save the King! Will no man say amen?
> Am I both priest and clerk? Well then, amen.
> God save the King! although I be not he,
> And yet amen, if heaven do think him me.
>
> (i.167-75)

Richard and Christ are similarly confident that they can call on God to rescue them. As Christ puts the question to his tormentors, "Do you think that I cannot appeal to my Father, and he will at once send me more than twelve legions of angels?" (St. Matthew 26:53). Richard, in like manner, similarly announces that "For every man that Bollingbroke hath press'd / To lift shrewd steel against our golden crown, / God for his Richard hath in heavenly pay / A glorious angel: then if angels fight, / Weak men must fall, for heaven still guards the right" (III.ii.58-62).

The Gospels of St. Matthew and Luke also announce that in immediate anticipation of his death, Jesus laments: "O Jerusalem, Jerusalem, killing the prophets and stoning those who are sent to you! . . . Behold, your house is forsaken and desolate . . . . Nation wlll rise against nation and kingdom against kingdom; there will be great earth-quakes, and in various places famines and pestilences . . . . Alas for those who are with child and for those who give suck . . . " (St. Matthew 23:37-38; St. Luke 21:10-11, 23). Similarly, Richard, from the battlements of Flint Castle, prophesies:

> Yet know my master, God omnipotent,
> Is mustering in his clouds on our behalf
> Armies of pestilence, and they shall strike
> Your children yet unborn and unbegot,
> That lift your vassal hands against my head,
> And threat the glory of my precious crown.
>
> (III.iii.85–90)

And, in associating Henry with the instigator of war described in the third and fourth verses of the sixth book of the Apocalypse, Richard thunders:

> Tell Bollingbrook . . .
> That . . .
>   . . . [h]e is come to open
> The purple testament of bleeding war;
> But ere the crown he looks for live in peace,
> Ten thousand bloody crowns of mother's sons
> Shall ill become the flower of England's face,
> Change the complexion of her maid-pale peace
> To scarlet indignation, and bedew
> Her pasters' grass with faithful English blood.
>
>   (III.iii.91-100)[25]

Each king is come for in the dark of night and each, though agonized, humbly submits to his fate. St. Mark records that upon the Mount of Olives, in the moments before his arrest, "[Jesus] fell on the ground and prayed . . . 'Abba, Father, all things are possible to thee; remove this cup from me; yet not what I will, but what thou wilt'" (14:35-36). Likewise, Richard, upon the castle heights, in the moments before his arrest, resigns himself to delivery into the hands of his enemies: "O . . . that I could forget what I have been! / Or not remember what I must be now! / . . . What must the King do now? Must he submit? / The king shall do it . . . / The king shall be contented . . . " (III.iii.136, 138-39, 143-45).

Each man is delivered to those who cry out for his life by timid governors who are themselves anxious to avoid antagonizing powerful adversaries: Pilate, governor of Judea, literally ablutes himself of responsibility for Jesus (St. Matthew 27:24); similarly, York, the Lord Governor of England, when faced with an angry rebellion, capitulates to the demands of the rebel mob and indifferently dismisses his guardianship of the king: "Things past redress are now with me past care" (II.iii.171). And during his trial, it is York, among others, whom Richard most bitterly accuses by an iconographic recollection and equation of his own inquisition with Jesus's trial: "Though some of you, with Pilate wash your hands, / Showing an outward pity, yet you Pilates / Have here deliver'd me to my sour cross, / And water cannot wash away your sin" (IV.i.239-42). In an ominous portent of future disaster, Northumberland arrogantly dismisses Richard's warning of ruin by blithely invoking a curse upon himself (a curse that, in its fulfillment, shall destroy him and his whole house in *1 Henry IV*): "My guilt be on my head, and there an end" (V.i.69)—a grievously ignorant invitation to disaster that is chillingly reminiscent of the cry of the mob at Jesus's trial: "His blood be on us and on our children!" (St. Matthew 27:25).

The fearfully anticipated death of each king invites other predictions of calamity. Jesus counsels the mournful women who accompany him on the road to Calvary: "Daughters of Jerusalem, do not weep for me, but weep for yourselves and for your children. For behold, the days are coming when they will say, 'Blessed are the barren, and the wombs that never bore . . . !'" (St. Luke 23:28-29); in like form, the Bishop of Carlisle pleads for Richard, lest the consequences of his deposition provoke the wrath of God and the destruction of the kingdom:

> My Lord of Herford here, whom you call king,
> Is a foul traitor to proud Herford's king,
> And if you crown him, let me prophesy,
> The blood of English shall manure the ground,
> And future ages groan for this foul act.

> Peace shall go to sleep with Turks and infidels,
> And in this seat of peace tumultuous wars
> Shall kin with kin and kind with kind confound.
> Disorder, horror, fear, and mutiny
> Shall here inhabit, and this land be call'd
> The field of Golgotha and dead men's skulls.
> O, if you raise this house against this house,
> It will the woefullest division prove
> That ever fell upon this cursed earth.
> Prevent it, resist it, let it not be so,
> Lest child, child's children, cry against you
>   "woe!"

(IV.i.134-49)

Finally, Richard's meditations on his fate recall the instruments of Christ's death which similarly assure the king's own: in words evocative of Christ's crucifixion, Richard muses upon the liberating possibilities of the prison's iron spikes which, if put to alternative use, could free rather than imprison him, " . . . how these vain weak nails / May tear a passage through the flinty ribs / Of this hard world, my ragged prison walls; / And for they cannot, die in their own pride" (V.v.19-22). Furthermore, as Jesus is pierced by a spear to hasten his death (St. John 19:34), so Richard is speared (V.v), and in dying, Richard announces that he rises to eternal life: "Exton, thy fierce hand / Hath with the King's blood stain'd the King's own land / Mount, mount, my soul! thy seat is upon high, / Whilst my gross flesh sinks downward, here to die" (V.v.109-12). As G. Wilson Knight understates, "In the world of Shakespearian tragedy . . . the Christ sacrifice can, if we like, be felt as central" (*Shakespearean Production* 158).

A marked and important difference between Richard and Christ, however, is to be discovered in the results occasioned by each king's death. James George Frazer, in *The Golden Bough: A Study in Magic and Religion*, demonstrates that in many religions and cultures, the death of the king is believed to accomplish salutary and life-giving effects for the community (308-30), a point which Joseph Campbell expands upon by recording that in some cultures and mythologies, the king does not accomplish his life-transforming purpose by death but rather assures it by the promise of return from a kind of sleep (a mimesis of death), from which he "will arise in the hour of destiny" (one notes especially the Arthurian legend as an apt British literary example of this myth).[26] Other societies presume, too, that the dead king preserves or sustains the vitality of the community by continuing to live among them in another form (358).

Manifestly apparent in such mythologies are reflections of the varied yet similar ways by which Christianity has attempted to interpret and define Jesus's death: in accord with Frazer's observation of the purpose of the death of the king in some cultures, he died, according to Saint Paul, that others might live (Rom. 14:9); Campbell's example of the king's triumphant return from death is illustrated by the Matthean interpretation which proposes that Christ, unvanquished by death, shall return at some unspecified future time to fulfill his purpose: " . . . then will appear the sign of the Son of man in heaven . . . and they will see the Son of man coming on the clouds of heaven" (St. Matthew 24:30). Applying Campbell's observations of some faith communities' belief in the continuing, if hidden, presence of the king among his people, one Gospel points out that though he shall no longer be recognizable according to his former self, Christ yet assures his community of his continuing presence among them: " . . . and lo, I am with you always, to the close of the age" (St. Matthew 38:20).[27] Furthermore, as Mircea Eliade writes of such acclaimed deities as Christ who perish *in extremis,* "the violent death of these divinities is *creative.* Something of great importance for human life appears as a result of their death. Nor is this all: the new thing thus shares in the substance of the slain divinity and hence in some sort continues his existence" (99).

Clearly, however, Richard's death accomplishes no purpose similar to that defined by Eliade. Richard's death, unlike the death of mythic kings, fails to achieve any regenerative outcome; rather, it occasions generations of bloodshed, almost a hundred years of civil war—virtually the same amount of time required, under the Tudors, to consolidate the dynasty and secure the establishment of the English Reformation in perpetuity. Richard's death does not renew the commonwealth but promises, like the protracted effort to expel the Roman Church from dominion in England, to drench England in the anti-sacramental spilling of the nation's lifeblood; and Henry Bolingbroke, like the new Church which he, in figure, represents, mourns this dreadful conflict: "Lords, I protest my soul is full of woe / That blood should sprinkle me to make me grow" (V.vi.45-46). The redemption of the realm, which might have been achieved had Richard been a different type of king, is deferred; the redemption must be won by a true king— and fittingly enough in the iconography of the Christian drama, he comes to us in the succeeding play as little more than a child, but one in whom true majesty resides, albeit concealed, awaiting the appointed time of his glorious epiphany (*1 Henry IV* I.ii.197-217).

Notes

[1]Noel Purden also suggests that the quality of Shakespeare's iconography is quite distinct from that of such dramatists as Marlowe, Peele, Lyly, Jonson, et al. "Shakespeare," writes Purdon, "preferred to inlay [his] icons more fluidly with the verbal aspects of his plays. Shakespeare makes it appear that the spectacle, the emblem, arise out of the language, rather than vice-versa . . ." (159).

[2]The idea that the king ruled by divine right was a Tudor commonplace, though its origin as a social doctrine was not original with the Tudors (see the more extensive discussion of this concept later in this chapter). It is to this acclaimed authority which Richard ("God's deputy anointed in his sight" [I.ii.38]) appeals in his impassioned denial that any authority on earth can rightly depose a king consecrated to royal government ("Not all the water in the rough rude sea / Can wash the balm off from an anointed king" (III.ii.54-55]), a claim energetically supported, too, by the Bishop of Carlisle (IV.i.121-29).

[3]Henry Ansgar Kelly's citation from John Gower's *Cronica Tripertita* (c. 1400) is especially revealing of this principle as it applies to Richard:

> The English people unanimously deposed Richard, and in so doing gave praise to Christ, who had led them out from captivity under the Herod-like Richard and brought them to a glorious kingdom . . . . God . . . fixed the day on which Henry was to be

blessed . . .; accordingly, he was declared king on the feast of Edward the Confessor. God had predestined him for the title so that he might bring justice to the realm. (15)

[4] R. Alan Kimbrough makes note in this regard of the especial achievement of visual iconography in the Royal Shakespeare Company's production of *Richard II* for the BBC. Kimbrough points especially to the director David Giles' "adroit use of the crucifix . . . and the shadows of the prison bars . . . to pick up and affirm the many religious images in the script that encourage attention to . . . Richard as God's anointed king" (120-21).

[5] Many other authorities, such as David Evett, also see Shakespeare as a fairly representative Anglican, one who "suppressed the doctrinal resonances [of his sources], though not to the point of inaudibility" (151), and Rowse himself elsewhere adds, in his study of Shakespeare's life and thought, that "Shakespeare's was the view of the . . . Protestant, but the reverse of the Puritan; conservative, carrying on the phrases of as older England, 'by our Lady', 'by the Mass', 'priests' not 'ministers', a proper respect for saints and saints' days" (74).

Somewhat surprisingly, however, although it is common knowledge that Shakespeare was baptized into the Anglican faith in 1564, was married in an Anglican parish church, baptized his children into the Anglican faith, and was himself buried with Anglican ceremony in an Anglican parish church (at Holy Trinity in Stratford-on-Avon), there yet remain some scholars, such as John Cowper Powys, who insist that Shakespeare, in fact, was no Anglican but one who "held in sober earnest what the Catholic Church claims in dogmatic theory" (217), a judgment with which others surprisingly concur (see, for example, John H. de Groot [*The Shakespeares and The Old Faith,* New York: King's Crown P, 1946], T. F. Thiselton-Dyer [*Folk-Lore of Shakespeare.* 1883. New York: Dover, 1966], and Heinrich Mutschmann and K. Wentersdorf [*Shakespeare and Catholicism.* New York: Sheed and Ward, 1952]).

Others, somewhat less convinced of Shakespeare's supposed "closet Catholicism," claim, however, that the great dramatist of Elizabethan England was repelled equally by Catholic and Calvinist pieties and was generally dissatisfied with the Church of England as well (Coleman vii). Thomas Carter even argues that Shakespeare was a Puritan [*Shakespeare: Puritan and Recusant.* 1897. New York: AMS, 1970]. Wibur Sanders, though dismissive of any argument which presumes to link Shakespeare to any particular confession of the Christian faith, yet acknowledges that a religious character of a kind is discernible in Shakespeare's work: Sanders, however, suggests that this religious character is merely an equivocal expression of what finally is no more than a "timid and unoriginal Christianity," unfathomable in its confessional particulars (361).

[6] Although for our purposes, attention necessarily must be focused on the iconographic rhetoric embedded within the play, the contribution of distinctive visual iconography to the Shakespearean stage cannot be overlooked, though scant evidence of those visual icons or hieroglyphs which Shakespeare may have employed in his own sixteenth-century direction is available. Alice Venezky, however, is convinced that the iconography of medieval and Renaissance *tableaux vivants* (non-dramatic scenes of posed, immobile actors presented during an interlude of a play's performance,

reflecting or representing important themes) suggested both subject and theme to Shakespeare and other dramatists of the age (164-65); but it may be as or more likely that Shakespeare utilized such an iconographic tradition of the theatre as the *tableau vivant* less as an inspirational source than for actual recreative representation within the body of his own larger drama. Consider, for example, the probable staging of the fourth scene of the final act of *1 Henry IV* (an iconographic construct discussed more fully in the eighth endnote of the following chapter). Dieter Mehl confirms that "many [Elizabethan] plays reflect this tendency to portray events on the stage in such a manner that they form significant and often emblematic images of the play's meaning" (51), and iconologist Huston Diehl notes that even the patterns of stage violence in such works as Thomas Kyd's *Spanish Tragedy* and Shakespeare's *Titus Andronicus* "allude to existing iconographic traditions of the Renaissance [that, in theatrical production, become] symbolic icons which express widely understood moral and ethical precepts" ("The Iconography of Violence" 30).

Furthermore, the lack of costume, theatrical properties and the use of a non-representational stage in Renaissance England required that Elizabethan dramatists rely upon figurative language to conjure up those images which relatively barren and unpropertied theatres such as the Globe could otherwise but little provide. Lisa-Lone Marker has observed that Renaissance rhetoricians were aware of the affinity for iconographic illustration which was shared by the linguistic and mimetic arts (97-98); and this reciprocal relationship between the oratorical and theatrical arts is perhaps best attested to in Renaissance example by Desiderius

Erasmus who, in his essay *De Utraque Verborem ac Rerum Copia (On Copia of Words and Ideas* [1518]), demonstrates his own reliance on dramatic example to instruct students of oratory in the illustrative power of language. He argues:

> We shall enrich speech by . . . description . . . when we do not relate what is done, or has been done . . . but place it before the reader painted in all the colours of rhetoric so that at length it draws the hearer or reader outside himself as in the theatre. The Greeks call this . . . painting the picture of things. (47)

Shakespeare's contemporary, George Puttenham, in *The Arte of English Poesie* (1589), also expresses much the same conviction as Erasmus:

> . . . matter and occasion leadeth us many times to describe and set forth many things, in such sort as it should appeare they were truly before our eyes though they were not present, which to do it requireth cunning: for nothing can be kindly counterfait or represented in his absence, but by great discretion in the dooer. (238)

[7] Henry V, as we shall see, demonstrates a number of Anglican propositions. For example, apart from echoing the Anglican baptismal liturgy in the rhetoric of the *Book of Common Prayer* (I.i.25-37) and adopting the distinctly Protestant conviction that revelation is closed and "miracles are ceas'd" (I.i.67), the play promotes an Anglican stance on baptismal theology (I.ii.31-32) and trumpets the proposition that one's justification is not accomplished by works (IV.i.302-03), a conviction which, derived from Lutheran dogmatic theology, becomes the cornerstone of Reformation doctrine in England.

[8] Bryant, I think, is correct. Every tragedy illustrates man's struggle to redeem himself within a universe iniquitous because of the conditions introduced by man's rebellion against his created perfection. Tragedy, therefore, is not inimical to the Christian view of history; indeed, rather than repudiating it, the Christian vision confirms it: man is what he is and lives in such a world as he does as the consequence of his own disordered, egocentric choice; Oedipus's fall could occur as fully within a Christian universe as in a pagan one. Tragedy is thus not an impossible framework within which a dramatic artist of Christian conviction may work.

[9] Richard is the tragic interpreter of his own fall even as it occurs. While yet on the throne, but dazed by a mystic melancholy, he would "sit upon the ground / And tell sad stories of the death of kings" (III.ii.155-56), "make dust [his] paper, and with rainy eyes / Write sorrow on the bosom of the earth" (III.ii.146-47); he surrenders his power even as he calls upon heaven to arm his name against "a puny subject [who] strikes at [his] great glory" (III.ii.86-87).

And although this puerile inconstancy of mind and temper compounded by an almost maudlin self-pity may diminish some of our sympathy for Richard (Webb 14), yet, as G. Wilson Knight recognizes, "whatever we think of Richard, [during the course of the play we sense that] some sacred essence, at once pastoral and royal, is being wronged (*The Sovereign Flower* 31). Concurring with much of this interpretation, Joseph Porter observes that in Richard II,

> Richard [does] not so much express ... as parade ... his
> sorrow. Typically, instead of something like "I am
> sorrowful" (as Hal later says "I am exceeding weary"
> he says something *about* his sorrow: rather than

> predicating "grief" of himself he uses a kind of
> assumed predication . . . . Such a mode is generally
> characteristic of Richard; almost always, instead of
> merely expressing an internal state, he refers to it. (29)

[10] It is interesting to note that the substance of Richard's delusion is shared by yet another Shakespearean king of questionable legitimacy. Claudius, too, appeals to his presumed participation in a sacramental bond between heaven and earth as the guarantee of his personal security: "There's such divinity doth hedge a king / That treason can but peep to what it would" (*Hamlet* IV.v.124-25).

[11] All citations and quotations are taken from The New Oxford Annotated Bible and hereafter will be included in the text.

[12] From this doctrine, which probably was formulated first by the Norman Anonymous shortly after the Norman Conquest of Britain (Sommers), the Tudor jurists formalized their position regarding the king's role *jure divino*—an extension, Kantorowicz explains, of the ancient Norman assertion that

> the power of the king is the power of God. This
> power, namely, is God's by nature and the king's by
> grace . . . . The king is a twinned being [*gemina
> persona*], human and divine . . . although the king is
> two-natured and geminate by grace only . . . and not
> by nature [who] *becomes* a twin personality through
> his anointment and consecration. (*The King's Two
> Bodies* 42, 49)

As Shakespeare's contemporary, Francis Bacon, confirms in his *Case of the Post Nati in Scotland*, "There is in the king not a Body natural alone, nor Body politic alone, but a body natural and body politic together: *corpus corporatio in corpore naturali, et corpus naturale in corporo corporato*" (231). Such a concept disallows the possibility of the king's perishing ("The king is dead. Long live the king!") for the king's nature, *jure divino,* is eternal; his Dignity is imperishable, and the king's Dignity, united with his humanity, form a fraternal bond, from which only the humanity is separable by time. Eric La Guardia concurs. He points out that "in terms of medieval political theology, the head of state is subject to the infirmities of nature in his temporal condition, but in his regal condition as *imago Christi* or *vicarius Dei* he is under the 'halo of perpetuity'" (68).

Ernst Kantorowicz provides one of the more appealing formulations addressing this doctrine of the dual nature of the king as one who bears a mortal humanity and an immortal Dignity:

> We thus have to recognize [in the king] a *twin person,* one descending from nature, the other from grace . . . one through which, by the condition of nature, he conformed with other men: another through which, by the eminence of [his] deification and by the power of the sacrament [of consecration], he excelled all others. Concerning one personality, he was by nature, an individual man: concerning his other personality, he was, by grace, a *Christus,* that is, a God-man . . . . (*The King's Two Bodies* 46)

The doctrine, conceivably, may be linked to or derived from the Church's historic understanding of the relationship of Christ to his Church in which an eternal king rules over both his Church Militant and Church Triumphant, or it may also be correspondent to the ancient doctrine of Christ's nature wherein it is confessed by the Church in the *Quincunque Vult* (also known as the Athanasian Creed) that Christ possesses two distinct natures, divine and human, which co-exist in one individual essence (ὁμοούσιον).

[13]No orthodox Elizabethan, however, irrespective of his dislike of or contempt for any authority, would countenance rebellion or disobedience against such authority due to his subscription to the Tudor doctrine of passive obedience; consequently, the doctrine of passive obedience, accompanied by strictures against rebellion, was promulgated by the Tudors. As Lawrence Stone exhaustively documents (*The Crisis of the Aristocracy: 1558-1641.* Oxford: Clarendon, 1965), the requisite conditions for disorder, rebellion, and the collapse of the dynasty were present in a hundred forms during the reign of Henry Tudor and his descendants. Furthermore, the Tudors could appeal to a number of Scriptural passages in order to offer Christian sanction to their policy, e.g., St. Matthew 5:38-48: St. Matthew 22:17-21; St. Mark 12:14-17; St. Luke 6:27-36; St. *Luke* 20:21-25; Romans 13:1-7; Titus 3:1-2; 1 St. Timothy 2:2, and 1 St. Peter 2:13-18. Such authoritative reproofs to rebellion, it was believed, could well serve to inhibit and discourage rebellion and encourage passivity in lieu of the lack of contraint which had been allowed by the weakness of the doctrine of divine right, the authority of which, given the displacement of Richard by the Lancasters, had obviously offered little credible deterrent to those who elected to challenge the established government.

[14]J. Waterworth translates from Chapter Four of the Roman Church's *Decree Concerning the Most Holy Sacrament*

of the Eucharist, promulgated at the thirteenth session of the Council of Trent:

> . . . because that Christ, our Redeemer, declared that which He offered under the species of bread to be truly His own body, therefore has it ever been a firm belief in the Church of God, and this holy synod doth now declare it anew, that, by the consecration of the bread and of the wine, a conversion is made of the whole substance of the bread into the substance of the body of Christ our Lord, and of the whole substance of wine, into the substance of his blood; which conversion is, by the holy Catholic Church, suitably and properly called Transubstantiation. (78)

[15]Percy Schramm attests that mere reception of the crown was never regarded in the medieval, pre-Reformation world as an act which could, of itself, bestow the character of monarchy upon the recipient, for valid coronation required much more than mere reception of the crown could impart; as he writes in *A History of the English Coronation,*

> [Coronation] is far more than drama: for God is looking down upon it, asking whether the crown has been passed on from head to head as it should be. Only if the forms have been truly observed, and nothing has been omitted, does the coronation have its due effect. (10)

[16]As Richard protests,

> . . . well we know no hand of blood and bone
> Can gripe the sacred handle of our scepter,
> Unless he do profane, steal, or usurp.
>
> (III.iii.79-81)

[17]In commenting upon this configuration of monarchy which dismisses the suggestion of the king's responsibility to any authority other than God himself, Fritz Kern notes that the adherents of this claim declare that "the king owes exclusively to God not only the essential content of his power but also his subjective and personal claim to the throne. Since the community has not given this to him, it can neither question or withdraw it" (11).

[18]Such a concept of authority and the ordered succession thereof, defined by Roman rather than Anglican standards, is, by its many shared presumptions, closely linked to the concept of the Divine Right of Kings, a notion which left Tudor theologians and practioners of statecraft uncomfortable— although the idea, like the historic episcopacy, was never altogether repudiated by the formulators of monarchial authority in Tudor England; a doctrine of divine right, modestly defended, could, after all, help preserve monarchial government and offer the enticing prospect of continuity and stability in the *saeculum* by its proclamation of rightful succession by direct continuance, but such a doctrine could obviously not serve as the cornerstone of Tudor authority. An emphasis upon monarchy by hereditary succession as the mechanism by which divine right was mediated was a doctrine of limited utility to the Tudors who needed to nurture a different or at least more eminent doctrine to confirm their authority. For as the defenders of divine right maintained,

> *Hereditary right is indefeasible* . . . . The right acquired by birth cannot be forfeited through any act of usurpation, of however long continuance, by any incapacity in the heir, or by any act of deposition. So long as the heir lives, he is king by hereditary right,

even though the usurping dynasty has reigned for a thousand years. (Kern 5)

Obviously, appealing as the doctrine might appear in theory, the Tudors could not embrace or prosecute such a doctrine of monarchy's authority without significant reservation, for, as noted earlier, although divine right offered some promise of security through its provision of an ordering metaphysical construct for a kingdom seemingly perpetually threatened by division and crises of authority, the Tudors themselves were only too distressingly aware of their own weak claim to the throne; the Tudors, after all, had claimed the Crown in 1485 by the power of the sword on Bosworth Field and had consolidated their claim by securing a marriage of expedience and commissioning an historically unprecedented propaganda to justify their dubious claim to the throne. Because the doctrine of divine right abrogated the possibility that a king could lose his mandate, the authority of the principle enshrined in law, if too insistently urged, would unquestionably mandate that the Tudors surrender the throne to their rival Yorkist claimants—the heirs of Richard II who were displaced by the change of dynasty following the Lancastrian usurpation in 1399.

Furthermore, such a doctrine of divine right implied, given its insistence upon hereditary indefeasibility, that even if a sovereign's mandate were to be withdrawn, only God, as he had conferred it, could revoke it and He alone, accordingly, would be the only one to know that He had done so. Therefore, absent any direct revelation to the contrary, the doctrine of divine right proclaimed that legitimate monarchy extends in perpetuity to a rightful king's issue, irrespective of who may actually occupy the throne, should the succession be interrupted. Consequently, the Lancastrians, beginning with Henry IV, sensibly dismissed their claims to the throne based on the arguments of rightful succession by direct continuance (Figgis 84) and ordered the formulation of a new standard to govern orderly succession. The promulgation, under the Tudors, of the doctrine of passive obedience and renewed emphasis upon the elective character of monarchy served well the Lancaster-inspired purpose of ridding England of a successionist doctrine that compromised both Lancaster and Tudor claims, but the emergent philosophy of monarchy which replaced the old notion of divine right also, and not coincidentally, contributed to the development of a happy correspondence between Tudor philosophy and Anglican theology (Booty 13).

[19]The Papal Bull *Apostolicae Curae*, promulgated in 1896 by Pope Leo XIII, declared Anglican orders to be "absolutely null and utterly void," a judgment based upon a consideration which most modern theologians of both Roman and Anglican confessional adherence agree to have been trivial and suspect in the extreme (the Bull declared Anglican orders "defective" because, "between 1550 and 1662, the words used at the actual conferment of the priest's orders did not specifically mention what order was being conferred" [Chadwick 147]).

[20]Concise yet thorough explications of the process by which episcopal election was accomplished in Elizabethan England are offered in Stephen Neill's *Anglicanism* (New York: Oxford UP, 1958) and Gregory Dix's *The Shape of the Liturgy* (London: Dacre P, 1945); in the latter work, see especially the

chapter on "The Reformation and the Anglican Liturgy" (613-734). See also Claire Cross's study of the interrelationship of episcopal and monarchial models of government in England in her study of *The Royal Supremacy in the Elizabethan Church* (London: George Allen and Unwin, 1969).

[21]The medieval superstitions surrounding and attendant upon the theory which proclaimed the divine right of kings—such as the supposed provision of mystical qualities upon the royal blood—were less troublesome difficulties to the Tudors than were the consequences which followed a study of the logical consequences of strict adherence to the practice of a succession so determined and justified: the pragmatic Tudors recognized the vulnerability of their claim, were they to urge the arguments of divine right with too much insistence (Morris 66-67). Therefore, in a magnificent demonstration of the Anglican and Tudor principle of government which eschews pre-Tudor and Roman justifications of royal authority, Hal, in *2 Henry IV*, justifies his father's right to the Crown in the words of one untroubled by disagreeable theorizing on the point: "My gracious liege, / You won it, wore it, gave it me; / Then plain and right must my possession be" (IV.v.220-22).

[22]Suspicion about Richard's sexual orientation was perhaps provoked by the king's reluctance to marry until late in his reign. Yet Richard's eventual, if late, marriage is no confirmation of heterosexuality either, for Richard's queen, Isabella, was not born until late in Richard's reign and, contrary to her frequent depiction in Shakespearean productions as a mature and regal woman, she was, in fact, only seven years old when Richard married her and was but ten years old when her husband was deposed (Evans, et al. 816n.)

The likelihood that the king's marriage to this child was ever consummated—even if Richard were inclined to have it so—is therefore highly doubtful.

It is also likely that in an effort to undermine loyalty to Richard or subvert sympathy for his cause, Shakespeare might have provided the allusion to Richard's supposed misconduct or derelict character to link him to Edward II, another English king of notorious reputation (Merchant, [Introduction to *Edward II*] ix-xii), with whom the English public would be familiar because of Marlowe's contemporary play about the wretchedly misguided monarch. F. P. Wilson persuasively suggests, however, that Shakespeare may have effected the dramatic connection between the two kings in order to serve a purpose higher than mere exploitation of the sensational or scandalous: in short, the dereliction of Richard and Edward, he proposes, may not have had anything to do with their apparent homosexuality. Rather, Shakespeare's Richard, like Marlowe's Edward, writes Wilson, "illustrate[s] weakness, not strength. Both kings expend themselves on unworthy favourites, forfeit the allegiance of exasperated nobles, are driven to reluctant abdication, and at the end are murdered in the prisons [to which they had been condemned]" (23). For more information and detail on this latter subject, see my yet-unpublished study, "The Rhetoric of Kingly Grief: Bathos in the Depositions of *Edward II* and *Richard II*."

[23] The allusion made by John of Gaunt in this passage is to the conventional Christian iconography of the pelican, a bird which draws blood from its side in order to feed its young—an observation (based, of course, on popular tradition, not zoological fact) which Christians eventually

emblemized in art as a sign of the wounded Christ who eucharistically nourishes his children with his own blood. This sacramental icon of the pelican, as Martha Fliescher notes, also has much been associated with the monarchial role (193), though with the diminishment of Christian monarchy in the late twentieth century, the symbol is less commonly used in Christian art and naturally is less recognized or understood when it is.

[24]There are those who disagree and do not see the Catholic Anglicanism of Hooker to be the definitive Anglican tradition upon which Shakespeare relied. Roland Frye states that "[t]he Church of England was broad and inclusive; it encompassed such Lutheran views as those of Tyndale, such 'Catholicism' as that of Henry VIII, such Puritanism as that of the great popular preachers of London, [and] such Calvinism as was influential in bishops and others . . . (*Shakespeare* 4). Edward Dowden contends that "as a historical fact, the Church of England has been Calvinist, and Arminian, and Latitudinarian, and Evangelical, and Sacramentarian" (*Puritan and Anglican* 78); Richard Dunn declares that the doctrinal content of the Anglican confession of faith, the Thirty-nine Articles, "affirmed all the chief Lutheran tenets" (37) and William Maxwell writes that liturgically, at the time of Shakespeare, the Church of England inclined to Lutheranism (144).

[25]Apocalypse 6:3-4 reads: "When he opened the second seal, I heard the second living creature say, 'Come!' And out came another horse, bright red; its rider was permitted to take peace from the earth, so that men should slay one another; and he was given a great sword."

[26]As the *Le Morte D'Arthur* reads,

> In many parts of Britain it is believed that King
> Arthur did not die and that he will return to us and
> win fresh glory and the Holy Cross of our Lord Jesus
> Christ . . . [Yet even among those who think Arthur
> entombed at Glastonbury] . . . inscribed on his tomb,
> men say, is this legend: HIC IACET ARTHURUS,
> REXQUONDAM, REXQUE FUTURUS. (502)

[27]Other suggestions in Scripture propose that Christ offers a continued presence among his community by the mediation of the Spirit of God, the Holy Spirit, e.g., St. John 15:26 and 16: 7-14.

ﾟ৯

The Mass of Saint Gregory by Albrecht Dürer in *The Complete Woodcuts of Albrecht Dürer*. 1927. Ed. Willi Kurth (New York: Dover), plate 263.

"As a work of art [*Richard II*] stands . . . close . . . to the Catholic service of the Mass. . . . "

— J. Dover Wilson ([*Introduction to Richard II*] xiii)

CHAPTER THREE

Henry the Fourth, Part One:

The Ascent Begins

"Let wonder seem familiar"—*Much Ado About Nothing*

Just as the Shakespearean romance *Cymbeline* is not really about Cymbeline, so Shakespeare's first play of *Henry IV* is not really about Henry IV. Indeed, no single figure exclusively commands our attention in *1 Henry IV*, for *1 Henry IV* is peopled with many characters of interest: the duplicitous king, the wayward prince, the impetuous young rebel, the vagabond knight. Herschel Baker suggests that both plays of *Henry IV* "trace the slow and ultimately successful efforts of the Lancastrian usurper to secure his hold upon the throne . . ." (842), but the play of *1 Henry IV* is rather more particularly attentive to the threats which jeopardize Henry's continued reign than it is to the king's "ultimately successful efforts to secure" that reign.

To a considerable degree, *1 Henry IV* "involves a thorough examination of the nature of kingship [and] is a study of the development of Hal" (Claeyssens 20); hence, writes Tillyard, Shakespeare "makes the world of Bolingbroke not so much defective as embryonic . . . , ready to grow to its proper fullness in [Hal]" (*Shakespeare's History Plays* 206); for it is through these plays of Henry IV's failure and Prince Hal's success that we see England emerge from brokenness and sin to attain both the promise and fulfillment of its destiny—the redemption of the kingdom from its ruined state—ruin eloquently mourned by John of Gaunt in *Richard II* ("That England, that was wont to conquer others / Hath made a shameful conquest of itself" [II.i.65-66]). Indeed, Gerald Cox observes that in *1 Henry IV*, "the metaphor of redemption is both central and pervasive" (130), and it is none other than Hal who promises that redemption: "I'll so offend, to make offense a skill, / Redeeming time when men least think I will" (I.ii.216-17). Even his enemies recognize his promise: as Sir Richard Vernon reports to the rebel camp at Shrewsbury: ". . . but let me tell the world, / If he outlive the envy of this day, / England did never owe so sweet a hope" (V.ii.6567).

Consistent with his typological use of historical figures to demonstrate that history is not merely an indifferent account of events but a form of progressive revelation (Rivers 149), Shakespeare begins to make use of Hal for his ultimately redemptive purpose in this play, but it is a use which he largely defers and more fully exploits in the last two plays of the tetralogy. Hal (especially as Henry V) will, in fact, become the tetrology's perfect representative type of the Church, but Shakespeare carefully preserves the usefulness of this image in this cycle of plays by never making it appear to be securely in the possession of someone other than the king—although whether even the regnant king always possesses this sacred mark is sometimes called into doubt by Shakespeare, e.g., in *Richard II* II.i.112.

Shakespeare, indeed, always invests his monarchs with this typological identity, irrespective of their personal merits or ability to sustain that identity. Consider, for instance, the example of Henry Bolingbroke in this play. Usurper though he may be, condemned to forfeit his throne in consequence of his sin, he nonetheless is the chief steward of England, and he is preserved on his throne, though perhaps only to enable the accession of his son to the full dignity of the Crown. Hence, Richard can betray his sovereign commission for selfish gain, but in doing so, he sullies more than himself; he corrupts the Church of which he is representative. Subsequently, when Prince Hal eventually redeems and purifies the monarchy in its rightful function as the beneficent seat of temporal authority in the Church of England, he does so by expiating his father's and Richard's sins and vanquishing the foreign (and Catholic) enemy. But before Hal can become the Anglican ideal, his father must at least be its imperfect type.

Henry Bolingbroke, because of his regicidal stain, cannot fulfill the messianic destiny for England which has been reserved for his son, but he can and does affirm that destiny and struggles for it, just as Lancelot, because of a different stain, cannot find the Grail, though he perseveres in quest of it. For example, having momentarily quelled the turmoil in the land, Henry, in Act I, aspires to guide his kingdom to the restoration of its unity in order that all may "[m]arch one way" (I.i.15) "under [the] blessed cross" (I.i.20) and thereby "chase these pagans in those holy fields" (I.i.24). In this passage, therefore, as an anachronistic bearer of the Church's standard, Henry would be recognized by the Elizabethan audiences as the personification of English Christendom not only because he is King and therefore Head of the Church, but also because it is his expressed intention to unify the Church in England and expel the influence of foreign pagans—whom Elizabethans would

associate with the Roman ecclesiastical order, especially in
the persons of its Italian representatives. (For an appraisal of
Elizabethan resentment against Italians [the British loath-
ing of Spaniards and the French at this time is equally
notorious], see Hallett Smith's introduction to *Cymbeline*
in *The Riverside Shakespeare* [Boston: Houghton Mifflin],
1974: 1517-20). Henry, also, in good Anglican form, defies
foreign "magicians" (I.iii.83), and he resists the occasion to
rescue a traitor and import a foreign threat (I.iii.85-87), acts
which correspond to the English Church's defiance of and
refusal to acknowledge the Roman priesthood or sanction
its activities in a land from which this priesthood had been
all but eliminated by the Act of Uniformity in 1559 (Lockyer
173-74; Meyer 21-22).

Henry's fears for his continuance on the throne due to
his culpability for the violent displacement of the previous
sovereign (III.ii.4-11) would also mirror the anxieties of
Anglican prelates and even the Queen herself (see Elizabeth
I's poulter-coupleted verse, "The Doubt of Future Foes,"
wherein she mingles apprehension with confidence when
reflecting upon the dangers of a Catholic insurrection and
restoration).[1] Henry knows that sympathy and support for
rebellion needs little stirring up in his kingdom, for entreat-
ies to rebellion against him, he tells us, have been "proclaim'd
at market-crosses" and even "read in churches" (V.i.73).
The King thunders that his opponents are traitors and liars
who deceive and misrepresent, and therein forfeit any claim
to the name of Christian (V.v.2-10); and such a defiant
posture would probably be recognized by Shakespeare's
audience as reflective of the denunciatory rhetoric of the
homilists of the late sixteenth century, who, with equal

fervor, would excoriate Catholic heresy, apostasy, and trea-
sonous attempts to recapture the English throne and make
it once more subject to the Roman See.[2] Henry's embodiment of Christian (and therefore English Reformation)
virtue appears clearly in his passionate oratory which
denounces the rebels' lack of faith and right religion in the
same breath that denounces their treason. It is important to
see, however, that neither here nor elsewhere does Shakespeare endow Henry with a deeply-layered iconography or
sanctity;[3] he is careful to reserve the fuller application of
near-deific character to Henry V, the successor to Henry IV
who is uncontaminated by the foul effects of his father's
crime. Indeed, as James Simeon says, "*In Henry V* . . . the
play seems bent on directing attention to the 'Mirror of all
Christian Kings' and through him, to the noble virtues of
which he is the 'pattern' or living icon" (77).

Henry IV comes to power upon Richard's fall, "riding,"
as John Marriott puts it, "the wave of a conservative
reaction" (101). But Henry's cause is not entrenchment or
regressivism. "Like the Tudors, [Henry] inaugurates a new
era," writes Charles Barber ("Prince Hal" 6a), not a conservative restoration such as that of the Bourbons in France.
Moreover, Henry rises, in the opinion of Arthur Humphreys,
more by the hand of beneficent destiny than by personal or
collective design ("The Unity and Background" 20). But
whether by design, fate,[4] or popular enthusiasm of the
moment, Henry's reign is brief and insecure. His government, as Shakespeare demonstrates, is troubled by an inability to acquire legitimacy or resolve turmoil with finality.
Joan Webber suggests that whatever the reason in historical
fact, in Shakespeare's rendering of the pragmatic and plain-

spoken king, the royal failure is attributable to Henry's inability to "control [his subjects'] sense of reality through his own control of language and ceremony . . . . He does not know how to direct and control their imaginations" (531, 533). Henry's failure to cloak himself in the mythic as well as the literal robes of state invites and nourishes the crises of confidence in *1 Henry IV* which provide the anxiety and rebellion that so devastatingly mark his reign.

Though Henry is assuredly more practical than Richard (Bradbrook 124), he can but little more effectively "trim . . . his land" (*Richard II* III.iv.56) than could his predecessor. Absent the signs of rightful monarchy and hence unable to conjure the monarchial ideal, Henry, in his "heroic endeavor," in the view of Ivor Morris, "[is] transformed into the spectacle of self-love declining upon limited good in the compulsive seeking of a mundane omnipotence . . ." (434). As the Archbishop of York illustrates the crisis in words derived from Christ's Parable of the Wheat and the Tares (St. Matthew 13:24-30), "He cannot so precisely weed this land / As his misdoubts present occasion. / His foes are so enrooted with his friends / That plucking to unfix an enemy, / He doth unfasten so and shake a friend . . ." (*2 Henry IV* IV.i.203-07). However, according to Holinshed, such was Henry's fate for having fractured the realm by regicide; indeed, Holinshed declares that not only Henry but "his lineal race were scourged afterwards as a dire punishment unto rebellious subjects . . ." (*Holinshed's Chronicle* 96)—a perspective which implies the Lancastrian adventure to have been only a qualified success, if not an outright failure.

Shakespeare seems determined in *1 Henry IV* to illustrate this royal failure, not only through the person of

Henry, but in the persons of several of the nobility and the rogue antic companions of Sir John Falstaff, for in the last analysis, Henry IV is distinct from the other rebels only in degree, not in kind. Indeed, the rebellion which Henry faces in *1 Henry IV* is but the continuation of rebellion against corrupted monarchy which he himself had commenced against Richard.[5] Thus we see that what Shakespeare presents us in this tetralogy is not just drama but myth: it is not rebellion which commands our attention but Rebellion;[6] the search is not just for *a* king but *the* king—one who can unify his people and then lead them to their appointed destiny, their national salvation. That Henry Bolingbroke is not this king is evident, for he lacks the fullness of sacred speech and figure that will be manifest in his son, a Shakespearean king of truly divine election. That greater king to come, Henry V, in many respects, will be twin to Arthur and Christ, kings both, who, like their antitype Hal, emerged from unpromising origins, later however to be revealed as the providentially anointed bearers of their people's destinies.

Hal, indeed, is an unexpected deliverer. We hear almost nothing of him in the first play of the tetralogy, and what we do learn is not encouraging, for he is alleged to be a frequenter of the taverns, companioned with a dissolute lot, a "young wanton and effeminate boy" (*Richard II* V.iii.10). In *1 Henry IV*, he fares little better in our introduction to him, but he quickly affirms to us that his manner is but a guise from which his glory will later emerge when the time comes for him to fulfill his purpose (I.ii.208-17). In this respect, Shakespeare draws out the iconography of Christ as the Bearer of a Messianic Secret with which none but a few should be privileged with knowledge until the time for its disclosure to the world,[7] and with this iconography Shakespeare yokes the young Prince of Wales. Hal thereby becomes the bearer of a messianic secret, too—the resolve to save his people when the appointed time arrives—and, like Christ, Hal is the bearer of a destiny that is specially known to his father (III.ii.133-37).

Distinguishing that which is real from that which is not is not just a problem in this play; the motifs of mistaken identity and purpose permeate *1 Henry IV*. Confusion between appearance and reality is pronounced and contributes to the heightened sense of fundamental disorder which convulses the England of Henry IV. For example, not only is the King mistaken about the person of his son— Henry thinks Hal a profligate and libertine — one in whom "riot and dishonor" stain the royal brow (I.i.85)—but the King also fancies that as punishment for his own "mistreadings," God may have made Hal for him as "a revengement and a scourge . . ." (III.ii.7). Hal, too, is much misunderstood by Falstaff, for in the fat knight's fond belief, the Prince is a rascal (I.ii.80), a coward (II.iv.142,146), and a rogue (II.iv.124). Falstaff's arrogant confidence in his own misplaced judgment ironically leads him to declare that Hal cannot conceal himself from the scrutiny of Jack Falstaff: "By the Lord, I kn[o]w ye as well as he that made ye" (II.iv.267-68); but in fact, in this play, it is rather Hal who alone seems to know who he is and who his associates are. As Hal soliloquizes of the loutish fellows of Eastcheap: "I know you all, and will a while uphold/ The unyok'd humor of your ideleness" (I.ii.195-96). And, like Falstaff and his low companion on Kendal Green, Hotspur, the fiery-tempered son of the Earl of Northumberland, is similarly "in the dark" with respect to Hal: young Percy is yet another who is unable to discern rightly the regal character of the Prince. Hotspur, for example, thinks Hal no soldier, a mere "sword-and-buckler" Prince (I.ii.230), unloved by his father and disgraced by common company (I.ii.231-33). Such thoroughly deceived characters as Falstaff and Hotspur prove that Hal is one whose destiny will be hidden until a transfiguring event reveals his hidden royalty, and Shakespeare pointedly nurtures this familiar iconography of the messiah-in-waiting in shaping the man who, in the fullness of his glory, the Chorus will declare to be no less than "the mirror of all Christian kings" *Henry V* II. Chorus 6).

As if to underscore Henry IV's illegitimacy and Hal's concealed but promised majesty, *1 Henry IV* abounds in even more suggestions that appearances cannot be relied upon to betoken reality. For instance, Hal and Points appear to participate in a robbery of the King's Exchequer (II.ii), although their real purpose is to expose Falstaff rather than pillage the treasury; Owen Glendower boasts of imagined dark powers by which he can "call spirits from the vasty deep" and even "command the devil" (III.ii.53; III.i.55-56); Henry confesses to Hal that it was by chicanery, deceit, and opportunistic daring that he came to the crown (III.ii.39ff.); the rebellion misinterprets the King's power and resolve (IV.i.113ff.); the conspirators question the sincerity of the King's suit for peace (IV.iii.107-13); the "liberal and kind offer of the King" (IV.ii.3) is traitorously withheld by Vernon and Worcester, while a never-uttered "bid [to] battle presently" (V.ii.30) is delivered in its place. Northumberland imperils and ultimately dooms the rebellion by feigning sickness and withholding his forces

(IV.i.31-38). Hotspur perseveres in mistakenly regarding the Prince as a vile reveller, untutored in the ways of war (V.ii.70-74); Henry multiples doubles of himself on the field at Shrewsbury so as to deceive the rebel commanders as to his true whereabouts (V.iii.25); Hal acknowledges, following Prince John's triumph at Gaultree Forest, that he was mistaken about his brother's soldierly resolve (V.iv.16-20); and Falstaff first counterfeits death on the battlefield and then counterfeits honor (which he thinks too costly to earn) by his unworthy claim to have killed Hotspur (V.iv).

Shakespeare does not directly indict Henry IV with respect to the malignancies of his kingdom, but he crowds the play of *1 Henry IV* with references to lies, sorcery, sickness, and death—contaminants which suggest the man whose monarchy spawns them. Because of the proliferation of such examples of royal malfeasance and misdirection, *1 Henry IV*'s formative imagery, in the appraisal of Madeline Doran, though less "direct" and "explicit" than that of *Richard II*, is yet "richer in implicit suggestion" (113), not so much evocative of a kingdom graced by sacramental speech and signs of right order and harmony as one in which such speech and signs of divine favor are absent or disfigured. Consequently, Shakespeare's Anglican audience would have been attracted to Henry IV as the embodiment of holy responsibility and a sacred office but repelled by him as a profaner of that to which he had been entrusted in sacred charge. He is beheld *perspeculum in enigmate*, cloaked in mystery and ambiguity: a king, but like Richard before him, little more than a king of show.

The principal threat to Henry's maintenance of the throne for the House of Lancaster is Henry Percy, also known as Hotspur, the brash young warrior son of Bolingbroke's old confederate, Northumberland. Hotspur is a proven soldier and a questor after honor (I.iii.201-07), and though he has been a loyal son of England, when Henry mounts the throne and will not ransom Mortimer, he and his father become the King's chief adversaries. The manner in which Shakespeare depicts this rivalry is significant, for his method not only supplies his play with indifferent history but furthers his Anglican apologetic.

Henry IV, although tainted by sin, functions as the foremost symbol of Anglicanism in the play because he possesses an office which becomes, in Shakespeare's time, the seat of the temporal head of the Church of England. Any rebel against that sacred office would therefore assuredly be correspondingly identified with either Roman Catholicism or Puritanism, the two principal indigenous threats against the Anglican Church of the time. In *1 Henry IV,* Shakespeare therefore not only provides us with a representative, in Henry IV, of the Anglican Church, but he provides us with representatives of Anglicanism's adversaries and contestants: Hotspur becomes a figure not only of insurrection but of Catholic insurrection, and Falstaff is modeled into a parody of the Puritan threat.[8]

As was demonstrated in the previous chapter, Richard II acquired the dimensions of Roman Catholic identity by his aggressive incorporation of a host of features which distanced him from conventional English and Anglican character expectations; consequently, Richard, for Shakespeare's audience, lost any natural sympathy which the spectators of the play might bring with them by his envelopment in alien and un-Anglican qualities of symbol and speech that connected him to a bygone and discredited era and faith. Hotspur functions in a similar if less detailed capacity in *1 Henry IV*. As Thomas Greene points out, Shakespeare's Hotspur in a "relic of a perishing [medieval] ideology" (227); he is an anachronistic vestige of a disturbed former time, the eclipse of which is signaled, in this tetralogy, by the accession of Henry Bolingbroke, "whose businesslike efficiency replaces the medieval ceremoniousness [and] formality . . . of the court of Richard II" (Barber, "Rule and Misrule" 67). As Barber continues, Hotspur represents an older way of life; his home is in the north of England, "more feudal and catholic than the south-east" (68); and he rejects the ideals of the Tudors (69). Furthermore, like the sixteenth-century Catholic cause of which he is an anachronistic type, Hotspur refuses to acknowledge the new authority in England which has displaced the old order (I.iii.213-16); he explicitly aligns himself with Richard's defeated cause (I.iii.170-76); he intimates that Henry is an agent of the devil's purposes (I.iii.124), and he excoriates the King for having overthrown the rightful succession (IV.iii.93-96), thereby inviting the present disorder.

But it will not be Hotspur who overcomes this disorder; it will be Hal. In repelling Hotspur's insurgent, reactionary threat and by atoning for his father's sin and perfecting his father's imperfect government, Hal will reveal himself to be the appointed hope of the English nation and the promise of sacred order for the future.

Even as Hotspur personifies the insurrectionist threat of Roman Catholicism to Elizabethan England, so Falstaff represents the growing danger of Puritanism—of which the besotted knight is the vehicle of much lampoon. Irving

Ribner proposes, for example, that Falstaff is a satirical study in the religious hypocrisy of the Puritan" *(The English History Play* 173-74); Richmond Noble agrees with this evaluation (169); and L. M. Oliver similarly contends that Shakespeare pointedly mocks Puritanical hypocrisy in his creation of John Falstaff, a fictional character who, Oliver suggests, was inspired by Foxe's characterization of John Oldcastle, a notorious Lollard of infamous pride, gluttony, lechery, and avarice (179-83). The suggestion is credible; Shakespeare may provide an embedded reference to the disreputable old heretic in Hal's adumbration of John Falstaff as "my old lad of the castle" (I.ii.41-42).

Poins also alludes to Falstaff's hypocritical, irreligious character early in the play when he suggests that Falstaff has sold his soul to the devil—and "on Good Friday"—in contemptible exchange for "a cup of Madeira and a cold capon's leg" (I.ii.114-17). The pointed reference to Good Friday suggests that Falstaff, in impious disregard, fails to observe the liturgical calendar of orthodox Christendom's holy days—Good Friday being a solemn day of *fasting* and *abstinence* in Anglican tradition—and Falstaff's cold defiance of holy tradition also suggests that he is Puritanically irreverent and possessed of too much self-conceit and not enough humility. In short, he is an assailant against the virtues of reverence and duty; "thou judgest false," as Hal says of him (I.ii.63); he is the enemy of order and the steward of anarchy. Falstaff, therefore, as the tempter, may provide mirthful company, but he offers a decidedly poor moral example. In such a demonic vein, Falstaff, as Hal tells us, for all his surface merriment, is yet an "old white bearded Satan" (II.iv.463), "the father who begets [lies]" (II.iv.225), a "devil who haunts [Hal in the likeness of an old fat man" (II.iv.447), "a villainous abominable misleader of youth" (II.iv.462), and one who "live[s] out of all order" (III.iii.20).

Falstaff's recurring association with Satan in this play places him outside the sacramental order; he embodies all that is low and disreputable, while Hal is representative of that which is lofty and noble. Hal is all spirit ("fire and air" as the Dolphin will express it in *Henry V* [III.vii.21]); he "rise[s] . . . like feathered Mercury" (IV.i.106); but Falstaff is all flesh, torpid and phlegmatic, "free from all censorship from conscience, morals, or custom . . ." (Hibbard, "'Henry IV'" 2). As James Leverett points out, "Henry's decay is the decay of state, [but] Falstaff rots for all mankind" (98); from Falstaff it therefore is not surprising to hear the plaintive, self-pitying excuse for his weakness that is allusive of the Anglican *Book of Common Prayer's* prefatory instruction for administering the Sacrament of Confirmation:

> Dost thou hear, Hal? Thou knowest in the state of innocency Adam fell; and what should poor Jack Falstaff do in the days of villainy? Thou seest I have more flesh than another man, and therefore more frailty.

(III.iii.164-67)[9]

Falstaff, however, is assuredly not just a devil and an oafish if clever hypocrite, but he also, in a similar vein, is derived in part from medieval comic theatrical traditions. For example, in the opinion of R. Chris Hassler, he is Shakespeare's pre-Lenten Shrovetide Rioter (122), yet he also is the sinister, medieval Vice, complete with "dagger of lath" (II.iv.137). He is the foolish companion of the morality Prodigal (Mendl 88)—(the latter role being one to which Hal's character in *1 Henry IV* is also substantially indebted): Falstaff also is Shakespeare's Lord of Misrule who yet, in death, resembles "an Anglican Everyman" (Baker, "The Christian Context" 81). He is a comic devil (Rossiter, *English Drama* 158). He is also the Elizabethan counterpart of the Roman braggart soldier, both Don Quixote and Sancho Panza, and the jealous owner of an abundance of petty appetites (Tillyard, *Shakespeare's History Plays* 289-90).[10]

Hypocrite that he is perhaps above all else (and therein an example of the worst in Puritan temperament and conduct), Falstaff is a portly paradigm of many uncensored weaknesses and faults which he (contrary to Christ's instruction in St. Matthew 7:3-5) is all too enthusiastically ready to point out in others. Yet, despite his malicious disregard and abuse of his sometime friends—witness his many attempts to indict others for conduct into which he himself has initiated them—Falstaff dares to suggest that those who think ill of him judge him wrongly. Like *Twelfth Night's* Malvolio (another dramatic exercise in Puritanical hypocrisy), pleading for sympathy from those whom he has scorned and abused, Falstaff declares himself to be singled out among sinners for reproof when throughout all the world are ruffians more accursed than he (II.iv.470-74).

As a critic, too, Falstaff is more often wrong than he is right, for the examples that this play provides of his self-serving use of others confirm that he is governed by a doctrine which is so individualized and particularistic that it precludes the possibility of nurturing authentic love for another or for the world. His affection for Hostess Quickly, for example, is mere sham; his association with her, as with Hal, is almost purely mercenary. And of humanity? What thinks he of it?

> There is nothing but roguery to be found in villain-
> ous man . . . . if manhood, good manhood, be not
> forgotten upon the earth, then am I a shotten
> herring. There lives not three good men unhang'd in
> England, and one of them is fat and grows old, God
> help the while! a bad world, I say.
>
> (II.iv.124-25,128-32)

As a discerning critic of his own and others' natures, therefore, Falstaff lacks all credibility, but his misguided appraisals are not the result of wilted or unformed intellect but attribut-able to his heretical dismissal of respect for all others' dignity except his own; [11] he lacks respect because he lacks humility, and he lacks humility because he cannot see himself as but one member of a common humanity: in him there is no urgency to amend his misshapen life and small inclination to renounce his sordid past "Well, I'll repent, and that suddenly, while I am in some liking" [III.iii.4-6]). He fears only men, not God ("Nothing confutes me but eyes, and nobody sees me" [V.iv.126-27]). Given this contradiction between orthodox teaching and heterodox presumption in the person of Jack Falstaff, Robert Stevenson's understated comment that Shakes-peare "can be presumed to have disliked puritans" (56) would seem well-founded and fittingly established in the caricature of Puritanism that is Sir John Falstaff, a judgment which David Bevington affirms (9) and with Eduard Eckhardt agrees: "Shakspeare wurzelt aber durchaus im Protestantismus, [aber] er ist freilich kein protestantischer Fanatiker . . . sogar [ist er] ein Gegner der Puritaner . . . " (236).[12]

Falstaff's un-Anglican personality is also established by his willful distortion of Prayer Book rhetoric, the disfigurement of which alerts the audience to Sir John's antagonism to the Church and right order. Falstaff several times alludes to passages of the *BCP*, among them portions of the Anglican Catechism (I.ii.104-05), the aforementioned preface to the Rite of Confirmation (III.iii.164-67), and the Marriage Service (III.iii.164-65).[13] Even the Prince's suggestion that Falstaff amend his life (a summons derived, in itself, from the opening sentences of the *Book of Common Prayer*'s rites of Morning Prayer, Evening Prayer, the Litany, and the Exhortation from the Communion Service, as well as from the Communion Service proper), is a summons rejoined by Falstaff's tortured reconstruction of the Catechism: "Why Hal, 'tis my vocation, Hal: 'tis no sin for a man to labour in his vocation" (I.i.104-05).

If Hotspur, therefore, is the archetype of Roman Catholic rebellion and Falstaff a figure of the Puritan threat, then Worcester, in this play, is a Renaissance icon of Judas Iscariot. In his failure to inform the rebels of the King's offer of peaceful settlement, he lays upon himself the responsibility for the cataclysm which follows and types himself as a Judas figure whose kiss given to the King (V.i.36) signifies not affection but betrayal and bad faith (cf. with St. Luke 22:47: "But Jesus said to him, 'Judas, would you betray the Son of man with a kiss?'") Even Falstaff says of Worcester's treachery—as Christ's own disciples might have said of the Zealot partisan— "Rebellion lay in his way, and he found it" (V.i.28).

The Battle of Shrewsbury in *1 Henry IV* invites other associations of English history with Christian iconography.

Noble persons die in a conflict wherein many valiant lives are sacrificed for the sake of the people, and these persons' deaths thereby in part assume a character of sacrificial dignity and significance that do not attend ordinary heroic demise. Indeed, in the Shakespearean histories, many of these scenes of death which focus upon the ignoble slaying of a sacrificial victim evoke comparisons with Calvary, thereby incorporating dramatic iconography of the Atonement into the play. As Martha Fleischer attests, Shakespeare's associations of these contemporary events with the events of sacred history bring such "history visibly close to its origins in Christian iconography" (236). In *1 Henry IV*, the slaying of Sir Walter Blunt especially evokes such associations, for Blunt dies garbed in the robes of the king; he perishes, a righteous innocent whose solemn death prompts Honor Matthews to assert that such death was probably designed by Shakespeare in order not just to elicit associations with Calvary but also to nurture the audience's familiarity with the ritual murder of innocents which Elizabethans would recall from their acquaintance with the story in Scripture (St. Matthew 2:16-18) as well as through such "Herod scenes" as that of *The Massacre Of the Innocents* in the Chester cycle of mystery plays (121).

Through such characters and dramatic associations in *1 Henry IV*, Shakespeare constructs a Christian universe, in miniature, by which the grand design of the world's redemption is reenacted and applied to the circumstances of English history. Led through a period of national darkness by the unprepossessing Prince, England convulses in the throes of illicit and corrupted monarchy to emerge, in *Henry V*, a nation purified of its sin and delivered to greatness by the examples of steadfast faith and perseverance in suffering. But Shakespeare is not yet done with illustrating the character of spiritual malignancy beneath the surface disorder and turmoil in the England of *1 Henry IV;* in *2 Henry IV* he invites us to descend into the maelstrom of horror that draws England even closer to oblivion and the threat of annihilation.

Notes

[1]The doubt of future foes exiles my present joy,

And wit me warns to shun such snares as threaten mine annoy.

For falsehood now doth flow, and subject faith doth ebb,

Which would not be, if reason ruled or wisdom weaved the web.

But clouds of toys untried do cloak aspiring minds.

Which turn to rain of late repent, by course of changed minds.

The top of hope supposed, the root of truth will be,

And fruitless all their graffed guiles, as shortly ye shall see.

The dazzled eyes with pride, which great ambition blinds,

Shall be unsealed by worthy wights whose foresight falshood finds.

The daughter of debate, that eke discord doth sow

Shall reap no gain where former rule hath taught still peace to grow.

No foreign banished wight shall anchor in this port,

Our realm it brooks no stranger's force, let them elsewhere resort.

Our rusty sword with rest, shall first his edge employ

To poll their tops that seek such change and gape for joy.

[2]In order to confirm Tudor absolutism, consolidate the gains of the Reformation, and suppress any resurgent sympathy for the restoration of Catholic supremacy, the Elizabethan Homilies regularly proclaimed the virtues of passive obedience and warned of the grave consequences attending civil rebellion. J. A. Bryant cites such a supporting passage from the *Sermons and Homilies* (a shortened form of reference to the *Certain Sermons or Homilies Appointed to be Read in Churches in the time of Queen Elizabeth of Famous Memory* [1574]): "The violence and injury that is committed against authority is committed against God" (*Hippolyta's View* 23)—meaningful not only because it was proclaimed in the service of Anglican monarchy but especially because of its prohibitive counsel against rebellion which was founded upon the assumption that blasphemy attended that which otherwise (as in our century) might be considered a purely secular act of armed defiance.

[3]One will recall, however, that the Duchess of York, in *Richard II*, had acclaimed Henry "a god on earth" (V.iii.136) when he forgave her son, Aumerle, of his conspiracy to murder the king at Oxford, though this is one of the few occasions employed by Shakespeare to demonstrate a quality of Christ-like character in Henry apart from the exercise of his natural authority. Still, it is a significant moment (although some of the events immediately precedent to it— e.g., Aumerle's pleading, York [that "fussy, incompetent old gentleman"]'s humiliation (Rossiter, "*Angel With Horns*" 27), and the Duchess's protracted and hysterical wailing for pardon—are almost ridiculously comic). Of the quality of Henry's extension of pardon to Aumerle, Ernest Gilman has perceptively written that "Aumerle is forgiven under a new

dispensation of mercy, and his pardon is the emblem of a regenerate kingdom . . . . English history [in this act] recapitulates spiritual history as a redemptive movement from sinfulness to grace" (112-13).

⁴Whether due in part to an ambivalence, indecisiveness, or lack of a definite perspective on the workings of fate in this tetralogy and elsewhere in Shakespeare, the absence of a precise definition of fate may be less attributable to Shakespeare's evasiveness or uncertainty on the subject than simply due to a contradictory posture with respect to fate or fortune which he shares with other Renaissance dramatists. For example, consider Mortimer Junior of Christopher Marlowe's *Edward II* and Edmund of Shakespeare's *King Lear*. Each claims to be in control of his own destiny, making "Fortune's wheel turn as he please[s]" (*Edward II* V.ii.53), yet each, contrary to his expectations, is finally mastered by fate: Edmund mutters in his dying gasp, "Th' hast spoken right, 'tis true. / The wheel is come full circle, I am here" (*King Lear* V.iii.174-75), in manner much like Mortimer's own tragic anagnorisis: "Base fortune, now I see, that in thy wheel / There is a point to which men aspire / They tumble headlong down" (*Edward II* V.vi.59-61).

⁵As Lewis Owen writes, Henry never appears able to command even the respect of his lesser subjects; and for all his able "pretending," he is, as a king, but a poor "player." His political ascent is marked by a simultaneous decline in his personal authority (13); for even though Henry had at least feigned obedience to Richard at Flint Castle (*Richard II* III.iii.187-88), his own rebellious nobility (governed, like Henry, by personal conceit and ὕβρις) do not, as Martha Fleischer points out, even pretend to acknowledge

Henry's supremacy by their exercise of due ceremony when withdrawing from his presence (80). Furthermore, such failure by English subjects to perform even token gestures of respect would not be perceived by a Shakespearean audience to constitute just a breach of courtesy or etiquette (Wright, "'Lord of His Love'") but would more ominously signify the absence of the King's Dignity in its supposed possessor.

[6]As *The Mirror for Magistrates* (1559) declares, in defining civil rebellion as rebellion against the divine authority of the civil order, "Whoever rebelleth against any ruler either good or bad rebelleth against God . . ." (178). Refer also to endnote 2.

[7]See, for example, the following passages in the Gospel of St. Mark: 1:25; 1:34; 1:43-45; 3:12; 5:43; 7:24; 7:36; 8:26; 8:30; 9:09; and 9:30. See also *The Messianic Secret* (J. C. G. Grieg's translation of William Wrede's seminal study, *Das Messiasgeheimnis in den Evangelien*), esp. pp. 24-81.

[8]Although George Becker is one who does not see Hotspur and Falstaff as representatives of the two rival religious traditions struggling for the soul of England, he does concede that "both are shown to be out of bounds in their behavior. Therefore both are dangerous to the realm and are potential misleaders of youth. They are the Scylla and Charybdis between which Hal must steer his course . . ." (33). Furthermore, as if to underscore the significance of the moral ground on which Hal finds himself with respect to these two contestants, Shakespeare, tableau-like, positions the Prince directly between the two adversaries on Shrewsbury Field—but Hal, notably, is the only one among the three who stands. Both Hotspur and Falstaff lie crumpled before Hal; one is dead; the other feigns death. The iconography,

of course, is Calvary: the bloodied lord looks down and aside to gaze upon broken, dead, or dying mankind, over which he pronounces words of benediction.

⁹ Peter Milward offers more evidence, in connection with this passage in Act III, which suggests that Shakespeare is governed by an Anglican sensibility in the composition of this play. As he remarks,

> there is a prefatory instruction [in the *BCP*] about the time of ministering the sacrament [of Holy Confirmation], "when children come to that age, that partly by the frailty of their own flesh, partly by the assaults of the world and the devil, they begin to be in danger to fall into sundry kinds of sin." It is possibly this sentence which is parodied by Falstaff in his attempt to excuse himself: "Thou seest I have more flesh than another man and therefore more frailty." (11)

Milward reminds us elsewhere that "in the plays . . . we find evidence of a familiarity with the Anglican services, such as [Shakespeare] could hardly have gained from hearsay. His frequent allusions to the *Psalms* . . . usually follow the version . . . used in the *Book of Common Prayer*. He also refers, explicitly or implicitly, to almost all the ceremonies prescribed in the Prayer Book and echoes many passages of the Elizabethan *Homilies* . . ." (104).

¹⁰The corpulent knight, lithe in his maneuverings if not in his movement (II.ii.12-13), is indeed adroit in amalgamating conventional roles from the medieval dramatic tradition. Wells and Gouda are among the many who concur with those scholarly appraisals which suggest that both Hal and Falstaff are creations derived from medieval drama: as

they observe, Falstaff, in particular, is "the devil of the miracle play, the Vice of the morality and the Riot of the interlude" (55).

[11] Falstaff, for instance, routinely insults Hostess Quickly by refusing even to acknowledge her personhood:

> How now, Dame Partlet the hen? have you inquir'd yet who pick'd my pocket?
>
> (III.iii.52-53)

> ... thou art a beast ... an otter ... neither flesh nor fish, a man knows not where to have her.
>
> (III.iii.122,125,127-28)

> There's no more faith in thee than in a stew'd prune, nor no more truth in thee than in a drawn fox, and for womanhood, Maid Marian may be the deputy's wife of the ward to thee. Go, you thing, go.
>
> (III.iii.112-15)

[12] Shakespeare, as a playwright and actor, would also likely find Puritanism especially offensive, writes Russell Fraser, not inconsiderably because of Puritanism's particular hatred and intolerance of the theatre which succored the fanatical desire of many to suppress the drama. Fraser cites John Rainolde, a Puritan contemporary of Shakespeare who summarizes in sweeping generalization the Puritan attitude toward dramatic art in *Thoughts Touching the Holie Scripture* (1584): "all Plaies, as carnall, be obscene and ridiculous . . ." (9). The result of the triumph of this ideo-religious tyranny of opinion under Oliver Cromwell in 1642 was, of course, the criminalization of all dramatic performance in England and the destruction of such great national theatres as the Globe.

[13]Falstaff's references to the *BCP* are usually, though not always, put to ill use. For example, Naseeb Shaheen points out that Falstaff's petition at I.ii.152-54 ("Well, God give thee the spirit of persuasion and him the ears of profiting, that what thou speakest may move and what he hears may be believ'd") is likely drawn from the collect following the Offertory of the Anglican Communion Service (141) and substantially preserves the spirit of the original. Furthermore, Stella Brook observes that such a petition as Falstaff's imitates "the rhythms and balanced construction of some of the Collects" (204). Other scholars also comment on some of Falstaff's perhaps more orthodox utterances: for example, Falstaff's "concern with age and death, however ironically expressed it may be, links him to that attitude of self-examination which marks the Christian outlook before Easter" (Baker, "The Christian Context" 77), and Falstaff's final words, in Baker's appraisal, "recall a Lenten service whose purpose was to summon the sinner to just such a change of life, the Commination in the *Book of Common Prayer*" (78)—a liturgy which, as H. W. E. Slade tells us, is intended for the "solemn denunciation of . . . grave sins" (qtd. in Adams 12); as a restorative rite of the Church, it is appropriately applied by Shakespeare to Falstaff's last moments in order to consolidate the audience's perception of Falstaff's repentant and Anglican end.

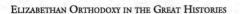

The Four Riders of the Apocalypse by Albrecht Dürer in *The Complete Woodcuts of Albrecht Dürer*. 1927. Ed. Willi Kurth (New York: Dover, 1963). plate 109

"Tell Bollingbrook .../That .../[h]e is come to open / The purple testament of bleeding war."

(*Richard II* III.iii. 91-94)

Chapter Four

Henry the Fourth, Part Two

The Ascent Continues

"Come hither, England's hope"—*Henry the Sixth, Part Three*

The accelerated decline of the kingdom under Henry Bolingbroke forms the principal theme of the second play of Henry IV. The infection which attacks England in *1 Henry IV* spreads with virulent fury in *2 Henry IV*. The inoculation against the disease is provided, however, by Prince Hal, who, in the final act, purges the kingdom of its sickness by his dispersal of the renegade band of corruption and its malignant leader, Falstaff, and he succeeds, as well, in overcoming the crisis of legitimacy wrought by his father's unconventional accession. England's collapse into almost total ruin is therefore dramatically reversed by the intervention of the Prince who becomes a King and lifts England to unforseen heights and unexpected promise.

When *Henry the Fourth, Part Two* opens, the first character to speak is Rumor—a Shakespearean variant, for this play, of the traditional Chorus—and appropriately enough for a play whose first voice is Rumor—"the creator and defeater of expectations, par excellence" (Holland 411)—Robert Hapgood warns us that "the central mode of speech in *2 Henry IV* is that of true and—almost as frequently—false report" ("Shakespeare's Thematic Modes" 43).

Indeed, rumor and question are dominant rhetorical modes in *2 Henry IV;* uncertainty and error govern the speech of the entire play. The inquiry, for example, of "What news?" pervades the play and is asked no less than seven times (I.i.7; II.i.133; II.i.164; II.i.170; II.iv.354; IV.i.18; V.iii.l01). "I hear" and "they say" are even more frequently urged upon listeners (I.i.188; I.ii.62; I.ii.103; I.ii.107; I.ii.203; II.ii.66; II.ii.113; II.iv.60; II.iv.239; III.i.95; III.ii.78; IV.iii.77; V.iii.140), and the question, "Dost hear?" is also repeatedly asked (II.iv.79; II.iv.82; II.iv.305).

Among the examples of disfigured speech, Hostess Quickly's utterances are so given to malapropism (. . . "he's an infinitive thing upon my score" [II.i.24]; " . . . you cannot bear with another's confirmities" [II.iv.57-58]) that Richard Brinsley Sheridan might worthily have used the Hostess as a model for his somewhat more famous figure of humorously inaccurate speech—and doubtless, if he had, she would think herself therefore "in good name and fame with the very best" [II.iv.75]—just as the ruffian Poins naively thinks himself a gentleman "well spoke on" [II.ii.65]).

Continuing the patterns of deceit and false report in *2 Henry IV,* lies about Justice Shallow's mistaken virility are so abundantly proffered by the Justice as to rival the ribald fancies of Falstaff himself. Prince John deceives Archbishop Scroop with the promise of a gracious hearing of the rebels' grievances ("My lord, these griefs shall be with speed redress'd, /Upon my soul they shall" (IV.ii.59-60); yet he reneges on his princely assurances and delivers the Archbishop and his fellows to the headsman ("Some guard [these traitors] to the block of death, / Treason's true bed and yielder-up of breath" (IV.ii.59-60). False accounts of the events at Shrewsbury circulate throughout the kingdom (Induction 6-10): Lord Bardolph's "certain news from Schrewsbury" (I.i.12) could hardly be less certain; and Henry IV deludes himself with an "atoning" death in a chamber named for the holy city to which he had deceived his countrymen into believing that he would pilgrimage— confessing on his deathbed that, despite his public assurances to the contrary, he had never intended to make any such journey at all (IV.v.204-15). Even the Epilogue begs pardon for his speech which is "marr[ed]" and "weary" (Epilogue 6,33).

The impact of this new rhetorical framework for this third play of the tetralogy is considerable and significant, for it underscores the continuing deterioration of a kingdom which, delivered from one evil, is repeatedly seduced into accepting another. As James Calderwood tells us, "Falstaff's lie at Shrewsbury [his claim to have defeated the ambitious Hotspur] is sustained in *2 Henry IV*, fittingly lodged in that lie-ridden, rumor-governed play in which Shakespeare spins out the consequences of the fall of sacramental speech" (89). And as Harold Toliver writes of King Henry, "after he becomes king . . . he begln[s] searching for a rhetoric to weave his momentary purposes into larger configurations; [but] he never grasps the potential mythic and ritual dimensions of the office" ("Shakespeare's Kingship" 71).

Unlike Henry's speech, Richard's ornate speech complements the majesty of the office which he occupies, although its rich, poetic character is designed more meaningfully to closely approximate Richard's own lofty, resplendent, ethereal person ("...look not to the ground / Ye favorites of a king, are we not high?" [*Richard II* III.ii.87-88]) more than the dignity of the Crown. Richard's fanciful and elevated oratory evokes the figure of a remote, detached king who dwells in such transcendent aloofness that he emerges insufficiently familiar with the hard machinery of coarse political reality sufficiently to maintain his government. Henry's lines, in contrast, while usually stately and dignified, are rarely and only imperfectly imperial; he speaks tersely and with an abbreviation which connotes the brute efficiency and studied pragmatism of his nature. With little poetic utterance therefrom, Henry Bolingbroke's tongue bespeaks his anchoring in the world, the *saeculum*, and suggests one who nurtures a machiavellian persona which eschews the sublimity of imagination in favor of the more practical and bodily arts which lead to material acquisition and the consolidation of political power. As Richard concedes of him, "they well deserve to have / That know the strong'st and surest way to get" (*Richard II* III.iii.200-01).[1]

Underscoring the rhetoric of uncertainty and the broader themes of illegitimacy and wrongful identity, confrontation and confusion also characterize the language of the play. Much like *Hamlet*, which open on a question ("Who's there?" [I.i.l]), the Induction of *2 Henry IV* accusatorally opens with " . . . which of you will stop / The vent of hearing when loud Rumor speaks?" 2). The very first lines of Act I also thrust forward a series of questions:

> Lord Bardolph. Who keeps the gate here ho?
> Where is the Earl?
> Porter. What shall I say you are?
>
> (I.1.1-2)

In fact, ten of the first twelve scenes of *2 Henry IV* open with questions.

Threats of chaos, disorder, and bloodshed permeate the play also. Not only does Henry's kingdom erupt from within, but it discovers itself to be threatened by rebellion in the North and in the East, as well. We hear from Lord Bardolph that "[t]he times are wild, contention, like a horse / Full of high feeding, madly hath broke loose, / And bears down all before him" (*2 Henry IV* I.i.9-11), and from Northumberland, the nobleman who earlier had backed Henry's deposition of Richard in order to "[redeem from broking pawn the blemish'd crown" (*Richard II* II.i.293), comes now the contrary, bellowing cry to " . . . let order die! / And let this world no longer be a stage / To feed contention in a ling'ring act; / But let one spirit of first-born Cain / Reign in all bosoms . . ." (*2 Henry IV* I.i.154-58). Northumberland's thundering invocation, therefore, is a summons to civil war—that like Cain against Abel, brother might lift up hand against brother and soak England in her own blood. Blood therein assumes an anti-sacramental significance in this play; it becomes the sign of a covenant broken rather than a covenant sealed, for blood, in *2 Henry IV*, betokens slaughter and disunion rather than fraternity and the empowering, sacramental bond which it acquires in the regal voice of Henry V: "For he today that sheds his blood with me / Shall be any brother . . ." (*Henry V* IV.iii.61-62).

Images of fragmentation, the impotence of age, the crippling power of disease, and the deeds of official malfeasance cloak the play with gloom and despair so dark and wrenching that it hardly surprises us that the comic vitality of *1 Henry IV* is so slightly recurrent in *2 Henry IV*. The Archbishop testifies of England's woe under Henry's insecure reign: "O thoughts of men accurs'd! / Past and to come seems best; things present worst" (I.iii.107-08). The Archbishop similarly comments upon the fractured government of an almost-ruined king, seeing the people nourished not by spiritual food but sating themselves, instead, on "dead vomit" (I.iii.99). Henry himself accompanies every single appearance of his in this play with lamentation either on the heaviness of his office, the weariness of his age, or the sorrow of his spirit.[2] Falstaff, too, is mocked by Doll Tearsheet as one who ought to give up "fighting o'days and foining o' nights, and begin to patch up [an] old body for heaven" (II.iv.232-33). Even Hal confesses, "Before God, I am exceeding weary" (II.ii.i). And Henry, declining in power and favor, observes the concomitant decline of his land as he affirms what his nobles already know:

> . . . you perceive the body of our kingdom
> How foul it is, what rank diseases grow,
> And with what danger, near the heart of it.
>
> (III.i.37-40)

That Henry's personal health and the health of England simultaneously decline at accelerated speed throughout this play reinforces our sense of the continuing absence of a spiritual strength that is bestowed by legitimacy (Frye, *Northrop Frye* 80)—legitimacy such as earlier was forsaken by Richard in order that he might live as though England were his own personal possession. Throughout Henry's reign, however, rebellion is not quelled but continues unabated, and ever-renewed uprisings intensify the lack of national renewal, the counterpart of which lack once was thought might be fostered by Henry's reign; indeed, the recurrent conspiracies among the English nobility magnify and parallel the similarly subversive activities perpetrated by Falstaff and his fellow low-born anarchists. Henry's inability to heal himself and his broken land and his failure to bind up his family's and country's wounds reveal the lingering lack of legitimacy in Henry's monarchy that suggests the intimate relationship between king and country is poisoned by crime.[3]

As James Winney reminds us, "The king [in Shakespeare] is an archetypal image invested with powerful associations" (44). As such, Henry's peril in England's peril, and his loss of power intimates his lack of a divine mandate and godly authority. As Harold Toliver acknowledges,

> the monarch in Shakespeare is often assumed to represent a natural and providential order that transcends normal politics. He is the manifest of providence in whom we can gauge the working of inscrutable forces . . . . As an archetypal symbol, he stands in a closed and articulate universe whose divine and cosmic influences converge in the action he performs. ("Falstaff" 59)

Accordingly, Henry's loss or surrender of any sovereignty he might have had invites a search for the repository of the divine will.[4] Clearly, by the end of Act IV, we know that Henry has utterly compromised his personal claim to authenticity and rightful monarchy, although Shakespeare apparently does not believe that Henry's crimes nullify his son's candidacy for the succession: in *2 Henry IV* IV.v.184, Henry repeats his confession of *1 Henry IV,* allowing that he had achieved the crown by "by-paths and indirect crook'd ways"; but Hal's act of repentance in *Henry V* IV.i.292-94 ("Not to-day, O lord, / O not to-day, think not upon the fault / My father made in compassing the crown!") and subsequent triumph at Agincourt would suggest that Hal (like the Reformation Church of which he is an icon), although the product of a contaminated history, can, nonetheless, be elected by God to embrace the demands of royal office.

Thomas Hyde also argues Henry IV's lack of a divine commission. Writes Hyde: the monarchy loses (or at least does not regain) its legitimacy under Henry IV; he is but a player-king who either discovers or confesses on his death-bed that [all his] reign hath been but as a scene" (IV.v.197) (107). John Bromley agrees, suggesting that reflective of this "player" image, Henry may possess some external public quality, but little private virtue (61). Henry, indeed, is the consummate politician; we rarely see him as anything else. Reality is nearly always defined politically by Henry: "Even Henry's griefs are political," Bromley continues; "he mourns the absence of the prince far more than he mourns the absence of the son" (61). Even in such a supposedly sacred quest as Henry's promised journey to Jerusalem, Henry repeatedly admits the calculated division between his public and private self, even encouraging Hal to assume a similarly evasive strategy and thereby deflect the questions of legitimacy surrounding the Lancasters' irregular acquisition of the royal title: "Therefore, my Harry / Be it thy course to busy giddy minds / With foreign quarrels" (IV.v.213-15).

Henry Kelly suggests that the divine wrath which falls on Henry comes in the form of his unease on the throne and adds that Henry's periodic respites from his sufferings signal the occasional and incremental return of God's favor to the royal family. He asserts that God's "punishment [of] the Lancasters] must be said to end whenever his [Henry's] fears are relieved" (232). But Kelly's equation of a subjective frame of mind with an objective state of grace cannot be supported by the text. Such momentary relief from unrelenting anguish as Henry may occasionally enjoy demonstrates instead his frequent and false apprehension of divine favor—false, especially inasmuch as none of Henry's brief moments of relative calm (*1 Henry IV* III.ii; *1 Henry IV* V.v; *2 Henry IV* IV.iv.; and *2 Henry IV* v.v.) establish any enduring tranquility for either Henry or England. In any case, not even Hal's exemplary reign as a model of the monarchial ideal is uncompromised by sin and error or distress of mind. Contrary to Kelly, Shakespeare therefore appears to confirm Henry Bolingbroke's inadequacy as a sovereign not only by Henry's distress and inability to reunify England but by the revelation from Hal himself, once established on the throne as Henry V, that his father went "wild into his grave" (*2 Henry IV* V.ii.123) and that "what in [Henry Bolingbroke] was purchas'd / [Has f]all[en] upon [him] in a more fairer sort" (IV.v.199-200).

In support, Norman Sanders observantly points out that both *1 Henry IV* and *2 Henry IV* are filled with sordid reminders of the unhappy events that followed Henry Bolingbroke's theft of the crown. He notes that

> [t]hese allusions [to the consequences of Henry's theft] are further reinforced by the cumulative effect of the imagery of sickness, weariness, and sleeplessness associated with Henry's reign . . . . The rebels against this diseased rule are similarly devalued; for throughout both parts they are characterized by division, bickering, and weakness. (32)

The fullness of the imagery of decay and death in *2 Henry IV* is indicative of a national state of decline that has been induced by repeated sacrilege against the Crown. As Roy Battenhouse affirms, "Bolingbrooke's sin [is] no single crime but a responding variation of Richard's sins" ("Revising Tillyard" 32).

The disease motif of *2 Henry IV* has not gone unnoticed by other scholars. Kenneth Muir and Sean O'Laughlin emphasize its pervasiveness (109-11). One can even find it in the comic scenes:

Poins.	And how doth the Martlemas [Falstaff], your master?
Bardolph.	In bodily health, sir.
Poins.	Marry, the immortal part needs a physician. But that moves him not; though that be sick, it dies not.

(II.ii.101-105)

Bullcalf.	O Lord, sir, I am a diseas'd man.
Falstaff.	What disease hast thou?
Bullcalf.	A whoreson cold, sir, a cough, sir, which I caught with ringing in the King's affairs upon his coronation-day, sir.

(III.ii.179-83)

As Shakespeare therefore intimates through Bullcalf, the anniversary celebration of Henry's accession brings sickness, not health.[5] The implication of Bullcalf's remark can hardly be mistaken: Henry's government is an infection in the land, his pretension to monarchy a domestic plague of state. Lord Bardolph acclaims that, like a fever, "the times are wild" (I.i.9), and even the King himself lacks immunity from the contagion which he spreads; as the Duke of Clarence tells us: "Th' incessant care and labor of his mind / Hath wrought the mure that should confine it in / So thin that life looks through and will break out" (IV.iv.118-20). Henry's illness, then, is not unlike Richard's or even Arthur's before him, for Richard, ruined, plunged into near-bathetic despair and Arthur, too, according to legend, unable to nurse his land to health, suffered the fragmentation of the kingdom in the ravages of body and soul.

If, then, as Anglican theology declares, a sacrament is an outward sign of an inward grace (Hooker 261), Henry, lacking his Dignity, is no embodiment of the sacramental ideal nor is England graced by its "reception" of him in this play. And, if the consequence of unworthy reception is judgment (286-87), then England, under Henry, embroiled in civil war and troubled by the threat of invasion, is duly judged.

Henry, adds Herbert Coursen, is nothing but "a pragmatic man who becomes a king *de facto*, not *de jure*. Even his projected crusade . . . an effort to place himself and his reign back within the sacramental system, turns out, as he tells us in his dying words, to have been merely a political device . . . " ("Sacramental Elements" 9). In his rhetoric, he similarly fails: Henry, writes Joan Webber, "is out-talked, upstaged, and left off stage for whole acts at a time, and, save for several significant exceptions, his rhetoric is alternately blunt and pedestrian, and hackneyed. We rarely see or hear majesty in him . . ." (531).

Henry's failure to restore himself to the "sacramental system," however, may largely be attributable to the fact that he might never have been in it to begin with. Given, as we have seen, the vital significance of blood, by which the sacramental union is sealed, Henry, as Shakespeare depicts him, can be representative of little other than a copious bloodletting. "The place of Bolingbook in the action of the play," writes J. A. Bryant, "is . . . that of a man who sets out to slay the murderous Cain and does so, only to find that he himself has the blood of Abel on his hands" (*Hippolyta's View* 30). Furthermore, as David Sundelson contends, such an ancient theme from salvation history as that of brother against brother (recall Northumberland's cry for Cain-like rebellion in the kingdom) supports the tetralogy's drama of national disintegration as a house divides against itself, noble-man and commoner alike, to the ruin of the whole (33).

The lower characters in *2 Henry IV*—Mouldy, Wart, and Feeble—also personify the sickness and decay of the realm; Falstaff is afflicted with gout and the pox (he cannot decide which is the cause of the other); he nonetheless resolves to "turn diseases to commodity" (I.ii.248); and the Archbishop of York, prior to his capture by Prince John, observes and prophesies:

> . . . we are all diseas'd
> And with our surfeiting and wanton hours
> Have brought ourselves into a burning fever,
> And we must bleed for it; of which disease
> Our late King Richard (being infected) died.
>
> (IV.i.54-58)

The contagion which infects the realm is also manifest in England's official corruption. Justice Shallow, for example, is a whoremonger and a liar who dances naked in taverns and bears little concern for his reputation and duty as a justicer of the realm (III.ii.302-28). Justice Silence is a companion and colleague of Shallow's who is given to heavy drinking and songs which celebrate the irresponsible, epicurean life:

> Do nothing but eat, and make good cheer,
> And praise God for the merry year,
> When flesh is cheap and females dear,
> And lusty lads roam here and there . . . .
>
> (V.iii.17-20)

This malfeasance which corrupts justice in the kingdom reflects infidelity, impotence, and anarchy as well. Nobles do not keep faith, oaths are forsaken, treason and insurrection bedevil the kingdom. The riots of Sir John Falstaff, in contrast to his happy, roguish antics in *1 Henry IV*, reveal more than a merely lazy humor: they reflect an abandonment of station and a cold contempt for civility and order to which neglect of office he likewise hopes to seduce the prince, as well. His antagonist is government and decorum itself: as he irreverently queries of Hal in *1 Henry IV*: " . . . shall there be gallows standing in England when thou art king? and resolution thus fubb'd as it is with the rusty curb of old father antic the Law?" (I.ii.59-61)

Davy, too, reveals the corruption and lack of an impartial justice in England during Henry's reign when he pleads with Justice Shallow to "countenance" one William Visor against Clement Perkes, despite the admitted villainy and knavery of the former. In Act Five, Davy entreats,

> An honest man, sir, is able to speak for himself, when a knave is not. I have served your worship truly, sir, this eight years; and if I cannot once or twice in a quarter bear out a knave against an honest man, I have but a very little credit with your worship. The knave is mine honest friend, sir . . . . (i.45-50)

To this plea, Shallow gives his assent and assures Davy that he shall find for his friend, the guilty party, against the innocent man: "Go to, I say, he shall have no wrong" (V.i.52)—a cruel reminder of the wicked judge of St. Luke 18—although the judge of Christ's parable at least later repents of his evil; Shallow, in perverse contrast, celebrates his.

Illustrating, too, the motif of theft as another extension of malfeasance in the realm (proceeding, of course, from Henry's theft of the throne), Falstaff swindles Shallow out of a thousand pounds, then promises him, in exchange, the preferment of the new king who ascends the throne upon the death of Henry IV: "Master Robert Shallow, choose what office thou wilt in the land, 'tis thine . . ." (V.iii.122-24). In such respect, Falstaff attains the full moral likeness of Henry IV: pretenders both, each fancies himself a king (recall Falstaff's mimicry of Henry in the tavern at Eastcheap), but each is rather a thief with kingly pretensions. Hal, notably, sees through both of them, however (*1 Henry IV* I.ii.195-96; *Henry V* IV.i.292-95), and he rejects them both, although Freudians would eagerly—and I think persuasively—suggest that Hal's rejection of his father cannot (and therefore does not) occur during his father's life. His rejection of Falstaff, therefore, substitutes for the deferred rejection of his now-deceased father, the father of lies (Stewart 191). And when Hal adopts a new "father"—for so he addresses him—his choice is the eminent and revered Lord Chief Justice (*2 Henry IV* V.ii.140).

All of the comic pickpockets and lie-abouts of *1 Henry IV* become the coarse and vicious criminals of *2 Henry IV*. They are not the devil-may-care roisterers of the first Henry play but savage, violent hoodlums. Falstaff's vagabond ways and grossness of character are not endearing qualities in *2 Henry IV*; rather, his dereliction is repeatedly and severely chastised, reproved, and described with unsympathetic attention in the third play of the tetralogy. A new low-born ruffian, Pistol, degrades the general company by his mercenary nature and arrogant, quarrelsome attitude. The jolly, whimsical, spirited attendants of Falstaff's happy, ragged band of *1 Henry IV* assume dark and menacing identities: gone are the laughable buffoons of the tavern in Eastcheap; in are sinister, vile creatures with names like Fang, Snare, and Shadow, villains whose names bear ample testimony to the invidious quality of their persons. Doll Tearsheet, an acid-tongued whore and murderess (yet the "Helen of [Falstaff's] noble thoughts" [V.v.33]) is added to the company of these new, otherwise-male disreputables; and Hostess Quickly's lighthearted, good-humored character of *1 Henry IV* is transformed in *2 Henry IV* into that of a sullen, contemptible gull who comes under the scrutiny of the police for operating a disorderly house from which Doll is finally hauled away to prison. Thieving justices, such as Silence and Shallow, reflect the corrupt and dissolute state of Henry's stolen kingdom. Paltry in their peccadilloes and insignificant in their persons, they are lechers and conspirators, nonetheless, who, accompanied by the harsher creatures of their association, demonstrate the present fulfillment of the Bishop of Carlisle's earlier prophecy: "Disorder, horror, fear, and mutiny shall here inhabit . . . if you raise this house against this house" (*Richard II* IV.i.142,145). Falstaff and his fellow menaces' thefts and Doll's complicity in the murder of her patrons are unmistakable parallels to and consequences of Henry's own usurpation of the throne and complicity in sacrilegious murder; as such, they demonstrate the ripple effect of royal crime which spreads its taint on all the kingdom.[6]

Falstaff becomes a figure of particular contempt in *Henry IV* as his temperament recoils into a state of sometimes violent degeneracy. He draws a sword on Pistol and wounds him in a drunken brawl over Doll Tearsheet (II.iv). He accepts bribes from would-be draft dodgers, thereby releasing able men from the king's service, although he relentlessly presses lesser and poorer men into military duties for which they are not fit (III.ii). A master of the rhetoric of evasion, he turns aside Mistress Quickly's demands for settlement and eventually persuades her to dismiss her lawsuit against him (II.i); he avoids responding to the inquiries of the Lord Chief Justice while simultaneously attempting to swindle him out of his money (I.ii)—a ruse which he later succeeds in practicing upon the unsuspecting Justice Shallow.

These detestable qualities of the lower orders are magnified in *2 Henry IV* not only to underscore the increasingly distorted state of England under Henry's reign but also to prepare us emotionally for these persons' separation from and repudiation by Prince Hal when he ascends the throne as King Henry V at the end of the play. In fact, much in contrast with *1 Henry IV*, Hal appears with Falstaff only once during the entire play of *2 Henry IV*, and this meeting is not an especially friendly one, altogether lacking the indolent humor characteristic of their former association (II.iv.287-90; 300-03; 306-15). Even though Arthur Colby Sprague sees the brief interlude of Falstaff and the Prince as reflective of a kind of lighthearted merriment (which is surprising, because Hal's repeated rebukes of Sir John are severe and not at all funlike or conducive to laughter), he acknowledges a diminished quality in Hal and Falstaff's relationship with each other when he writes that "[t]he mere sight of the fat knight amuses [Hal] still—witness his joking about Sir John's grave— but amusement is one thing, the affectionate equality of friendship another" (90). A. P. Rossiter also suggests that Falstaff, as a devil of disorder, is innately comic in all his doings—not because he is especially witty or playfully innocent in *2 Henry IV*—but because he reflects the disorder of Hell; Falstaff's underworld of roguery "is comic," writes Rossiter, "as the Devil's world must be—since it is the negation of human dignities" (*English Drama* 158).

To distinguish himself from the rowdy commons and the implication that he has forsaken his responsibilities as heir apparent and Prince of Wales, Hal has to demonstrate, in *1 Henry IV*, to his father's satisfaction, that his mingling with the revelers of Eastcheap has not corrupted his high intentions or subverted his sense of royal purpose. Yet the prince, in effect, repeats this reconciliation with his father in *2 Henry IV*, and one might be constrained to question why. Hal pronounces,

> The tide of blood in me
> Hath proudly flowed in vanity till now.
> Now doth it turn and ebb back to the sea,
> Where it shall mingle with the state of floods
> And flow henceforth in formal majesty.
>
> (V.ii.129-33)

In an interpretation consistent with the frequently-noted character of Hal as a royal fifteenth-century incarnation of the Prodigal Son who forsakes his dissolute ways and returns to this rightful place at home (St. Luke 15:11-32), Arthur Morgan interprets this second reconciliation as correspondent to Hal's prodigality; in short, he sees Hal as a relapsed wanton in *2 Henry IV* who must beg the forgiveness of his father a second time (9). Others, such as G. X. Hunter, maintain that Hal's reformation in *2 Henry IV* is merely an imitative nod to the first popularly-received Henry IV play, of which *2 Henry IV* is but a sequel and a typical example of the conventional Elizabethan two-part play (238-48). Irving Ribner, however, while conceding in the first part that Hal's second reformation is probably ahistoric, somewhat less cynically than Hunter concludes that Shakespeare probably believed that another drama-tized illustration of the reformation of Hal's spirit could enhance his audience's appreciation of the significance of the process of princely renewal: " . . . all that this [Hal's dual reformation of character in *1 Henry IV* and *2 Henry IV*] really indicates is that for Shakespeare the didactic is far more important than the factual. Each of the reformations is a ritual process to be taken more symbolically than literally" (170).

Hal, in each Henry IV play, is able to establish his autonomy from both his father and the lowly criminal underlings of Falstaff's company of which Hal's usurping father is both royal personification and cause. Indeed, such may be the reason that explains why Hal takes his father's crown from his father's bedside before his father has actually died: the prince takes the crown because his father, the regicide, has no authority to bestow it (although Henry clearly thinks himself wronged by Hal's supposed impatience and insensitivity in words reminiscent of Christ at Gethsemane: "What, canst thou not forbear me half an hour?" [IV.v.109] mourns the disconsolate king). As Norman Sanders suggests,

> [I]t is plain that the prince conceives himself to be solely responsible for making his way to the crown in an environment that has nothing of the normal security and aids which an heir might expect to be available to prepare himself for future kingship. His society is sick; established authority is riddled with guilt [and] the opposition to this authority is doubly guilty . . . . (31)

In this respect, it is easy to see how aptly Hal, even before his accession, resembles, at least in part, the Reformation Church of which he, among other things, is the visible icon. Struggling to assert its primacy over the nuisance of Puritanism and the resurgent threat of Roman Catholicism, the Church of England similarly could not acknowledge or follow any conventional or recognized form for assuming authority in the kingdom; yet the absence of traditional or recognized channels for such assumption could not deter the Church from "taking" that authority from an already corrupt establishment when the moment seemed opportune and fitting.

Furthermore, as noted in the previous chapter, inasmuch as Hal functions in part as this Shakespearean vehicle of Reformation virtue, Falstaff is counterposed as a parody of Puritanical sensibilities. His description is, as Eileen Cohen remarks, "strikingly similar to Hooker's description of the sixteenth-century left-wing reformers" (190). He demonstrates no regard for the law or the Church; he attempts to excuse his many faults with circumlocutious renderings of Scripture and abasements of the *Book of Common Prayer*; he swaggers with the bravado and confidence of the pompously self-rlghteous.

Although Shakespeare stages many such Puritanical attributes as these for broad comic effect and ridicule (one recalls Shakespeare's similar success in drawing his *Twelfth Night* portrait of the puffed-up Puritan, Malvolio, as a comic subject for common abuse), Falstaff is gradually transformed from a cowardly buffoon into a diseased renegade and impious threat to order ("Let us take any man's horses, the laws of England are at my commandment!" [V.iii.135-37]).[7] Hal must repudiate this threat—not only as bearer of the Crown but as Shakespeare's anachronistic occupant of an office which in Shakespeare's century shall be declared to hold the temporal head of the Church of England. Hal, therefore, in rejecting Falstaff, disavows not only the treason but the heresy which Falstaff represents. It is the King of England to whom Shakespeare gives over the functions of God's Vicar in the fifteenth-century events of the play, thereby pre-empting the authority of Rome to define and expel heresy and anachronistically placing it, instead, in the hands of a monarch whose descendants will succeed to this sacred authority in a later century.

In rejecting heresy and treason by casting Falstaff aside, Hal, as Henry V, allows *2 Henry IV* to "culminate in a sacrificial act with the new king acting as personal viceregent for destiny" (Toliver, "Falstaff" 4), thereby revealing in his newly-consecrated person that mark of "the Royal Supremacy [which] was the cornerstone of [the] Reformation" (Sykes 18). Hal performs, therein, an essential mimetic function of divine rule through which "the bond between heaven and England is maintained symbolically, ritualistically, ceremoniously" (LaGuardia 78). As Edward Berry also suggests, "The curse Richard brings upon England, aided by Bolingbrook, is the curse of living in a fallen world.... When Hal banishes Falstaff at the end of *2 Henry IV*, this fallen world is reordered" (106).

The romantic critic has always disparaged Henry V and treated rather more sympathetically the character of Falstaff, especially in Henry's excoriation and banishment of the fat knight at the conclusion of *2 Henry IV* (V.v. 47-70), although such critiques generally overlook Shakespeare's purposes in crafting and developing the characters of Hal and Falstaff as he has. When one considers the grave purposes imparted through Shakespeare's frequently comic medium, Falstaff simply cannot be vindicated, for as Harold Jenkins reminds us, despite Falstaff's conveyance of much humor and merriment, he is "none the less the tempter whom the virtuous gentleman of Renaissance courtesy first indulges and then subdues; the private will impeding public good; the riotous disorder which the wise ruler must bring under control" (13-14). Given our contemporary political allowances for eccentricity and nonconformity because we live in a relatively stable society to which such individual curiosities as Falstaff provoke little fear, we are perhaps much less indignant about or threatened by characters such as Falstaff than was Shakespeare; for Shakespeare wrote at a time, in marked contrast to our own, of relative political fragility when difference of opinion often suggested disloyalty or at least inspired suspicion. Much of modernity's hostile reception of Falstaff's banishment may be attributable, therefore, as Robert Ornstein observes, to our contemporary tendency to sentimentalize that, however, which would have been perceived as an impious challenge to order and tranquility in Shakespeare's day (9).

In any case, despite the new king's banishment of him, Shakespeare confers on Falstaff a noble, Anglican end, which would seem to suggest that even Shakespeare was not altogether indifferent to the gentler side of the old ruffian. Hostess Quickly tells us that Falstaff, having died, is "in Arthur's bosom, if ever man went to Arthur's bosom" (*Henry V* II.iii.9-10);[8] and, reports the hostess, he "went away and it [as if he] had been any christom [newly baptized] child" (II.iii.ll-12). She also reports that, at the end, he "babbl'd of green fields" (II.iii.17)—a probable allusion to the Psalmist's " . . . he maketh me to lie down in green pastures" (Ps. 23:2) and part of the Anglican burial liturgy. And, in response to the nameless boy's remark in *Henry V* that "the dev'l would have him [Falstaff] about women" (II.iii.35-36), we are informed by Hostess Quickly that Falstaff "did in some sort, indeed, handle women, but then he was rheumatic, and talk'd of the whore of Babylon" (II.iii.36-39)—a certain reference to one of the cruder Elizabethan appellations for the Roman Catholic Church, which was commonly believed among Anglicans of the day to be "the scarlet woman of Revelation 17:3-6" (Evans, et al. 945).[9] Falstaff, therefore, for all his faults, is not abandoned in utter disrepute by Shakespeare, for he at least departs this life properly disregarding the claims of the "old faith" and embracing a traditional Anglican piety (Wunderli and Broce, 259). Christopher Baker also has recognized that "[i]n his last hour, there is only one Falstaff, one which an audience would have recognized from countless religious contexts which counseled amendment of life, among them the Anglican liturgy . . ." (69).

Apart from renouncing ties to Falstaff, Hal, like the moralities' Youth who must renounce Vice and eventually embrace Virtue (the latter represented, in this instance, by the Lord Chief Justice), also must sever his equally contaminated connection with his father. He must, as Robert Pierce says, part from his father and attain maturity to achieve his destiny (172). And as the English Reformation Church separated itself from a paternal authority and bound itself to a canonical confession in the form of the Thirty-Nine Articles, so Hal separates himself from his paternal authority and embraces the rule of law in the person of the Lord Chief Justice (*2 Henry IV* V.ii.103-06). Hal declares therein that the willfulness which characterized reigns of both his predecessors, Richard II and Henry IV, will not characterize his: he submits himself to the law, as Christ, too, humbled himself under the Law (Phil. 2:8). In fact, Matthew Wikander hears echoes of the vows of obedience of the marriage ceremony in Hal's acceptance of a new authority for himself in the realm. Following the offer of his hand to the Lord Chief Justice, Hal declares "I do" and "I will" before his spiritual father (V.ii.104,113,117,118,120), and this suggest the vows of matrimony, writes Wikander; "in effect, Hal vows to divorce Falstaff and marry his kingdom" (22).

In the opinion of R. J. Dorius, England's change of direction under the newly-crowned Henry V is also reflected in the rhetorical patterns which characterize the play following Hal's assumption of the throne. Consistent with the Anglican tone of this play following Hal's accession, Dorius notes that the rhetoric near the close of *2 Henry IV* is "of an almost high church language that becomes more organ-like in parts of *Henry V*" (Introduction 10). Harold Toliver substantially agrees, for he asserts that, in general, the rhetoric of history (as distinguished, for example, from the rhetoric of comedy) is "more openly incantational . . . and ritualistic [in that it] engages the emotions of its participants and fuses them into an harmonious community" ("Falstaff" 68). By way of example, one need only look back to Richard's apostrophes to the earth upon his arrival in Wales (*Richard II* II.ii.4-22), or to Falstaff's gentle, subdued protest of Hal's promised banishment of him, wherein the fat knight attempts to caress the prince's sympathy by attributing to his own wanting person qualities which he does not possess—as if the mere invocation and repetition of virtue's name could invent the reality (*1 Henry IV* II.iv.519-27). In *2 Henry IV*, this desire for reconciliation and harmonious union recurs in the new king's extension to his people of a Christlike invitation to embrace him as one who shall "live to speak [his] father's words" (V.ii.107), yet "be your father and your brother too" (V.ii.57). "Let me but bear your love, I'll bear your cares" (V.ii.58), he continues, promising to convert present sadness into expectant joy (V.ii.60-61)—a promise achieved in its fullness in the following and final play of the tetralogy.

The guiding purpose of *2 Henry IV* is the advancement by trial of a son who, triumphing over his adversaries, attains to the promise of his father, establishing himself finally in his appointed sphere of radiant glory and majesty. This son, Prince Hal, England's celebrated Henry V, like the English Church of which he is representative, renounces his bondage to the tyranny of imperial disorder and forsaken legitimacy (Roman Catholicism) as well as to popular anarchy and that which mocks all pretense to established order (Puritanism). Hal, England's hope, secures his rightful post as the representative of the Anglican *via media* by rejecting his dependence and reliance on the figurative embodiments of England's right- and left-wing ecclesiastical threats: his father, Henry IV—illicit bearer of the wreck of the *ancien regime,* who can no more "weed his garden" than Richard—and Falstaff, the portly parody of Puritanism, "kill'd by [our] hard opinions" (Epilogue 32-33), who threatens the sanctity of the realm with his irreverent and impious reck-lessness. In rising above them both, Hal establishes himself as the emblem of the Anglican ideal, the advent of which promises English redemption, restoration, and deliverance from trial.

Notes

[1]And yet there are some startling similarities in the two kings' speech. Recall, for example, Richard's doleful laments when confronted with the imminency of his fall:

> Let's talk of graves, of worms, and epitaphs,
> Make dust our paper, and with rainy eyes
> Write sorrow on the bosom of the earth.
> Let's choose executors and talk of wills:
> . . . yet . . . what can we bequeath
> Save our deposed bodies to the ground?
>
> *(Richard II* III.ii.145-50)

Compare them with Henry Bolingbroke's mournful complaint to his son whom he thinks would have him in his grave:

> And bid the merry bells ring to thine ear
> That thou art crowned, not that I am dead.
> Let all the tears that should bedew my hearse
> Be drops of balm to sanctify thy head;
> Only compound me with forgotten dust;
> Give that which gave thee life unto the worms,
> Pluck down my officers, break my decrees,
> For now a time is come to mock at form.
>
> *(2 Henry IV* IV.v.111-18)

[2]As Donald Stauffer expands,

> The scenes in which Henry IV figures are artfully colored by a mood of melancholy meditation—on poorest subjects and uneasy crowns, on sleep and conscience, chance and change, time and necessity;

"inward wars" and thwarted pilgrimages, on "golden care," disloyalty and sorrow, on greatness and "forgotten dust," sanctity and guilt, sages, apes and wolves, "indirect crook'd ways" and the fear of God . . . . (97)

[3]Caroline Eckhardt notices that this doctrine of interdependence of king and country, so prominent in the Arthurian legends, was not lost on the Henry of history. Indeed, she notes, in order to promote his legitimacy and diminish his culpability for usurping the throne, Henry declared himself to be Merlin's prophesied "Boar of Commerce," the promised deliverer who would unify the kingdom (119).

[4] Henry Bolingbroke, though hardly an unblemished bearer of God's standard in 2 Henry IV, is still used (much as is the tyrant, Richard of Gloucester, in *Richard III*) as both scourge and minister of the divine will in this play. Though he essentially is one who is to prepare the way for the surprising epiphany of his son, he is also the appointed instrument of God's wrath against Richard II. Of him it surely can be said,

> There is some soul of goodness in things evil,
> Would men observingly distil it out.

(*Henry V* IV.i.4-5)

[5]Bullcalf is not saying that he has been ill since Henry took the throne in 1399 (else, in real time, he would have suffered from his cold for nearly a decade). Rather, in saying that he caught his cold "with ringing in the King's affairs upon his coronation-day" (III.ii.182-83), he announces that he became ill while ringing church bells, a practice which marked, and continues to mark, the anniversary celebration of an English sovereign's coronation.

[6] R. J. Dorius comments extensively upon the imagery of decay, corruption, disease, sloth, waste, excess, and ruin which colors, in relative degree, the first three plays of the Lancaster cycle. He remarks that "the general movement of *Richard II* and of the cycle through *2 Henry IV* is from youthful or springtime luxuriance to aged or wintry barrenness," a movement of contrasts—a "pervasive imagery of extremes" ("A Little More" 14)—which is expressly created to fix within the reader or audience an impression of ravenous dissolutes of both princely and homely character, all of whom would seem to lack any purpose other than, as Hal declares, to "fe[e]d[e]d upon the body of my father" (*2 Henry IV* IV.v.160).

[7] J. Dover Wilson concurs. In *Shakespearean Dimensions*, he observes that "Falstaff, in the two parts of Henry IV, starts as a comedic figure, but his humor changes into an anti-social threat" (24). As such, he must be suppressed, for even as Falstaff signifies misrule, so Hal must emerge to signify right rule (Barber, "Rule and Misrule" 51-70); and just as the rebel lords must be overruled to preserve the civil order, so Falstaff must be overruled; for Falstaff, in the last analysis, is an instigator of riot and the very personification of anarchy, modeled as he is after John Oldcastle, the Lollardist companion of Henry V in the days of his dissolute youth (Humphreys 34-36), a renegade and rebel whom no Elizabethan would sentimentalize, aware as the Elizabethan public was of the strictures against rebellion promulgated by such sermons as the homily, *Against Disobedience and Willful Rebellion.*

[8] The Hostess, given her propensity for malapropism, obviously means not "Arthur's bosom" but rather "Abraham's bosom" (St. Luke 16:22), yet the "mistake"

reinforces our perception of Falstaff's death as an Anglican end. It would hardly be the last time, either, that a British poet would acclaim heaven graced and even ennobled by its reception of a countryman. One need only recall the second stanza of Rupert Brooke's "The Soldier":

> And think, this heart, all evil shed away,
>> A pulse in the Eternal mind, no less
>>> Gives somewhere back the thoughts of
>>>> England given,
>> Her sights and sounds; dreams happy as her day;
>> And laughter, learnt of friends; and
>>> gentleness,
>>>> In hearts at peace, under an English
>>>> heaven.

[9] It is not insignificant to note, as does John King, that Renaissance art usually depicted the Babylonian whore to be wearing a papal tiara (*Tudor Royal Iconography* 116). Such imagery was derived, in part, from the account in the Apocalypse wherein St. John the Divine records that he

> . . . saw a woman sitting on a scarlet beast which was full of blasphemous names, and it had seven heads and ten horns. The woman was arrayed in purple and scarlet, and bedecked with gold and jewels and pearls, holding in her hand a golden cup full of abominations and the impurities of her fornication; and on her forehead was written a great mystery: "Babylon the great, mother of harlots and of earth's abominations." And I saw the woman, drunk with the blood of the saints and the blood of the martyrs of Jesus. When I saw her I marveled greatly.
>
> (Revelation 18: 3-6)

Cain Kills Abel by Albrecht Dürer in *The Complete Woodcuts of Albrecht Dürer.* 1927. Ed. Willi Kurth (New York: Dover, 1963), plate 261.

> . . . let order die!
> And let this world no longer be a stage
> To feed contention in a ling'ring act;
> But let one spirit of first-born Cain
> Reign in all bosoms . . . .
>
> (*2 Henry IV* I.i. 154-58)

Chapter Five

Henry the Fifth:

The Summit Achieved

"The greatest grace lending grace"
— *All's Well That Ends Well*

A few readers of the fourth play of the Lancastrian Tetralogy, *Henry V*—most notably W. B. Yeats—believe that Shakespeare crafts more of a caricature than character of monarchy in *Henry V* (133). However, aware of Henry V's legendary reputation, and attentive to the Anglican character of Shakespeare's audience, other scholars agree with Fredson Bowers' contention that while Shakespeare was no critically indifferent playwright, he assuredly wrote not out of general contempt for his audience's political and theological convictions, but with respect and genuine deference to them; for Shakespeare, says Bowers, was "concerned to control for his own ends the reactions of his audience . . . manipulat[ing] and direct[ing them] into certain channels of belief" ("The Structural Climax" 310)—patterns of belief which would not subvert the political and theological orthodoxies of his day. Agreeing with Bowers, and commenting with respect to Shakespearean drama's theological character, John Shaw writes that "scenes in Shakespearean drama were related to one another with didactic intent . . . [a]nd the liturgically-minded playgoer . . . would have had eyes to see and ears to hear . . . parallels, contrasts, and juxtapositions." Paul Siegel, too, acknowledges Shakespeare's expert articulation of orthodox English theological convictions in his recognition that Shakespeare was no mere dramatic "recit[er of] trite commonplaces [but one who] . . . made familiar doctrine come alive" (*Shakespearean Tragedy* 84), a point with which Roland Frye agrees: "Shakespeare often referred to Christian doctrine, and whenever he did we should surely attempt to understand what is said; not to do so would be to deny ourselves the fullest understanding and appreciation of his plays" ("Theological and Non-Theological Structures" 134). More specifically, William Burgess writes that Shakespeare's theological views certainly were the orthodox Protestant views of his day (vii), and O. B. Hardison, expanding upon all these insights, contends that the larger purpose of Shakespearean drama in general, and of *Henry V* in particular, is the activation of the audience's theological sensibilities by associating a secular history with a sacred purpose and form:

> *Henry V* is a clear example of the use of ritual form for a secular subject. The play begins with challenge and conflict, turns on what Henry insists is the "miracle" of Agincourt, and ends with a political and social marriage—the union of France and England and the wooing of Katherine. The implications of the form are brilliantly realized in the imagery of death and peril, providential salvation, and finally, in Burgundy's speech, natural rebirth. (290-91)

Indeed, in *Henry V*, as in all of Shakespeare's other plays in the Lancaster cycle, the emphasis upon the king as the person through whom we are to comprehend the proper role of the Church in English society is evident in those associations with matters ecclesiastical which we, like Shaw's sixteenth-century "liturgically-minded playgoer," are invited to make while we watch ostensibly non-ideological historical drama unfold.

For example, comprehended within the familiar context of the sacred works from which they are substantially modeled, the Lancaster plays, in many respects, are to the Yorkist plays what the Old Testament is to the New: a rehearsal of the redemption of a people, prefigured in a monarch who, though imperfect, nonetheless represents those ideal qualities of public and private virtue which those weak kings that open each Shakespearean tetralogy possess in inverted proportion: Henry VI, the man of quiet virtue who is better fitted for a prie-dieu than a throne; and Richard II, the resplendent "king of show" whose dissipation and vain self-regard lose for him all but a "brittle glory"—the withered remains of the failed promise of his election to the throne. The unity of the tetralogies, then, is perhaps best identified through an extension of John Blanpied's suggestion that the ..."fundamental motive in the histories . . . is the need to make a future . . ." (15); for it is in their formation of one complete salvation history, roughly analogous to the testaments of the Scriptures, that the tetralogies, as the secular equivalents of their sacred predecessors, find the fullest expression of their unity. The Lancaster cycle, therefore, reads much like an "Old Testament" of England's fall and promise of redemption which requires the "New Testament" of the Yorkist cycle to complete its promise, for the Lancaster plays present Henry V as the Redeemer of his wayward people, although even Henry V looks forward to that more perfect deliverance to come at the end of the Yorkist cycle—the "New" Testament of the histories—when Henry Tudor, Earl of Richmond, defeats the Great Adversary, Richard of Gloucester, at Bosworth Field. This prophetic, heraldic, Davidic figure of Henry V appropriates the regenerative character of all the baptized in a coronation marked by allusions to the Anglican baptismal liturgy of the *Book of Common Prayer* and, especially in his holy cause to gain France, unites in himself the figures of the Old Testament prophet and captain—the interpreter of God's will and the bearer of God's divine commission against his enemies.

Shakespeare also attempts to amplify the Anglican voice and reify the Reformation consciousness of his audience through the use of a rhetoric grounded in the conviction that one should write in order to shape an audience's response rather than merely ornament or decorate one's work. Such a posture places him distinctively within the tradition of Aristotle's *Rhetoric,* Cicero's *De Oratorio,* and Quintillian's *Institutio Oratoria,* with respect to their shared advocacy of the persuasive rather than the decorative principle as the guiding consideration of the rhetorician; and since Shakespeare sees the history of England as something of a national liturgy, i.e., the "working out" (λειτουργία) of a national redemption, it therefore ought not surprise us to discover that Shakespeare uses Anglican liturgy and doctrine to impart persuasively his belief that in King Henry the Fifth, the embodiment of Reformation consciousness attains its fullest expression. Henry, like the England he represents, signifies in his person the achievements of Anglicanism. He is the patient deliverer of the national Church (an "unimpeachably English and patriotic" Church, in the words of J. J. Scarisbrick [186])[1] from its bondage to a tyrannical Roman authority—a tyranny personified by the affected and un-English Richard; and he is the repudiator of the fanaticism and hypocrisy of Puritanism—as parodied by the unregenerate Falstaff. Accordingly, Henry is an *exeplum*, the protagonist of a kind of morality play who, in Tillyard's words, "becomes less a man doing things than one who in doing them embodies certain virtues and vices in such a way that he stands as a great example, a figure of solemn didacticism" (*Shakespeare's History Plays* 28). Such an achievement was a significant accomplishment by Shakespeare, for as Horton Davies reminds us, "it was a continuing struggle [during the Shakespearean era] to affirm Anglican doctrine against the contentions of the Catholics on the right and those of the Puritans on the left" (xvi).

Furthermore, unlike any of his unhappy and unwise predecessors, Henry is perspicacious and possesses what Tillyard has called the king's "perfect knowledge of himself and of the world around him" (*Shakespeare's History Plays* 260): like the young Christ debating the scholars in the temple ("all who heard him were amazed at his understanding" [St. Luke 2:47]), so the young king amazes the leaders of the Church: "Hear him but reason in divinity, / And all admiring, . . . / You would desire the King were made a prelate" (I.i.38-40). Henry, like England, following the consolidation of its Reformation, is wondrously regenerated and born anew. "A true lover of the holy Church" (I.1.23), he inherits and wisely governs from a "sacred throne" (I.i.38).

Incarnate bearer of the nation's purpose that he is,[2] Henry's unambiguously Anglican character is affirmed almost at once in *Henry V*, for Shakespeare was acutely aware that the successful presentation of England's greatest national hero required every concession to the nationalistic sentiments of the people, and for most of them, their Anglican identity was an indivisible part of their sense of national self (Leary 253).

Elizabethans expected their national drama to reflect this theological awareness. In particular, Clark Cumberland tells us that "Shakespeare seems to have accepted the doctrine of Baptismal Grace as taught in the Church of England" (261), and there is probably no better illustration of this Anglican posture in Shakespeare than in the Archbishop of Canterbury's account of Henry's sudden and miraculous regeneration at the time of his accession. The imagery of Henry's accession in Act I, Scene 1, in fact, is awash in the rhetorical waters of the Anglican rite of Baptism. The Archbishop first tells us that following his "baptism" of coronation, Henry is not unlike a spiritually-washed babe, "full of grace and fair regard" (*Henry V* Chorus 5), and in the first scene of the first act, the Archbishop reports of Henry that

> The breath no sooner left his father's body,
> But that his wildness, mortified in him.
> Seem'd to die too: yea, at that very moment,
> Consideration like an angel came,
> And whipp'd the offending Adam out of him,
> Leaving his body as a paradise,
> T'envelop and contain celestial spirits,
> Never was such a sudden scholar made;
> Never came reformation in a flood,
> With such a heady currance, scouring faults . . . .
>   (I.i.25-34)[3]

A comparison of this, the Archbishop of Canterbury's account of Henry's regeneration, with the various petitions of an Anglican priest administering the regenerative Sacrament of Baptism (the latter uttering the words of the rite from the 1559 *Book of Common Prayer*) is revealing: ". . . his wildness, mortified in him / Seem'd to die too . . . " (I.i.26-27); ". . . we which are baptized die from sin, [and] continually mortify . . . all our evil and corrupt affections" (*BCP* 276); "Consideration like an angel came, / And whipp'd the offending Adam out of him" (I.i.28-29); ". . . grant that the old Adam in these children may be so buried . . " (*BCP* 274); "Leav[e . . .] his body as a paradise, / T'envelop and contain celestial spirits" (I.i.30-31); "Grant that all carnal afflictions may die in them, and that all things belonging to the Spirit may live and grow in them" (*BCP* 274). The image of this royal transfiguration is suffused with images of baptismal water: Hal's reformation, for example, like baptism, comes "in a flood," and the "heady currance" which inundates him "scour[s his] faults" (I.i.33,34); his is a watery transformation which, like H. E. Cain's classification of Hal's "second reformation before his father in *2 Henry IV*, is of a "sudden, complete and . . . almost miraculous kind" (qtd. in Schell 11).

The emphasis of the power of baptism to sanctify is developed further in the king's commission of trust in his spiritual fathers: "For we will hear, note, and believe in heart, / That which you speak is in your conscience wash'd / As pure as sin with baptism (I.ii.30-32), the cumulative effect of which speech is to assist in underscoring "the principal theme of *Henry V* . . . the establishment in England of an order based on consecrated authority" (Traversi,

Shakespeare 166)—though not the "consecrated authority" to which Richard appeals—a monarchy, instead, which "realiz[es] the whole sense of Elizabethan moral and religious order" (Fergusson, *Trope* 78).

J. H. Walter also contends that in the Archbishop's account of the prince's transformation, "the linking of significant words [such as] 'consideration,' 'angel,' 'paradise,' [and] 'celestial spirits' indicates that Shakespeare was undoubtedly thinking of repentance and conversion in the religious sense—especially because Henry's transformation into the apotheosis or monarchy is also accounted equally sudden and by divine initiation in the anonymous fifteenth-century *Vita et Gesta Henrici Quinti* (also known as the *Gesta Henrici Quinti*), a work which Walter believes that Shakespeare probably consulted, for it, like Shakespeare's *Henry V*, suggests that Henry was *felici miraculo convertitur* upon his consecration as monarch (157-58). Significantly, however, aware as he was that the *Vita* was a Roman Catholic chronicle (and, as such, suffused with non-Anglican theology), Shakespeare, for *Henry V*, thoughtfully decided to modify the *Vita* Archbishop's account of the wondrous change in the king, to conform, instead, to Anglican convictions regarding the nature of divine revelation. Consequently, following his unmistakable allusion to the *BCP's* baptismal liturgy in defining the character of Henry's elevation, Shakespeare's Archbishop of Canterbury—now speaking in an Anglican voice—breaks with the Roman account of the *Vita* and carefully reminds us that in contrast to Roman Catholic belief in open or continuing revelation, "miracles are ceased; / And therefore we must needs admit the means / How things are perfected" (I.i.67-69).

Henry therefore ascends the English throne through an act that is reshaped into an Anglican sacramental rite that releases the King from domination by his "old Adam." Henry, accordingly, "in putting on the new man . . . repudiated his past and had no more connection with it" (Prlor 321). And Raphael Holinshed, also invoking the Christian metaphor of the "new man," similarly records that at his coronation, "[Henry] determined to put on him [self] the shape of a new man" (*Holinshed's Chronicle* 70). No English spectator of this play could regard any such announced "reformation" as anything other than an event meant to be comprehended and defined within a religious context, heralded as it is not only by a voice intimately familiar with the liturgical formulae of the Anglican prayer book but delivered, as well, by no less authoritative Anglican voice than that of the See of Canterbury. Furthermore, as A. L. Rowse notes, "phrases [from the Prayer Book] had a different effect upon Elizabethans than upon us: to those of us who can remember them, they are nostalgic and tired; to Elizabethans they were new-minted and stirring, and printed themselves freshly upon the mind" (5).

Hal's sudden and unanticipated conversion from the feckless prince of the indolent mob to the radiant exemplum of high majesty was a familiar legend among Elizabethans. But according to Tillyard, the reputation of the madcap prince, dramatically turned warrior-king, originated even earlier, especially in such pre-Shakespearean drama as Richard Tarleton's *Famous Victories of Henry V* and the more contemporary *Shoemaker's Holiday* of Thomas Dekker (*Shakespeare's History Plays* 305). Henry's piety as king (as Holinshed especially attests) was also extensively documented by "any of the prose chronicles of England which Shakespeare consulted (311). Edward Hall, in fact, in the opinion of Henry Ansgar Kelly, is the only chronicler of medieval English history who does not personally drape Henry in the robes of piety, perceiving him rather as an "honor-craving hero ... virtuous in function of his magnaminity rather than [in exhibition of his] piety" (193).

Following the elevation of Henry to the proximate stature of a demigod in the opening scene of the play, the second scene of the first act of *Henry V* offers the Archbishop of Canterbury presenting the argument of the Church for the justification in law of Henry's ambition to reclaim the French crown for his posterity; the court then considers strategies for the conquest of France; and finally, Henry resolves, in defiant response to the Dolphin's insulting gift of the tennis balls, that with "God before, / We'll chide this Dolphin at his father's door" (*Henry V* I.ii.308-09). The unfolding of this extended, formal scene of state, according to Martha Fleischer, reinforces Shakespeare's intent to present Henry as an unblemished prince, for such a scene had served a similar purpose for the pre-Shakespearean author of *Edward III* (51). George Becker also maintains that in this scene, "[Henry's] words give evidence of moral superiority, of passions that are impersonal, essentially royal, emanating not from resentment at the affront to his person, but from concern for the well-being of his kingdom" (71), observations which are consistent with Henry's youthful declaration of royal intent in the first act of *1 Henry IV* (especially evident in lines 195-217 of the second scene).

Henry's desire, accordingly, is not for blind foreign conquest but for the restoration of unity to his kingdom;

France, after all, we are told, belongs to England "by gift of heaven" (*Henry V* II.iv.79). Henry's voice is "the voice of unity," Robert Hapgood writes. "[I]n a world of retrospection, his is the voice of the future; in a world of false report, his speech is direct and true; in a world of dispute, his call is to concord" ("Shakespeare's Thematic Modes" 47-48). Sidney Shanker likewise suggests that "*Henry V* is a devoutly conceived plan for English unity . . . , for governance by a transcendent king who could make the commons love him" (68), an "ideal king [who] embodies in himself and projects upon his state the ideal metaphysical order" (Zimbardo 17).

The ideality of Henry's reign is characterized, therefore, not only by shrewd politics but by a spiritual quality as well (Knight, *Shakespearean Production* 159), and of this reign's political character, many critics have had much to say. Attesting to its aggressively patriotic and conservative nature is Derek Traversi, who notes that *Henry V*, in its political voice, is a strongly conventional play ("Henry the Fifth" 62). Tillyard sees in the mature Henry a living emblem of the ideal Renaissance prince (*Shakespeare's History Plays* 277). Henry is a skilled politician to Margaret Labarge (187) and a studied hypocrite to the Marxist critic Stephen Greenblatt (41).[4] He is a study in political maturity to Tucker Brooke (332) and a man whose commanding vision was much needed at the desperate time of his accession (Churchill 89). Shakespeare, however, there can be little doubt, is much (and perhaps principally) concerned with a presentation of monarchy in his fourteenth-century histories of England which glorifies sixteenth-century Tudor precepts and ideals (Barber, "Prince Hal" 75). O. B. Hardison, in fact, compliments Shakespeare's use of creative anachronism in his depiction of the Lancastrian monarchs as an effective, if unconventional, form of verisimilitude which on occasion had been successfully employed before Shakespeare by medieval playwrights (246).

Shakespeare was not the first English dramatist to use the devices of his craft to propagandize for a particular religious order. Such distinction probably best belongs to the Protestant playwright John Bale (in support, see especially Jesse W. Harris's *John Bale, A Study in the Minor Literature of the Reformation* [Freeport, 1970] and Rainer Pineas's *Tudor and Early Stuart Anti-Catholic Drama* [Nieuwkoop, 1972]). Bale's theatrical work dramatically inaugurated the English stage's use as a vehicle for popularizing the Reformation and "protestantizing" medieval English Catholic drama,[5] but Shakespeare was the first to so intimately fuse Tudor political principle to Reformation sensibilities that one could conclude of the Shakespearean vision that to be authentically English was to be indissolubly Tudor and Anglican.[6] Of such kings as Shakespeare's Henry V, for example, Irving Ribner notes that these sovereigns were certain that in the performance of their political duties they also were "performing the will of God" (*The English History Play* 187); and, as we too have discovered, even the "political" scenes in *Henry V* reveal an undeniably Anglican character. But even if some reject this interpretation (as does Cornelius van der Spek, in his suggestion that the play reflects no thoroughgoing Anglican temperament [85]), many others (including, ironically, van der Spek himself) seem compelled to acknowledge that at least in Henry's determination to give precedence to his affairs of state rather than be dissuaded by prelates of possibly mercenary character,

"Shakespeare's standpoint regarding the supremacy of the sovereign proves to be that of the true Anglican" (85).

In any case, however, G. Wilson Knight presents a more interesting argument for concluding that Henry, though certainly a "worldly" king, is yet a more completely "spiritual" king—even in the exercise of his worldly offices ("We are no tyrant, but a Christian king" [I.ii.241], as Henry declares). Knight suggests that while Henry is a worldly king, that alone does not mean that the King is less reverend in his person or less significant in his vocation than if he were given to the purely "spiritual" life, but rather that he, in his Anglican personification of monarchy, consolidates the two to form an indivisible whole (*Shakespearian Production* 159). Within Knight's observation is contained a notable implication that if Henry were but a pagan monarch, he would be like any other sovereign, i.e., the representative of a community which collectively invests its identity and purpose in a designated individual. Henry, however, as a Christian king (and especially as an Anglican king), embodies, as Supreme Head of the Church, not just the communal but the universal. Even Derek Traversi (who would quarrel with this point) partially concedes it by acknowledging that [Henry's] conduct is marked . . . by a sense that the traditional sanctions of monarchy are no longer immediately valid, that the . . . royal office need[s] to be reconsidered in [the context of] a new world..." (*Shakespeare* 3).

Knight's conclusion about Henry is not far removed from that of Ronald Berman, who proposes that Henry V deserves to stand among the heroes of Thucydides, Herodotus, Homer, and Plutarch, with men such as Themistocles, Pericles, Odysseus, and Darius. All are heroes distinctive among the commonplace persons of their ages, individuals who demonstrate their abilities to surmount those limitations which restrain more ordinary men. They embody the ideals of their cultures and possess a kind of divinity of character which bestows upon them a dignity and majesty appropriate to their worth (9-10). In similarly demonstrating this conviction in Henry, Knight reminds us that "Shakespeare's conception of true royalty is very close to his conception of divinity" (*This Sceptered Isle* 28), an idea which reinforces observations that Knight records elsewhere (see the preceding references to Knight's commentary in this chapter) concerning his conviction that in Shakespeare, the ideal Christian king unites in himself the highest of royal and Christian virtues, emblemizing in his own person the character of England, a kingdom "marked out as an example of both religious wisdom and moral strength" (28). Holinshed, too, records of Henry that he, during his tenure on the throne, reigned as a royal ideal; in sharp contrast to his account of Richard's debauchery, Holinshed declares that Henry V

> ... was a king, of life without spot; a prince whome all men loued, and of noen disdained .... Wantonnesse of life and thirst in auerice had he quite quenched in him .... For bountifulnesse and liberalitie, no man more free, gentle, and franke, in bestowing rewards to all persons, according to their deserts .... A maiestie was he that both liued & died a paterne in princehood, a lode-starre in honour, and mirror of magnificence; the more highlie exalted in his life, the more deeplie lamented at his death, and famous to the world alwaie. (*Holinshed's Chronicle* 88-89)

John Barton's suggestion, therefore, that the scene of Henry and the Archbishop of Canterbury be played as comedy (92-93) seems altogether inappropriate, not only because it diminishes Henry's majesty but also because it scants the gravity of the council's deliberations in guiding the king to make a regal decision consistent with his princely promise to "redeem . . . the time"—a promise offered in *1 Henry IV*—and not likely made frivolously or insincerely, modeled as it is by Shakespeare after Saint Paul's admonition to the Ephesians: "Take heed, therefore, that you walk circumspectly, not as fools, but as the wise, redeeming the time: for the days are evil" (5:15-16).

Henry's consultation with spiritual authority may seem peculiar, comic, or ironic to some readers of *Henry V* who prefer to think that Shakespeare's occasional caricatures of the clergy as comic buffoons or dull-witted louts reveal an unyielding secularist's contempt for the sacred teaching office of the episcopacy. But those readers, perhaps too much governed by twentieth-century sensibilities, ought to be reminded that the very notion of man making an uninformed choice for the good—apart from considering that which had been *revealed* to be good—was unheard of by orthodox Elizabethans. Indeed, man's choices were properly limited to devising means by which he could better obey—not defy—eternal law; for example, to the Elizabethan Anglican, by the investiture of canonical authority in a teaching magisterium, Christians had established a formal hierarchy within the Church—not to circumvent or disregard revelation, but to provide a means for its continuing interpretation in faithful response to the divine promise: "He who hears you hears me" (St. Luke 10:16). As L. A.

Cormican writes, little of the nature of medieval ethics in Shakespeare can be apprehended without understanding the widespread acceptance of belief in the Church's aposto-licity ("Medieval Idiom in Shakespeare [II]" 301); and Richard Hooker's *Laws of Ecclesiastical Polity* contains extensive discussions of the nature of divine law, especially with regard to how it can be understood and effected in the lives of men (see especially the *Laws*' "Of the Natural Way of Finding Out Laws by Reason to Guide the Will unto That Which is Good").

Furthermore, as David Evett points out, "the image of the reformed Hal—so able to 'reason in divinity' that [the Archbishop of] Canterbury wishes he were a prelate—is consistent with a Protestant emphasis on the individual as his own theologian" (151); and the attribution of such a quality to Henry serves well the Shakespearean cause of sculpting the image, in Henry V, of a king who prefigures a monarch whose successors also shall govern as Defenders of the Faith in the Church of England. Therefore, not only does Henry demonstrate his piety and holy submission to anointed spiritual authority by deferring to his spiritual counsel, but he simultaneously projects himself as the repository of spiritual wisdom. As one who both proclaims God's will and bows to it (see especially I.i.25-37; I.i.37-52; I.ii.289-93; IV.viii.118-21; and IV.i.306-22), Henry becomes not just a "Renaissance and seventeenth-century common-place [of ideality in monarchy]" (Korshin 151) but a type of Christ and the genesis of such perfect kingship that he consumes all evidence of his origin; in him, we see mirrored the pragmatic monarch which was his father; we see the king who is brother to his lowest subjects (as he learned to be in the company of the revelers at Eastcheap); and we see in him the image of perfected Richard: the king who would consolidate popular myth and symbol and incorporate them both into his public self. We believe Henry, therefore, when he announces, in rhetoric which incorporates into himself and his purpose the iconography of the triumphant, resurrected Christ: "But I will rise . . . with so full a glory / That I will dazzle all the eyes of France" (I.ii.278-79).

Shakespeare attempts to achieve a variety of purposes in molding Henry into the likeness of Christ. He makes of him an ideal Renaissance monarch, a Davidic warrior-king, and a prototype of the Great Redeemer of England, Henry Tudor. As Ribner notes, by employing so much divergent imagery, Shakespeare does not attempt to forge any kind of allegorical drama (*The English History Play* 186); instead, he elects to offer his audience an unambiguously nationalistic spectacle of quasi-epic proportions, promote the Tudor myth of providential direction in English history, encourage the association of the English monarch with worldly and other-worldly kings of sacred history, and depict a king whose piety and government is specifically (if not pedantically or insistently) Anglican.

That such varied purposes inhere within *Henry V* ought not seem unusual; as Clifford Leech has observed of Renaissance English drama in general, and of religious drama in particular, the dramatist "is rarely content to represent life from a single viewpoint throughout a whole play" (187). Furthermore, that Henry should perform varied dramatic service as both antitype of Christ and prototype of Henry Tudor ought not startle the reader of English Renaissance drama: as Paul Korshin asserts, "in seventeenth-century England, when the doctrines of Church and state were closely linked and when civil instability constantly threatened, the urge to typologize the monarchy seems to have been greater than at any time in English history since the Reformation" (117).

Charles Barber recognizes the emergent typological character of the Prince of Wales in Henry IV: "In the *Henry IV* plays . . . it is Prince Hal . . . who typifies the Tudor monarchy; and the whole structure of *1 Henry IV* reflects the delicate equilibrium of late sixteenth-century English society" ("Prince Hal" 68). Hal, indeed, is the very embodiment of Tudor political philosophy and Anglican religious sensibility. He is one who relies on the sage, reverent counsel of others and manifestly is nothing like the unparliamentarian feudal absolutist that was Richard II. Hal, as the new king, Henry V, is not unlike the new English Church, for neither King nor Church poses as an autocratic dispenser of infallible, unchallengeable truths, but each humbly nurtures a position as mediator between God and man.

Henry, before God and his subjects, is thoughtful, reverent, and chastened by his responsibilities: must he, for example, answer for his soldiers on the Day of Judgment, as the soldier on the field at Agincourt asserts? (IV.i.134-41); must he atone for the sins of another? (IV.i.292-94). In confronting such questions, not only does Shakespeare create an icon of Christ in Henry, but he also shapes Henry into an example of monarchy which is evidently far removed from Richard. And if Richard is in part a personification of Roman Catholic tyranny, then in Henry's calm reflection upon his own limitations, preoccupation with thoughts of his holy responsibility, and desire to embrace rather than anathematize his detractors, he personifies the character of the new Church of England and becomes, in his functions as representative of both Christ and his Church, a living symbol of authority which practices both mediation and reconciliation.[7]

Hal's incarnation of perfect regality in medieval chronicles has not been overlooked by scholars. It often has been observed that Shakespeare, rarely original in his composition, relied extensively upon many sources in composing Henry V, and most of these sources were dedicated to the romanticization and idealization of Henry as a king who briefly brought a golden age to England and prefigured the fullness of English monarchy in Henry Tudor.[8] David Riggs acknowledges this transformation of historical fact into idealized fiction when he writes that Shakespeare's histories "begin in memory and end in myth" (160). Even more specifically, J. H. Walter has extensively documented the many particular ways in which such an ideal conception of royalty is fashioned in Shakespeare's creation of Henry V by tracing the influence of such interpreters of perfect kingship as Erasmus and Chelidonius in Shakespeare's play.

Using Erasmus's *Institutio Principis* (1516) and Chillester's translation of Chelidonius's treatise, *Of the Institution and first beginning of Christian Princes* (1571), Walter contends that Shakespeare sought to give precise scope and classical definition to his ideal monarch. In Walter's evaluation, among those characteristics of perfect royalty defined by Erasmus and Chelidonius and subsequently applied to the person of Henry by Shakespeare are the requirements that the ideal king shall be (1) a Christian

(I.ii.241); (2) one who supports the Christian Church
(I.i.23,73); (3) a learned man (I.i.32); (4) familiar with
theology (I.i.38-40); (5) committed to the establishment of
justice (V.ii.43-145; II.ii); (6) capable of exercising clem-
ency (II.ii.39-60; III.iii.54; III.iv.lll-18); (7) incapable of
exacting personal revenge (II.ii.174); (8) disciplined and
given to self-control (I.i.241-43); (9) governed by wise
counsel (I.ii.; II.iv.33); (10) acquainted with, but not
corrupted by, the commons (IV.i.85-235); (11) a defender
and preserver of the state (IV.i.236-90); (12) concerned,
even burdened, by the cares of state (IV.i.236-90); (13)
mindful of his realm, even when he might otherwise rest
(IV.ii.264, 273-74, 289); (14) one who orders his realm
with the efficiency of a colony of bees (I.i.183-204); (15)
one who unifies the functions of the state like the functions
of the body (I.i.178-83); (16) a ruler of obedient subjects
(I.i.186-87); (17) a severe punisher of idlers, parasites, and
flatterers (review the fates, for example of Bardolph, Nym,
Doll Tearsheet, et al.); (18) the possessor of a spirit that does
not rely on ceremony or insignia for the prince's validation
(IV.i.244-74); (19) one who avoids flattery and recognizes
it when it is proffered (IV.i.256-73; IV.i.267-9); (20) an
example of the supremacy of Christian monarchy (IV.vii.13-
53); (21) aware of the evils of war and the virtues of peace
(II.iv.105-09; III.iii.10-41; V.ii.34-62); and (22) honorably
married (V.ii)(154-55). David Riggs similarly acknowledges Shakespeare's reliance on Erasmus's treatise on
Christian government: "Henry V," he writes, "remains the
only play that [Shakespeare] could have written with Hall's
Union in one hand and Erasmus's *Institutio Principis* in the
other" (140).

Such sources as Erasmus and Hall serve Shakespeare's political and theological purposes well in his attempt to make Henry the Tudor/Anglican ideal, "the king that audiences at the Globe would have him be" (Stoll 130). Many critics of Shakespeare's depiction of Henry, however, do not see the king as a worthy model of monarchy, despite Shakespeare's extensive consultation and use of medieval and Renaissance authorities to define those features which typify the princely ideal. C. G. Thayer, for example, expresses some qualified reservations about Shakespeare's Henrician ideal:

> *Henry V* is a kind of political Utopia, and audiences and readers are by no means agreed on its attractiveness. But how many Utopias have been universally attractive? How many of us would really enjoy life in Plato's republic? One is reminded of Mark Twain's Satan, that the human conception of heaven includes everything they detest and nothing they like. Shakespeare's idea of order was scarcely Dionysian, and it certainly wasn't democratic; but I see no reason to doubt that he believed in it fully . . . .
> ("Shakespeare's Second Tetralogy" 6)

Henry seems curiously detached from his humanity in *Henry V*, perhaps due as much to a somewhat mechanical application of abstract virtues to the prince as to Shakespeare's deliberate attempt to make of Henry a steward of high majesty who is revealed by deeds rather than words. Richard had defined his government in richly textured lyric which, though reflective of the resplendence of his person, conformed little to the actual character of his government, except perhaps in its ability to reinforce the general impression that Richard's government was as glittery and airy a thing as his speech. Henry, in contrast—like his father (Gerald Cox, in fact, has said that Henry sometimes even "seems too much his father's son" [131])—is a prince of accomplishments rather than poetry: his purpose is to do rather than to be, and in this respect, his verbal economy and relatively simple, unadorned rhetoric (most of *Henry V* is composed in blank verse) reflect as much of his regal character as Richard's lofty but often vacuous speech reveals of his.

Henry V's less personable and more distant character in *Henry V* may also be attributable to the desire by Shakespeare that the king embody some elements of transcendence usually associated with divinity. Patricia Barry discerns such an attempt in Shakespeare's *Henry V*: "One device for characterizing royalty is to cause an ordinary king to imitate characters with extraordinary powers" (45); and certainly such characterization would not appear alien to the Elizabethan playgoer who would see in any monarch a type of divine kingship (Pierce 218-19). Furthermore, as an emblem of monarchy, Henry's occasional distance and abstraction as a character would not violate any established theatrical conventions in Elizabethan character portrayal. J. L. Styan, in fact, notes the particular usefulness of the dramatic practice of "pass[ing] between particularity and generality, between the real and the abstract" in the Elizabethan theatre, for it allows the playwright to invoke qualities or an identity which might be difficult to impart to a character otherwise defined too naturalistically (*The Shakespeare Revolution* 30).

Virginia Carr suggests, too, that some ambiguous responses to Henry may also, in part, be due to Shakespeare's "manipulation of a double perspective . . . in the person of Henry," for Henry compels us to look back to the golden age of Edward III at the same time that he foreshadows and invites us to look forward to the triumph of the Tudors (542). Perhaps as importantly, however, Henry sometimes also typologically functions as both Adam and Second Adam: bearing the burden of a blemished dynasty (IV.I.292-94), he simultaneously is about the business of rescuing a fallen people when they least expect it (*1 Henry IV* I.ii.212).

Character definition, in any case, is one of Shakespeare's principal tasks in *Henry V*; indeed, it is through his gradual revelation of the messianic persona in Henry by means of an iconography which reflects the sacramental union of God and man in Christ that Shakespeare accomplishes one of the chief purposes of his play. As E. E. Stoll points out, "Plot, indeed, is not the strong point of this 'history.' *Henry V* is . . . rather a series of tableaux . . . . There is even no external struggle, because there must be, in this patriotic drama, no enemy able to withstand him" (125). Indeed, in the effort to magnify a character, few devices other than the tableau could more effectively call an audience's attention to the king's supreme position among his nobility in Tudor drama, for the tableau's primary function, according to Sydney Anglo, is to depict hierarchy in its rightful orders (165). Therefore, to a dramatist interested in illustrating the union of divine purpose and mortal essence in a king (complementing, as well, the doctrine of the King's Dignity and other dualities), the selection of the tableau for such illustration would appear a natural choice.

Establishing Henry as a messianic figure within such a framework supports and enables Shakespeare's Anglican apologetic, too, for England thereby is depicted by Shakespeare as a divinely anointed land whose people are guided by a special providence in the person of an anointed king, a king whose very reason for being is that he might redeem his people from their captivity to evil and error (Morris 256-57).

In order to underscore this messianic, redemptive work of the son of the King, Shakespeare dramatizes by profuse example Henry's intimate relationship with, and reliance upon, God. Henry, for example, invokes God more than thirty times in the play—fourteen times in Act IV alone—a practice distinctly divergent from the prayerful character of Richard II who, in the play titled after him, invokes God but *once*—and then to mercilessly solicit the hasty death of John of Gaunt![9] As Joan Webber also notes, "[When] Henry prays to God rather than, like Richard, speaking for God ... he [achieves] another kind of importance by speaking for all his people. He becomes the spirit of England" (537); as an emblem of Christ the Mediator, Henry offers up in his person the prayers of his people.

Henry's reflection of the person of Christ in *Henry V* is one of Shakespeare's most carefully constructed sacramental icons, but as much is revealed of his redemptive purpose in Henry's government as in his person. One thinks of Richard's rule in contrast to Henry's: Richard's turbulent reign, like Herod's or Caesar's, was tyrannical, capricious, and preoccupied with the prerogatives of office ("Think what you will, we seize into our hands / His plate, his goods, his money and his lands" [*Richard II* II.i.209-10]), whereas Henry's government is an exercise in "willed and purposeful self-surrender" (Knight, *Shakespearian Production* 158);

he is conscious of a king's responsibility to God, and accountability before Him (*Henry V* I.ii.241). Henry, unlike the grasping Richard, reflects the sacrificial character of Christ the Redeemer: "For he to-day that sheds his blood with me / Shall be my brother; be he ne'er so vile, / This day shall gentle his condition" (IV.iii.61-63), a declaration which echoes Christ's promise to the thief who dies with him on Calvary: "Truly, I say to you, today you will be with me in Paradise" (St. Luke 23:43).

Nathan Scott has recognized the importance of this messianic construct in works similar to *Henry V*: "[They] who devote themselves to [the] work of redemption . . . initiated by Christ are . . . extensions of his Presence: in their action is contained a sacramental quality which we must apprehend" (qtd. in Cary 66). And Henry assuredly embodies a variety of such extensions of Christ: Henry, for example, does not eschew the morally specious and evil ways of the world but neither is he seduced by them; he does not abandon his worldly call (as his son, Henry VI, substantially does) in order to pursue or preserve an artificial or monastic holiness; in his refusal to be conformed to the world (witness Hal's resistance to the many riots of Falstaff and the other anarchist revels of the fat knight and his companions), Henry, like Christ, as Alvin Kernan has said of him, is *"in"* not *"of"* the world (29)—an emblem therein, too, of consubstantiationist eucharistic sacramentology; he sojourns awhile amidst his people, awaiting his hour to "redeem . . . [the] time when men least think [he] will" (*1 Henry IV* I.ii.210).

Henry also manifests his messianic character in the concealment, like Christ, of his messianic destiny; he would wait (as he indicates in his first soliloquy [*1 Henry*

IV I.ii]) until the moment of his apotheosis to kingly glory to be fully revealed. And, like Christ in the wilderness, Hal, in *2 Henry IV*, prepares for the challenge that awaits him by confronting the "necessity of subduing his own will . . . , making himself the instrument of a . . . justice which transcends all personal considerations and upon which his own authority . . . must rest" (Traversi, "The Historical Pattern" 108).

Also, in the manner of Christ on the eve of Calvary, so Hal, on the eve of Agincourt, removes himself from the company of his men that he might privately meditate and pray before embracing the next day's ordeal that will prove to be his greatest trial. The iconography of the scene evokes Gethsemane: the king, alone, prays to his God that his followers might remain steadfast (IV.1.289-90); secluded from others, he contemplates the events of the forthcoming day in darkness outside his camp, which lies just beyond the gates of a city where this king is to do battle and—in the face of apparent defeat—triumph over an adversary on a day that will be celebrated for eternity (IV.iii.56-59).

Within this scene, the king, anguished and penitent (IV.i.292-302), concludes his affecting prayer by anachronistically assuming the appropriate Reformation posture of one who recognizes that despite his attempts to right his predecessors' wrongs, "all that [he] can do is nothing worth" (IV.i.303), thereby repudiating confidence in any Roman Catholic and non-Anglican doctrine of penance which would assert one's ability to intervene meritoriously in an effort to remit another's guilt without the participation of that person in the act of atonement. Instead,

Hal, submissive and contrite, affirms, in good Anglican form, that his "penitence comes after all, / Imploring pardon" (IV.i.304-05). And, like the soon-to-be martyred disciples of Christ, outside the gates of Agincourt linger the "poor condemned English / Like sacrifices" (IV Chorus 22-23). There, they await the challenge of the day, while the men of the French army—like the Roman soldiers beneath the cross of Christ—"play at dice" (IV Chorus 19). Yet among them walks the king to bring them comfort, of whom the Chorus invites us to proclaim, "Praise and glory on his head!" (IV Chorus 31).

Furthermore, Henry's concealment of his royalty as he moves among and converses with his followers (IV.i) recalls Christ's own concealment of his resurrected divinity when he appears among his followers and talks to them on the road to Emmaus (St. Luke 24:13-31). In each case, the disguised king cloaks his true self, only to reveal it in all its glory at a later time. As the Chorus says of Henry, reminding us of the Lucan account of Christ's comforting presence among his devastated apostolate,

> . . . [He] who will behold
> The royal captain of this ruin'd band . . .
> Let him cry, "Praise and glory on his head!"
> For forth he goes, and visits all his host,
> Bids them good morrow with a modest smile,
> And calls them brothers, friends, and countrymen.
>
> (IV Chorus, 28-29, 31-34)

And, recalling the joy and consolation nurtured in the disciples by Jesus's resurrected presence among them (St. Luke 24:41), the Chorus acclaims a like response which Henry elicits from his men:

> Upon his royal face [he] . . .
> but freshly looks, and overbears attaint
> With cheerful semblance and sweet majesty;
> That every wretch, pining and pale before,
> Beholding him, plucks a comfort from his looks.
> A largesse universal, like the sun,
> His liberal eye doth give to every one,
> Thawing cold fear . . . .

(IV Chorus, 35,39-45)

This association of the king with the life-giving power of the sun is used elsewhere in *Henry V* as an Henrician metaphor, e.g., V.ii.162, and Henry himself declares his intent to "imitate the sun" (*1 Henry IV* I.ii.197) in the sudden revelation of his majesty. Shakespeare's development of this imagery is not particularly original (although, if we review the tetralogy from this advanced perspective, we notice that he employs it to unprecedented effect throughout the Henriad),[10] for the association of the sovereign with the sun had been imported to Europe from the Orient during the time of the Crusades (L'Orange 18-20) and was readily incorporated into the then-regnant series of medieval Western monarchial symbols (Patrides 69).

During the nighttime hours before the siege of Agincourt when Henry quietly moves among and discourses with his troops ("a little touch of Harry in the night" (IV Chorus 47), he is asked by one soldier if the king "hath a heavy reckoning to make" (IV.i.134) for leading men to death in battle. Henry declares that the king, though he order men to die in battle, is not responsible for the fate of their individual souls, for he is merely the executor of God's wrath:

> War is his [God's] beadle, war is his vengeance
> .... Then if they die unprovided, no more is the King
> guilty of their damnation than he was before guilty
> of those impieties for which they are now visited.
> Every subject's duty is the King's but every subject's
> soul is his own.
>
> (IV.i.169, 173-77)

Yet Henry, like Christ, feels the painful burden of his office as he, in anguish, contemplates the heaviness of his responsibility for others under his authority:

> Upon the King! let us our lives, our souls,
> Our debts, our careful wives,
> Our children, and our sins lay on the King!
> We must bear all. O hard condition . . . .
>
> (IV.i.230-33)

Lily Campbell, however, discovers an Anglican apologetic in Henry's defense of his unaccountability for the souls of soldiers who die in battle under his command. In her allegorical exegesis of the play, she suggests that Shakespeare inserts this otherwise perhaps inessential dialogue into the general action of the play in order to provide a royal rebuttal to the calls for insurrection against the Crown which were being published and distributed throughout England in the late sixteenth century by William Cardinal Allen—tracts which Allen distributed in the hope of inspiring a Catholic revolt against Elizabeth and restoring the throne to a Catholic occupant. Allen's tracts, for example, insisted that any soldier would be forever damned who died in an unjust war fought on behalf of an unjust cause or fought on behalf of an heretical prince—the implication being, of course, that anyone who died under Elizabeth's authority would be denied resurrection to life eternal. Consequently, the tracts urged Catholic rebellion as a goal and terrorism as a means to that goal by suggesting that when one finds oneself under heretical authority, the Catholic subject's holy duty is to rebel against that authority and refuse the commands of a non-Catholic sovereign (*Shakespeare's Histories* 273-80). By Henry's declaration, therefore, that every individual is responsible for his own salvation, Shakespeare, through the character of his anachronistically Protestant king, not only endorses an Anglican theological judgment but specifically repudiates and reverses the antagonistic Catholic suggestions of Cardinal Allen which threatened to break the domestic peace and undermine authority in the realm.[11]

Henry, nonetheless, is a king whose own government, in many respects, appears unaccountably fierce and disagreeable—if not altogether cruel—and it is Henry's apparent or at least perceived severity as a king that sometimes alienates him from those modern audiences that are inclined to applaud sanguine leaders of contemporary bourgeois democratic sympathies. Because Henry's harsh justice (IV.vii.63-65) and ferocious martial spirit (III.i.118; IV.vi.36-38) offend such liberal sensibilities, it is difficult for some to imagine that Shakespeare could truly have idealized this King, but Robert Hunter reminds us that "in considering the medieval and sixteenth-century attitudes toward the problems of mercy and forgiveness . . . , the virtue of justice was not notable for any admixture of benignity. Deeds of what seem to us abominable cruelty were regarded as praiseworthy when they were performed in justice's name" (12). Hunter illustrates this by referring to King Cambises's flaying alive of one of his councilors, an act which did not earn Cambises a reputation as a cruel and tyrannical prince, but which rather earned him the reputation of being a just and good king (12). What therein distances a modern reader from Henry would probably and ironically have invited the Shakespearean audience to embrace their King even more completely as an exemplum of the majestic ideal. Critics such as C. H. Hobday, who see Shakespeare subtly criticizing Henry as a warmonger (111), are therefore almost certainly mistaken in their conclusions, for their interpretation of the proper canons of monarchy is too far removed from the defining circumstances of Shakespeare's day to be persuasive, a point which J. H. Walter has demonstrated.[12]

Indeed, some examples of Henry's hard judgments *assist* Shakespeare's characterization of Henry as a Christlike monarch who sacramentally embodies a transcendent ideal in matters of justice. In Act II, for example, Henry summarily orders the execution of Lord Scoop, the Earl of Cambridge, and Sir Thomas Grey when they, traitors themselves in need of the king's mercy, argue that mercy ought to be denied a poor man whom Henry had earlier imprisoned for drunken, verbal abuse of the king. Henry declares to them in his condemnation that "the mercy that was quick is us but late, / By your own counsel is suppress'd and killed" (II.ii.79-80). The event reflects with remarkable likeness the Parable of the Wicked Servant in the Gospel of St. Matthew—a parable in which a king shows mercy to a servant who cannot pay his debt but subsequently imprisons that same servant whom he had forgiven when he discovers that the forgiven servant, upon his release, had seized, threatened, and shown no mercy to a poor man who likewise owed money to him (18:23-35).

Henry's alleged severity also might be ascribed to the capital punishment which he, through the Duke of Exeter, imposes upon Bardolph for his theft of a pyx (III.vi.39-45). However, such a seemingly draconian response to an act of relatively minor consequence in the midst of a kingdom beset by war actually reflects not vile harshness but the pious judgment of a wise prince to those of Elizabethan expectations. According to Tillyard, Elizabethans of the mind of the official Tudor historian, Polydore Vergil, would anticipate that one of their king's supreme duties, as temporal head of the Church, would be the protection of the faith from sacrilege (*Shakespeare's History Plays* 33), so Henry's charge that while in France, he "would have all such offenders so cut off" (III.vi.107-08) marks him, to Elizabethans, not only as a man of justice but a man of holy reverence, modernity's misgivings notwithstanding.

Henry's marriage to Katherine in Act V also invites consideration of Henry as the emblem of unity which seals those who have been adversaries in a bond of grace. Following the great English military triumph in Act IV, the rather passive character of Act V, devoted as it is to Henry and Katherine's marriage, may seem anticlimactic, given the astonishing character of the victory in Agincourt,[13] although to Barbara Palmer, the "verbal pageantry" of the concluding act aptly and necessarily complements the formal opening of the play (123). More importantly, however, Shakespeare's inclusion of the marital material reveals that despite appearances, it is not Agincourt which completes Henry's accession to ideality; that consummation is achieved by the oaths of the Treaty of Troyes and Henry and Katherine's marriage which join two Christian nations in the persons of their princes. Harold Toliver agrees: "Shakespeare likes to reinforce the seating of civil power . . . with the promise of national renewal and continuity in the marriage ceremony" ("Shakespeare's Kingship" 63). As Queen Isabel prays,

> God, the best maker of all marriages,
> Combine your hearts in one, your realms in one!
> As man and wife, being two, are one in love,
> So be there 'twixt your kingdoms such a spousal,
> That never may ill office, or fell jealousy,
> Which troubles oft the bed of blessed marriage,
> Thrust in between the [paction] of these kingdoms,
> To make divorce of their incorporate league;
> That English may as French, French Englishmen,
> Receive each other. God speak this Amen!
> (V.ii.359-68)

As J. H. Walter concludes, "It is this completion [the treaty and the marriage] that necessitated Act V; it [the completion] was not implicit in Agincourt" (167).

The marriage of Henry and Katherine also prefigures the fullness of English national unity in the post-Bosworth Field marriage of Henry Tudor to Elizabeth of York which effects a similar but, for Tudor England, a more immediately meaningful reconciliation that unites the warring houses of Lancaster and York and ends the Wars of the Roses. Henry and Kate's marriage therefore provides a formative metaphor for apprehending, in a Christian context, the means by which final reconciliation between enemies is achieved. As Ernest Gilman remarks, Henry and Katherine's union is an incarnational foreshadowing of the union of Henry [VII] and Elizabeth [of York which] " 'erected' fallen England to a state of sacramental integrity exemplified not only by 'man and woman in marriage' but by the union of the 'Godhed to the manhod' . . . ." (99). Consequently, Gilman continues, in the fullness of this imagery of conquest and marriage as unifying events, Henry Tudor's later victory over the tyrant, Richard III (fulfilling the destiny prefigured in Henry's glorious, but imperfect, conquest of France) and his consequent marriage to Elizabeth of York become "nothing short of an act of redemption, a national resurrection" (99).

Finally, Shakespeare's choice of a wedding to conclude *Henry V* also complements John King's Reformation emphasis upon marriage as a sacramental sign of hope for the "grace-full" reformation of human society (*English Reformation Literature* 202). Northrop Frye, for example, notes that especially in Shakespearean comedy—to which dramatic genre the final act of Henry V could persuasively lay claim— "the birth of [a] new society is symbolized by a closing festive scene featuring a wedding, a banquet, or a dance" (*A Natural Perspective* 72). Such a hope for international union and renewal is expressed no less expectantly in *Henry V* than by the French king who, in his commendation of his daughter to Henry, consigns to this union the peace of the world:

> Take her, fair son, and from her blood raise up
> Issue to me, that the contending kingdoms
> Of France and England, whose very shores look pale
> With envy of each other's happiness,
> May cease their hatred; and this dear conjunction
> Plant neighborhood and Christian-like accord
> In their sweet bosoms, that never war advance
> His bleeding sword 'twixt England and fair France.
>
> (V.ii.348-55)

In achieving the restoration of the kingdom to the unity which it had lost, Henry, however, becomes more than an historical symbol of what was and is but emerges as also a sign of what England is to be. Henry V, this "star of England" (Epilogue 6), is the fulfillment of English destiny at the same time that he is another herald and forerunner of it, for although "Fortune made his sword; / By which the world's best garden he achieved" (Epilogue 6-7), Henry's descendants will "los[e] France, and ma[k]e his England bleed" (Epilogue 12). Henry, therefore, like David to Christ, proleptically prefigures yet another and greater king to come: Henry Tudor, the royal bearer of English salvation, the nation's deliverer, another king emblemized by the sun (Anderson 122), the appointed scourge of God against the menace of demonic evil in Richard III; Henry V, therefore, both is and is to be. In the achievement of his destiny—the restoration, enlargement, and magnification of his kingdom—Henry V, like David before him, becomes a secular Christ as well as the sacramental embodiment of expectant hope: he becomes, in short, the incarnation of the royal ideal for his time as well as the promise of a greater glory yet to come, one in whom inheres "pure fire and air; and the dull elements of earth and water never appear . . ." (III.vii.21-22).

Notes

[1]Henry is patient and deliberate in a manner that sharply contrasts with Richard's hysteria and ungoverned passion, as wildly disordered as the turmoil which he cannot quell. In this context, a useful distinction between ordinary patience and Christian patience not only assists in illustrating Henry's virtue as one who patiently awaits his destiny but also advises us of his distinctly Christian character. John Danby, for instance, observes that ordinary or Stoic patience is a resignation characterized by indifference to fate that is accompanied by the impotence of an unfeeling passivity, whereas for the Christian, patience is instead an attitude of faith, born of the conviction that burdens are not empty, valueless sufferings but are instead redemptive opportunites for the bearer to share in the transfiguring life of God in Christ (*Poets on Fortune's Hill* 110). Such latter definition, of course, is not only the representative posture of Henry but also (and perhaps more notably) the model of patience which Edgar urges upon his father and the King in *King Lear*; for Gloucester and Lear, based as their dispositions are for much of the play either upon despair for the future or angry (if stifled) resistance to fate or circumstance, do not conform to that Christian attitude of expectant hope and patient endurance in the midst of strife which defines Edgar's sense of what it means to forbear.

[2]Rosemary O'Day reminds us of the quality of the Tudor public's understanding of the indivisible union between the king and the land (a union, as we have noted,

which was much enshrined in popular legend via the Arthurian tradition) in her emphasis that among Tudor Englishmen "the prince was his people." She also notably attests that especially in their exploitation of this mythology, "Shakespeare's history plays . . . provide good examples of this attitude" (6).

[3]Holinshed's account also reflects this reading, demonstrating Hal's transformation by its reminder to the chronicle's readers of the King's repudiation of his low, roguish, devilish companions at his coronation: "For whereas he had made himselfe a companion unto misrule mates of dissolute order and life, he now banished them all from his presence . . . inhibiting them upon a great paine, not once to approach, lodge, or soiourne within ten miles of his court or presence" (*Holinshed's Chronicle* 70).

[4]Greenblatt's indictment of what he perceives to be the moral bankruptcy of the English monarchy in the Henriad, especially as it is personified by Hal, is interesting, though we do not require Mr. Greenblatt to inform us of Hal's studied duplicity; Hal tells us of it himself (see especially *1 Henry IV* I.ii.197-217). In any case, to single out Hal as the paragon of treachery in the Lancaster plays seems selective—especially as the principal objects of Hal's deception—the King and Falstaff—are archetypes of deception themselves.

[5]See such representative works by John Bale as *King John; The Temptation of Our Lord by Satan;* and the *Comedy Concerning Three Laws, of Nature, and Christ, Corrupted by the Sodomites, Pharisees, and Papists.*

[6]Shakespeare was accompanied in this assertion by Anglican theologians and prelates. As Leonard reports, "Whether it was Cranmer or Hooker . . . Anglican churchmen

[of the sixteenth century] found themselves defining the mission of the church in terms of the needs of England as seen by the regnant civil power. Any opposition to the will of the monarch was, accordingly, both seditious and sectarian. A heretic was anti-English and [anti-Anglican] . . . " (32).

[7]Alan Velie concurs: "Shakespeare stresses that the temporal ruler should be very cautious in meting justice to his subjects. Unless they are definitely reprobates, he should show them the mercy he hopes to receive when he himself is judged by God" (45).

[8]Hal, for example, like King David of the Scriptures, is heir to a blemished dynasty, and as David's innocent son dies because of David's complicity in the death of Uriah the Hittite (2 Samuel 12:14), so Hal's pious, devout son, owing to the guilt incurred by *his* lineage, dies by the hand of Richard of Gloucester, who has been appointed by God the Yorkist scourge (" . . . die, prophet [says Richard to Hal's son, Henry VI], in thy speech / For this, amongst the rest, was I ordain'd [*3 Henry VI* V.vi.57-58]). But Hal, also like King David, is a sign of the great redeemer of the nation who is to come, and Henry VI, shortly before his murder at the hands of Richard III, confirms this promise: he prophesies of the infant Henry, Earl of Richmond—destined to become Henry VII, the deliverer of his people—in a scene iconographically modeled after the Lukan account of the infant Christ before the prophet Simeon (liturgically recalled in the Nunc Dimittis):

> Come hither, England's hope. If secret powers
> Suggest but truth to my divining thoughts,
> This pretty lad will prove our country's bliss.
> His looks are full of peaceful majesty,

> His head by nature fram'd to wear a crown,
> His hand to wield a sceptre, and himself
> Likely in time to bless a regal throne.
> Much make of him, my lords, for this is he . . . .
>
> (*3 Henry VI* IV.vi.67-75)

[9]Early in the play, Richard leads Bushy, Bagot, and Green in prayer: "Now put it, God, in the physician's mind / To help him [John of Gaunt] to his grave immediately! / Come gentlemen, let's all go to visit him. / Pray God we may make haste and come too late!" (I.iv.59-60, 63-64)

[10]One of Shakespeare's more original uses of this sun imagery is not in emblazoning Henry with the associations conventionally ascribed of one who compares himself to or is compared with the sun; instead, he uses it to advance a distinction between the relative strength of will which distinguishes Henry from individuals like Falstaff, men who are lesser beings than he. Falstaff, for example, by his own admission, is a creature of darkness, governed by the moon—unlike Henry, who not only labors in the light but identifies with the light and is inseparably united to and radiant of the light. In contrast to Hal's "herein will I imitate the sun" (*1 Henry IV* I.11.197), Falstaff revealingly cajoles Henry,

> Marry, then, sweet wag, when thou art king, let not us that are squires of the night's body be called thieves of the day's beauty. Let us be Diana's foresters, gentlemen of the shade, minions of the moon, and let men say we be men of good government, being governed, as the sea is, by our noble and chaste mistress the moon, under whose countenance we steal.
>
> (*1 Henry IV* I.11.23-29)

[11]Allen's fanaticism and treason were probably inspired, as Ken Powell and Chris Cook inform us, by Pope Plus V's Bull, "Regnans in Excelsis," in which Queen Elizabeth was excommunicated and all Catholics loyal to Rome were summoned by the Vatican to rise up and depose her (121).

[12]See once again Walter's criteria of ideal monarchy as these were enumerated by Erasmus and Chelidonius and subsequently borrowed by Shakespeare.

[13]Modern historians suggest that on the eve of Agincourt, Henry may have had no more than 5500 men under arms, many of whom were suffering from dysentery and malaria, and he was arrayed against a thundering French army, led by the Dolphin, of probably more than five legions' strength (approximately 30,000 soldiers). Yet he won, and in doing so, outslaughtered the adversary by a conservatively-estimated margin of at least 35-1 (Seward 160-69; Hibbert 77-117). Small wonder, therefore, that the English would have interpreted their victory as providential, especially when one considers it in light of the next century's seemingly invincible challenge to England by the Spanish Armada which, like Agincourt, produced an English triumph in the midst of what otherwise appeared to augur certain defeat.

Calvary by Albrecht Dürer in *The Complete Woodcuts of Albrecht Dürer*. 1927. Ed. Willi Kurth (New York: Dover, 1963), plate 192.

> . . . yet you Pilates
> Have here deliver'd me to my sour cross,
> And water cannot wash away your sin.
>
> (*Richard II* IV.i.240-42)

Conclusion

Shakespeare's history plays attempt to achieve far more than mere momentary entertainment, and they are even less reliable accounts of historical events than the unabashedly prejudiced prose chronicles of the day. Rather than document historical *fact*, Shakespeare's histories propose to establish historical *truth*, a truth which, in Shakespeare's era, to be compelling, was thought to be propositional and therefore quite distinct from our modern understanding of truth as that which can be verified and empirically documented as *actual*, derived from observation. Shakespeare's truths, therefore, as they are the truths of the Anglican Church and State of the sixteenth century, would have been considered by most spectators of Shakespearean drama to be the possessors of an independent validity, because their character would be thought holy, sovereign, and hence inviolate.

Shakespeare's plays, by continuing the didactic tradition of the medieval stage and Renaissance historiography, embraced the precepts of Tudor monarchy and applied those principles of absolute monarchy and Protestant theology to the Elizabethan stage. Shakespearean drama therefore interpreted history; it did not recollect it—except in the spirit of sixteenth-century imagination, harmonized with legend and myth.

Accordingly, in Shakespeare's Lancaster plays, Richard II is divorced from his time and sculpted into an ogre of almost imperial Roman tyranny and capriciousness and

endowed with all manner of foreign affectation. Consequently, like vanquished Catholicism under the Tudor
successors to the throne, Richard, when confronted by
rebellion, vainly invokes his perception of a divine and
immutable right to rule because of what he mistakenly
believes to be his personal and perpetual possession of an
indelible mark of sovereignty. Richard lacks the Protestant
conviction that, in the dereliction of his rule, he has
forfeited the royal prerogative once extended by a God who
will give and withdraw gifts as he pleases; Richard's fatal
error, like that of the medieval Roman Church of which is
he so much the personal icon, is in not realizing that his
commission is not his private possession; he is fundamentally unable to accept the evidence about him that the divine
mandate once conferred on him has been transferred to
another. In wildly passionate verse, bordering almost on
hysteria (and in truth succumbing to it), Richard flagellates
himself—not in penance, however, but in convulsions of
sentimentality and self-pity:

> I'll be buried in the king's high way,
> Some way of common trade, where subjects' feet
> May hourly trample on their sovereign's head;
> For on my heart they tread now while I live,
> And buried once, why not upon my head?

(III.iii.155-59)

On the other hand, utilizing the mechanics of the
medieval *de casibus* theme, Shakespeare crafts in Henry
Bolingbroke a man who is the quintessential opportunist
but also the bearer of talents for efficiency, economy, and
industry which better serve the realm than all of Richard's
impassioned fantasies of glory and celebrity. Shakespeare

therefore at once creates in this single play an image of impiety and treason in Richard and a picture of determination and resolve in Henry Bolingbroke, though Henry's reign, like the life of the early Reformation Church which he in many respects embodies, is marked by the absence of the traditional tokens of legitimacy and is beset by conspiracy and armed rebellion. Purged, however, of the excesses and frippery of the Plantagenet court, Henry Bolingbroke establishes a reign of austere, ambitious, and unmistakably English character. His rule is marked by temperance, generosity, and forbearance (he forgives Aumerle, for example, of his complicity with the would-be assassins at Oxford), and he is exceptionally aware of his responsibility for having overthrown his predecessor, though he never apologizes for the necessity of having had to do so. He is the early fifteenth-century's representative of the late sixteenth-century king: quick to seize the advantage of the moment from his enemies, supreme and self-consciously authoritative, yet humble and aware of his own imperfections, trimmed and tailored like the English garden which Richard's kingdom does not resemble (III.iv.55-57), and he is gravely conscious of his responsibilities.

Henry's kingdom declines in *1* and *2 Henry IV*, and Shakespeare therein emotionally detaches us from Henry, for Henry himself is less immediately the sign of God's anointed than the progenitor of a greater destiny which is to follow. Just as in *Macbeth*, when Macbeth is allowed to see the bloody abortion of his own brief reign and the ascendancy of the dynasty to be established by Banquo's heirs ("What, will the line stretch out to th' crack of doom?" [IV.i.117]), so Henry feels the frustration of his own purpose and fears the loss of his hard-won advantage. Beset by the apparent lack of character in his eldest son and by the comic sloth and indifference of Falstaff, Henry despairs of the future. Hal and Falstaff, representative of all derelict noblemen and commoners, are harbingers of no glorious destiny for the kingdom, but true to form, England, that "royal throne of kings" (*Richard II* II.i.40), acquires a measure of its future glory under the Tudors with the accession of the unlikely and unlooked-for deliverer, Prince Hal, who becomes Henry V. Furthermore, it is an accession accompanied (not unlike that of the Tudors) with a "reformation" swift and purifying, the king an embodied promise and promisor of a renewed state, one whose accession is effusively described by the attendant archbishop at Henry's coronation in words derived from the baptismal liturgy of the Anglican *Book of Common Prayer*—in itself, a sign of the purification which has come to the kingdom in the elevation of this "mirror of all Christian kings" (*Henry V* II Chorus 6) to the throne.

Finally, in *Henry V*, we see the young king attain the fullness of English monarchy, prefiguring the very apotheosis of English monarchy to be realized by the Tudors. Henry's brief tenure on the throne, however, in truth, was characterized less by the perfection of English government itself than by astonishing military success in France. Henry's triumph, like the defeat of the Armada under Elizabeth, was achieved more by unforseen good fortune than by military prowess, but both victories—stunning and remarkable each— were widely believed to have been providentially ordered, and Henry's conquest of Catholic France (perhaps in itself a dramatic type of the crushing defeat of Catholic Spain under Elizabeth), is so depicted by Shakespeare.

Henry's triumph over France and his marriage into the French royal family through his alliance with Katherine almost surely are conceived as anticipatory types of the unification of the two warring houses of York and Lancaster achieved in Henry Tudor's marriage to Elizabeth of York; yet unlike the later union, Henry V's momentary glory was rapidly eclipsed (as Shakespeare dramatizes in his succeeding [though earlier-scripted] Yorkist tetralogy) by the disaster of his son's reign following the young Henry VI's premature death. Failing to achieve any stable or secure government at home which could withstand the challenge to his son upon his death, Henry V, despite Shakespeare's characterization to the contrary, proved, in fact, to be a monarch whose reign was extremely fragile and ill-conceived, one who attempted to extend English hegemony over territories so vast that the need to consolidate authority at home was overlooked.

None of these fatal errors in Henry V's brief administration is even alluded to by Shakespeare, of course, but such politic silence is only too understandable when we consider that none of these compromising facts accommodated Shakespeare's agenda, which was to apply to those persons and events in English history a trans-historical significance not dissimilar to the prophetic, priestly, and kingly qualities applied to another Messiah by chroniclers of another, more ancient salvation history that was guided by yet another kind of messianism and refracted through the several lenses of experience and faith.

The Lancaster plays therefore, extensions of this Christian messianism, are obediently crafted not only in reverent compliance with the larger mythological character of that movement but in fealty to its particular confessional expression in Tudor England. To the end of demonstrating the providential guidance of the English nation within the theological context defined by Tudor historiography, Shakespeare becomes not only another but easily the best dramatic apologist for a Reformation which continues, some four centuries later, to define the Christian faith of an England "[r]enowned . . . [f]or Christian service and true chivalry . . . [d]ear for her reputation through the world" (*Richard II* II.i.53,54,58).

Bibliography

Adams, Caroline. *The Prayer Book Pattern*. New York: Macmillan, n.d.

Adams, John Cranford. *The Globe Playhouse: Its Design and Equipment*. 2nd ed. 1942. New York: Barnes and Noble, 1961.

Against Disobedience and Willful Rebellion. Ed. John Griffiths. *The Two Books of Homilies Appointed to be Read in Churches*. Oxford, 1859. 106-14.

Anderson, Judith H. *Biographical Truth: The Representation of Historical Persons in Tudor-Stuart Writing*. New Haven: Yale UP, 1984.

Anglo, Sydney. *Spectacle, Pageantry and Early Tudor Policy*. Oxford: Clarendon, 1969.

Anglo-Saxon Chronicle. Ed. and trans. James Ingram. London: J. M. Dent and Sons, 1912.

Aristotle. *The Rhetoric and Poetics of Aristotle*. Eds. and trans. W. Rhys Roberts and Ingram Bywater. New York: Modern Library, 1984.

Armstrong, William A. "The Elizabethan Concept of the Tyrant." *Review of English Studies* 22 (1946): 161-81.

Aronson, Alex. *Psyche and Symbol in Shakespeare*. Bloomington: Indiana UP, 1972.

Augustine of Hippo. Vol. 2 of *The City of God*. Ed. and trans. Marcus Dods. Edinburgh: T and T Clark, 1949. 2 vols.

Bacon, Francis. *Case of the Post Nati in Scotland*. Vol. 15 of *The Works of Francis Bacon*. Eds. Jamy Spedding, Robert Ellis, Douglas D. Heath. 1864. St. Clair Shores, MI: Scholarly P, 1968. 189-248. 16 vols.

Baker, Christopher. "The Christian Context of Falstaff's 'Finer End.'" *Explorations in Renaissance Culture* 12 (1986): 68-86.

Baker, Herschel. "Henry IV, Parts 1 and 2." *The Riverside Shakespeare*. Eds. G. Blakemore Evans, et al. Boston: Houghton Mifflin, 1974. 842-46.

Baldwin, William, et al. *The Mirror for Magistrates*. Ed. Lily B. Campbell. Cambridge: Cambridge UP, 1938.

Bale, John. *Comedy Concerning Three Laws of Nature, Moses and Christ*. New York: AMS, 1970.

—. *King Johan*. Ed. Barry B. Adams. San Marino: Huntington Library, 1969.

—. *The Temptation of Our Lord*. New York: AMS, 1970.

Barber, Charles. "Prince Hal, Henry V, and the Tudor Monarchy." *The Morality of Art: Essays Presented to G. Wilson Knight by His Colleagues and Friends*. Ed. D. W. Jefferson. New York: Barnes and Noble, 1969. 67-75.

—. "Rule and Misrule in 'Henry IV.'" *Twentieth Century Interpretations of Henry IV. Part One: A Collection of Critical Essays*. Ed. R. J. Dorius. Englewood Cliffs, NJ: Prentice-Hall, 1970. 51-70.

Barnaby, Andrew. "The 'Poet Historicall' and the Dream of History." Seventeenth Annual Conference, The Ohio State University Center for Medieval and Renaissance Studies, Columbus, 28 Feb. 1986.

Barnet, Sylvan. "Some Limitations of a Christian Approach to Shakespeare." *Tragedy: Modern Essays in Criticism*. Eds. Laurence Anthony Michel and Richard Benson Sewall. Englewood Cliffs: Prentice-Hall, 1963. 199-209.

Barroll, J. Leeds. *Artificial Persons: The Formation of Character in the Tragedies of Shakespeare*. Columbia: U of

South Carolina P, 1974.

Barry, Patricia S. *The King in Tudor Drama*. Salzburg: Institute für Englische Sprache and Literatur, 1977.

Barthes, Roland. *Writing Degree Zero and Elements of Semiology*. Trans. Annette Lavers and Colin Smith. New York: Hill and Wang, 1970.

Barton, John. *Playing Shakespeare*. London: Methuen, 1984.

Bates, Katherine Lee. *The English Religious Drama*. New York, 1893.

Battenhouse, Roy. "Revising Tillyard: How?" *Shakespeare Newsletter* 34 (1984): 32.

—. "Shakespearean Tragedy as Christian: Some Confusions in the Debate." *Centennial Review* 8 (1964): 77-98.

Beasley, Jerry C. "Early English Fiction: Historical Criticism, Old and New." *Studies in the Novel* 17 (Winter 1985): 335-54.

Becker, George J. *Shakespeare's Histories*. New York: Frederick Ungar, 1977.

Beckerman, Bernard. *Shakespeare at the Globe: 1599-1609*. New York: Macmillan, 1962.

Bede, the Venerable. *Ecclesiastical History of the English Nation*. London: J. Dent and Sons, 1910.

Benson, Jackson J. Steinbeck—A Defense of Biographical Criticism." *College Literature* 16 (Spring 1989): 107-16.

Beowulf, An Adaptation by Julian Glover of the Verse Translations of Michael Alexander and Edwin Morgan. Brunswick Road, Gloucester: Allan Sutton, 1987.

Bergeron, David M. "Civic Pageants and Historical Drama." *Journal of Medieval and Renaissance Studies* 5 (1975): 89-105.

Berman, Art. *From the New Criticism to Deconstruction: The*

Reception of Structuralism and Post-Structuralism. Urbana: U of Illinois P, 1988.

Berman, Ronald. Introduction. *Twentieth Century Interpretations of Henry V: A Collection of Critical Essays.* Ed. Ronald Berman. Englewood Cliffs, NJ: Prentice-Hall, 1968. 3-10.

Berry, Edward I. *Patterns of Decay: Shakespeare's Early Histories.* Charlottesville: UP of Virginia, 1975.

Bethell, S. L. *Shakespeare and the Popular Dramatic Tradition.* Durham, NC: Duke UP, 1944.

Bevington, David. *Tudor Drama and Politics.* Cambridge: Harvard UP, 1968.

Bible, The New Oxford Annotated, With the Apocrypha.

Blanpied, John. *Time and the Artist in Shakespeare's English Histories.* Newark: U of Delaware P, 1983.

Blickenderfer, James. *The Eighteenth Century.* New York: Scribner's, 1929.

Boethius. *The Consolation of Philosophy.* Ed. and trans. Richard Green. Indianapolis: Bobbs-Merrill, 1962.

The Book of Common Prayer 1559: The Elizabethan Prayer Book. Ed. John E. Booty. Charlottesville: U of Virginia, 1976.

Booty, John E. "Richard Hooker." *The Spirit of Anglicanism: Hooker, Maurice, Temple.* Ed. William J. Wolf. Wilton, CT: Morehouse-Barlow, 1979. 1-48.

Boris, Edna Z. *Shakespeare's English Kings, the People, and the Law: A Study in the Relationship Between the Tudor Constitution and the English History Plays.* Rutherford: Fairleigh Dickinson UP, 1978.

Bowers, Fredson. "The Structural Climax in *Henry IV, Part I.*" *William Shakespeare: Henry the Fourth, Part I: An*

Authorized Text, Cultural Contexts, Extracts from the Major Sources, Essays on Criticism, Bibliography. Ed. James L. Sanderson. Rev. Ed. New York: Norton, 1969. 309-16.

—. "Theme and Structure in 'King Henry IV, Part I.'" *The Drama of the Renaissance: Essays for Leicester Bradner.* Ed. Elmer M. Blistein. Providence: Brown UP, 1970. 42-68.

Bradbrook, Muriel C. *The Artist and Society in Shakespeare's England.* Brighton, Sussex: Harvester, 1982.

Bradley, A. C. *Shakespearean Tragedy.* 2nd ed. 1905. New York: St. Martin's, 1981.

Bray, Alan. *Homosexuality in Renaissance England.* London: Gay Men's P, 1982.

Brockett, Oscar G. *History of the Theatre.* 4th ed. Boston: Allyn and Bacon, 1982.

Bromley, John C. *The Shakespearean Kings.* Boulder: Colorado Associated UP, 1971.

Brook, Stella. *The Language of the Book of Common Prayer.* London: Andre Deutsch, 1965.

Brooke, Tucker. *The Tudor Drama.* New York: Houghton Mifflin, 1977.

Bruner, Jerome. "Myth and Identity." *The Symbolic Order: A Contemporary Reader on the Arts Debate.* Ed. Peter Abbs. London: Falmer, 1989. 174-79.

Bryant, J. A. *Hippolyta's View: Some Christian Aspects of Shakespeare's Plays.* Lexington: U of Kentucky P, 1961.

—. "The Linked Analogies of Richard II." *Sewanee Review* 65 (1957): 420-33.

Burckhardt, Sigurd. *Shakespearean Meanings.* Princeton: Princeton UP, 1968.

Buckle, Henry Thomas. *History of Civilization in England.*

Vol. 1. New York, 1874. 2 vols.

Bullough, Geoffrey. *Narrative and Dramatic Sources of Shakespeare*. New York: Columbia UP, 1960.

Burgess, William. *The Bible In Shakespeare: A Study of the Relation of the Works of William Shakespeare to the Bible*. 1903. New York: Haskell House, 1968.

Bush, Geoffrey. *Shakespeare and the Natural Condition*. Cambridge: Harvard UP, 1956.

Calderwood, James L. *Metadrama in Shakespeare's Henriad: Richard II to Henry V*. Berkeley: U of California P, 1979.

Campbell, Joseph. *The Hero With a Thousand Faces*. 2nd ed. Princeton: Princeton UP, 1968.

Campbell, Lily B. "English History in the Sixteenth Century." *Shakespeare: The Histories: A Collection of Critical Essays*. Englewood Cliffs, NJ: Prentice-Hall, 1965. 13-31.

—. *Shakespeare's Histories: Mirrors of Elizabethan Policy*. San Marino, CA: Huntington Library, 1947.

Tudor Conceptions of History and Tragedy. Berkeley: U of California P, 1936.

Canons and Decrees of the Sacred and Ecumenical Council of Trent. Trans. J. Waterworth. Chicago, 1848.

Carlyle, Thomas. "The Poet and the Prophet." *Victorians on Literature and Art*. Ed. Robert Peters. New York: Appleton-Century-Crofts, 1961. 17-24.

Carr, Virginia. "Once More Into the Henriad: A 'Two-Eyed' View." *Journal of English and Germanic Philology* 77 (1978): 530-45.

Carter, Thomas. *Shakespeare: Puritan and Recusant*. 1897. New York: AMS, 1970.

Cary, Norman R. *Christian Criticism in the Twentieth Century: Theological Approaches to Literature*. Port

Washington, NY: Kennikat, 1975.

Cauthen, I. B., Jr. "*Richard II* and the Image of the Betrayed Christ." *Renaissance Papers* (1954): 45-48.

Chadwick, Henry. "The Discussion About Anglican Orders in Modern Anglican Theology." *Apostolic Succession: Rethinking a Barrier to Unity.* Vol. 34 of Concilium: Theology in the Age of Renewal. Gen. Ed. Han Kung. New York: Paulist P, 1968. 141-49. 40 vols.

Chambers, Raymond Wilson. *Man's Unconquerable Mind.* London: J. Cape, 1939.

Champion, Larry S. *Perspective in Shakespeare's English Histories.* Athens, GA: U of Georgia P, 1976.

Chance, Jane. "The Medieval 'Apology for Poetry': Fabulous Stories and Narratives of the Gods." *The Mythographic Art: Classical Fable and the Rise of the Vernacular in Early France and England.* Ed. Jane Chance. Gainesville: U of Florida P, 1990. 3-46.

Chelidonius, Tigurinus. *A most excellent historie, of the institution and first beginning of Christian princes.* Trans. James Chillester. London, 1571.

Churchill, Winston S. *Churchill's History of the English-speaking Peoples.* Arr. Henry Steele Commager. New York: Dodd, Mead and Company, 1965.

Cicero. *De Oratorio: Cicero on Oratory and Orators.* Ed. and trans. J. S. Watson. Carbondale, IL: Southern Illinois UP, 1970.

Claeyssens, A. E. "'Henry IV, Part One.'" *Lectures on Four of Shakespeare's History Plays.* Eds. Lester M. Beattie, John A. Hart, Raymond E. Parshall. Pittsburgh: Carnegie P, 1953. 19-34.

Clemen, Wolfgang H. *The Development Of Shakespeare's*

Imagery. Cambridge: Harvard UP, 1951.

Cohen, Eileen. "The Visible Solemnity: Ceremony and Order in Shakespeare and Hooker." *Texas Studies in Literature and Language* 12 (Summer 1970): 181-95.

Coleman, Hamilton. *Shakespeare and the Bible*. New York: Vantage P, 1955.

Coleridge, Samuel Taylor. "Richard II." *Coleridge's Writings on Shakespeare*. Ed. Terence Hawkins. New York: Capricorn, 1959. 219-44.

Collins, Joseph B. *Christian Mysticism in the Elizabethan Age*. Baltimore: Johns Hopkins UP, 1940.

Cormican, L. A. "Medieval Idiom in Shakespeare (I): Shakespeare and the Liturgy." *Scrutiny* 17 (1950): 186-202.

Medieval Idiom in Shakespeare (II): Shakespeare and the Medieval Ethic." *Scrutiny* 17 (1951): 298-317.

Coursen, Herbert R., Jr. *Christian Ritual and the World of Shakespeare's Tragedies*. Lewisburg: Bucknell UP, 1976.

—. *The Leasing Out Of England: Shakespeare's Second Henriad*. Washington, D. C.: UP of America, 1982.

—. "Sacramental Elements in Shakespearean Tragedy." *Christianity and Literature* 23 (1974): 7-19.

—. "Theories of History in *Richard II*." Seventeenth Annual Conference, The Ohio State University Center for Medieval and Renaissance Studies, Columbus, 27 February 1986.

Cox, Gerald H. "'Like a Prince Indeed': Hal's Triumph of Honor in '1 Henry IV.'" *Pageantry in the Shakespearean Theatre*. Ed. David M. Bergeron. Athens, GA: U of Georgia P, 1985. 130-49.

Craig, Hardin. *The Enchanted Glass: The Elizabethan Mind in Literature*. New York: Oxford UP, 1936.

Cranmer, Thomas. "A Speech at the Coronation of Edward VI, February 20, 1547." *The Works Of Thomas Cranmer.* Ed. G. E. Duffield. 20-22.

—. "Of the Presence of Christ." *Writings and Disputations of Thomas Cranmer, Archbishop of Canterbury, Martyr, 1556, Relative to the Sacrament of the Lord's Supper.* Ed. John Edmund Cox. Cambridge: Cambridge UP, 1844. 51-200.

Crawford, John. "The Importance of the Supernatural in Shakespearean Politics." Division on Political Themes in Shakespeare, South Central MLA Convention, New Orleans, 31 October 1986.

—. ed. *Romantic Criticism of Shakespearean Drama.* Salzburg: Institut für Englische Sprache und Literatur, 1978.

Cross, Claire. *The Royal Supremacy in the Elizabethan Church.* Vol. 8 of Historical Problems: Studies and Documents. Ed. G. R. Elton. London: George Allen and Unwin, 1969. 8 vols.

Cumberland, Clark. *Shakespeare and the Supernatural.* London: Williams and Norgate, 1931.

Daly, Peter, et al., eds. 1 vol. to date. Toronto: U of Toronto P, 1988- .

Danby, John F. *Poets on Fortune's Hill: Studies in Sidney, Shakespeare, Beaumont and Fletcher.* London: Faber and Faber, 1952.

—. *Shakespeare's Doctrine of Nature: A Study of King Lear.* London: Faber and Faber, 1949.

Daniel, Samuel. *Archi-Episcopal Priority Instituted (sic) By Christ, Proven By Plaine Testimonies of Scripture Asserted By the Ancient Fathers: And Whereunto All the Moderne Divines of the Protestant Side Doe Fully Assent, Without*

Contradictlon of Any One Man. 1641. Ann Arbor: University Microfilms, 1967.

Dante. *The Banquet.* Ed. and trans. Christopher Ryan. Saratoga, CA: Anma Libri, 1989.

Davies, Horton. *Worship and Theology in England: From Cranmer to Hooker. 1534-1603.* Princeton: Princeton UP, 1970.

Dean, Leonard. "Tudor Theories of History Writing." *University of Michigan Contributions in Modern Philosophy* 1 (1941): 1-24.

Dekker, Thomas. *The Shoemaker's Holiday.* Ed. Gerald Eades Bentley. *The Development of English Drama.* New York: Appleton-Century-Crofts, 1950. 110-48.

Dickens, A. G. *The English Reformation.* New York: Schocken, 1964.

Diehl, Huston. "Iconography and Characterization in English Tragedy, 1585-1642." *Drama in the Renaissance: Comparative and Critical Essay.* Eds. Clifford Davidson, C. J. Gianakaris, and John H. Stroupe. New York: AMS, 1986. 11-20.

—. "The Iconography of Violence in English Renaissance Tragedy." *Renaissance Drama* 11 (1980): 27-44.

Dix, Gregory. *The Shape of the Liturgy.* London: Dacre P, 1945.

Dollimore, Jonathan. *Radical Tragedy: Religion, Ideology and Power in the Drama of Shakespeare and His Contemporaries.* Chicago: U of Chicago P, 1984.

—, and Alan Sinfield. "History and Ideology: The Instance of *Henry V.*" *Alternative Shakespeares.* Ed. John Drakakis. London: Methuen, 1985. 206-27.

Doran, Madeline. "Imagery in *Richard II* and in *Henry IV.*" *Modern Language Review* 37 (April 1942): 113-22.

Dorius, R. J. "A Little More than a Little." *Shakespeare Quarterly* 11 (1960): 13-26.

—. Introduction. *Twentieth Century Interpretations of Henry IV, Part One: A Collection of Critical Essays.* Ed. R. J. Dorius. Englewood Cliffs, NJ: Prentice-Hall, 1970. 1-11.

Dowden, Edward. "The Mood of Shakespeare's Last Plays." *His Infinite Variety: Major Shakespearean Criticism Since Johnson.* Ed. Paul N. Siegel. Philadelphia: J. B. Lippincott, 1964. 377-81.

—. *Puritan and Anglican: Studies in Literature.* 3rd ed. London: Kegan Paul, Trench, Trübner, 1910.

Downer, Alan S. "The Life of Our Design: The Function Of Imagery in the Poetic Drama." *Modern Shakespeare Criticism: Essays on Style, Dramaturgy, and the Major Plays.* Ed. Alvin B. Kernan. New York: Harcourt, Brace, and World, 1970. 30-40.

Dryden, John. *An Essay of Dramatic Poesy.* Oxford, 1899.

—. *Essays of John Dryden.* Ed. W. P. Kerr. Vol. 1. New York: Russell and Russell, 1969. 2 vols.

Dunn, Richard S. *The Age of Religious Wars, 1559-1689.* New York: W. W. Norton, 1970.

Eckhardt, Caroline D. "Prophecy and Nostalgia: Arthurian Symbolism at the Close of the English Middle Ages." *The Arthurian Tradition : Essays in Convergence.* Eds. Mary Flowers Braswell and John Bugge. Tuscaloosa: U of Alabama P, 1988. 109-26.

Eckhardt, Eduard. *Das Englische Drama im Zeitalter der Reformation und der Hochrenaissance.* Berlin: Walter de Gruyter, 1928.

Eliade, Mircea. *Myth and Reality.* New York: Harper and Row, 1963.

Eliot, T. S. "Tradition and the Individual Talent." *Selected Essays, 1917-1932.* Ed. New York: Harcourt, Brace, 1932. 3-11.

Elton, W. R. "Shakespeare Evangelized: Seven Types of Miscomprehension." *Shakespeare Newsletter* 14 (1976): 32, 36.

Elyot, Thomas. *The Governour.* Ed. Ernest Rhys. London: J. M. Dent and Sons, 1907.

Erasmus, Desiderius. *Institutio Principis Christiani.* Trans. Neil M. Chesire and Michael J. Heath. Vol. 27 of Collected Works of Erasmus. Ed. A. H. T. Levi. Toronto: U of Toronto P, 1986. 199-288. 66 vols.

—. *On Copia of Words and Ideas (De Utraque Verborem ac Rerum Copia).* Eds. and trans. Donald B. King and H. David Rix. Medieval Philosophical Texts in Translation 12. Milwaukee: Marquette UP, 1963.

Erikson, Erik H. *Young Man Luther: A Study in Psycho-analysis and History.* New York: W. W. Norton, 1962.

Esslin, Martin. Introduction. *Shakespeare Our Contemporary.* By Jan Kott. Garden City, NY: Doubleday, 1964. xi-xx.

Evans, G. Blakemore, et al. *The Riverside Shakespeare.* Boston: Houghton Mifflin, 1974.

Evett, David. "Types of King David in Shakespeare's Lancastrian Tetralogy." *Shakespeare Studies* 14 (1981): 139-61.

An Exhortation concerning good Ordre and Obedience to Rulers and Magistrates. Ed. John Griffiths. *The Two Books of Homilies Appointed to be Read in Churches.* Oxford, 1859. 139-47.

Fergusson, Francis. *The Idea of a Theatre.* Princeton: Princeton UP, 1949.

—. *Trope and Allegory: Themes Common to Dante and Shakespeare*. Athens, GA: U of Georgia P, 1977.

Fiedler, Leslie. "Archetype and Signature: A Study of the Relationship Between Biography and Poetry." *An Introduction to Literary Criticism*. Eds. Marlies K. Danzinger and W. Stacy Johnson. Boston: Heath, 1961. 262-68.

Figgis, John Neville. *The Divine Right of Kings*. 2nd ed. Cambridge: Cambridge UP, 1937.

Fitch, Robert E. *Shakespeare: The Perspective of Value*. Philadelphia: Westminster, 1969.

Fleischer, Martha Hester. *The Iconography of the English History Play*. Salzburg: Institut für Englische Sprache und Literatur, 1974.

Foreman, Walter C. *The Music of the Close: The Final Scenes of Shakespeare's Tragedies*. Lexington: UP of Kentucky, 1978.

Fraser, Russell. *The War Against Poetry*. Princeton: Princeton UP, 1970.

Frazer, James George. *The Golden Bough: A Study in Magic and Religion*. New York: Macmillan, 1922.

Frey, David L. *The First Tetralogy: Shakespeare's Scrutiny of the Tudor Myth: A Dramatic Exploration of Divine Providence*. The Hague: Mouton, 1976.

Frye, Northrop. *The Educated Imagination*. Bloomington: Indiana UP, 1964.

—. *The Great Code: The Bible and Literature*. New York: Harcourt Brace Jovanovich, 1981.

—. *A Natural Perspective: The Development of Shakespearean Comedy and Romance*. New York: Columbia UP, 1965.

—. *Northrop Frye on Shakespeare*. Ed. Robert Sandler. New Haven: Yale UP, 1986.

—. *The Secular Scripture: A Study of the Structure of Romance.* Cambridge: Harvard UP, 1976.

—. *A Study of English Romanticism.* Chicago: U of Chicago P, 1968.

Frye, Roland. *Shakespeare and Christian Doctrine.* Princeton: Princeton UP, 1963.

—. "Theological and Non-Theological Structures in Tragedy." *Shakespeare Studies* 4 (1968): 132-48.

Fuller, Reginald H. "Apostolicity and Ministry." *Concordia Theological Monthly* 17 (February 1972): 67-76.

Garber, Marjorie. "'What's Past is Prologue': Temporality and Prophecy in Shakespeare's History Plays." *Renaissance Genres: Essays on Theory, History, and Interpretation.* Ed. Barbara Kiefer Lewalski. Cambridge: Harvard UP, 1986.

Gesta Henrici Quinti: The Deeds of Henry the Fifth. Eds. and trans. Frank Taylor and John S. Roskell. Oxford: Clarendon, 1975.

Gildas. *The Ruin of Britain, and Other Works.* Ed. and trans. Michael Winterbottom. London: Phillimore, 1978.

Gillingham, John. *The Wars of the Roses: Peace and Conflict in Fifteenth-Century England.* Baton Rouge: Louisiana State UP, 1981.

Gilman, Ernest B. "'Richard II' and the Perspectives of History." *Renaissance Drama* 7 (1976): 85-116.

Girard, René. *Violence and the Sacred.* Trans. Patrick Gregory. Baltimore: The Johns Hopkins UP, 1977.

Goodrich, Michael. *The Unmentionable Vice: Homosexuality in the Later Medieval Period.* N.p.: Dorset, 1979.

Grabar, André. *Christian Iconography: A Study of Its Origins.* Princeton: Princeton UP, 1968.

Grafton, Richard. *Abridgement of the Chronicles of Englande.* Rev. ed. N.p., 1570.

Graves, Robert. *The White Goddess: A Historical Grammar of Poetic Myth.* New York: Farrar, Straus and Giroux, 1948.

Greenblatt, Stephen. "Invisible Bullets: Renaissance Authority and Its Subversion, *Henry IV* and *Henry V.*" *Political Shakespeare: New Essays in Cultural Materialism.* Eds. Jonathan Dollimore and Alan Sinfield. Ithaca: Cornell UP, 1985. 18-47.

Greene, Thomas M. *The Vulnerable Text: Essays on Renaissance Literature.* New York: Columbia UP, 1986.

Griffiths, Ralph A. "The Later Middle Ages (1290-1485)." Ed. Kenneth O. Morgan. *The Oxford Illustrated History of Britain.* Oxford: Oxford UP, 1984. 166-222.

Groot, John H. de. *The Shakespeares and The Old Faith.* New York: King's Crown P, 1946.

Hager, Alan. *Shakespeare's Political Animal: Schema and Schemata in the Canon.* Newark: U of Delaware P, 1990.

Hall, Edward D. *Hall's Chronicle, Containing the History of England, During the Reign of Henry the Fourth, and the Succeeding Monarchs, to the End of the Reign of Henry the Eighth, in Which are Particularly Described the Manner and Custom of Those Periods.* Ed. Sir Henry Ellis, London, 1809.

Hall, Thomas. English 303 classroom lecture. Valparaiso University, 7 December 1982.

Hapgood, Robert. "Shakespeare and the Ritualists." *Shakespeare Survey* 15 (1962): 24.

—. "Shakespeare's Thematic Modes of Speech: *Richard II* to *Henry V.*" *Shakespeare Survey* 20 (1967): 41-50.

Harbage, Alfred. *As They Liked It: An Essay on Shakespeare and Morality.* New York: Macmillan, 1947.

Hardison, O. B., Jr. *Christian Rite and Christian Drama in the Middle Ages.* Baltimore: Johns Hopkins UP, 1965.

Hardyng, John. *The Chronicle from the Firste Begynnyng of England.* Vol. 805 of The English Experience: Its Record in Early Printed Books Published in Facsimile. Amsterdam: Theatrum Orbis Terrarum, 1976. 964 vols.

Harnack, Harvey Andrew. "The Typological Divine: A Study in the Figural Expression of Renaissance Kingship." *DAI* 37 (1977): 5851-A (The University of Michigan).

Harris, Jesse W. *John Bale, A Study in the Minor Literature of the Reformation.* Freeport, NY: Books for Libraries, 1970.

Hart, Alfred. *Shakespeare and the Homilies.* Melbourne: Melbourne UP, 1934.

Hassler, R. Chris. *Renaissance Drama and the English Church Year.* Lincoln: U of Nebraska P, 1979.

Hazlitt, William. *Lectures on the Literature of the Age of Elizabeth and Characters of Shakespeare's Plays.* London, 1890.

Heninger, S. R., Jr. "The Sun-King Analogy in *Richard II*." *Shakespeare Quarterly* 11 (1960): 319-27.

Henke, James T. *The Ego-King: An Archetype Approach to Elizabethan Political Thought and Shakespeare's Henry IV Plays.* Salzburg: Institut für Englische Sprache und Literatur, 1977.

Hibbard, G. R. "George Chapman: Tragedy and the Providential View of History." *Shakespeare Survey* 20 (1967): 27-32.

—. "'Henry IV' and 'Hamlet.'" *Shakespeare Survey* 30 (1977): 1-12.

Hibbert, Christopher. *Agincourt.* New York: Dorset P, 1964.

Hind, Arthur M. *Engraving in England in the Sixteenth and Seventeenth Centuries.* 3 vols. Cambridge: Cambridge UP, 1953-64.

Hobday, C. H. "Imagery and Irony in *Henry V.*" *Shakespeare Survey* 21 (1968): 107-14.

Holderness, Graham. *Shakespeare's History.* Dublin: Gill and Macmillan, 1985.

Holinshed, Raphael. *Chronicle of England, Scotland, and Ireland.* Ed. Sir Henry Ellis. London, 1807.

—. *Holinshed's Chronicle as Used in Shakespeare's Plays.* Eds. Allardyce and Josephine Nicoll. London: J. M. Dent, 1927.

Holland, Norman. "Henry IV, Part Two." *The Design Within: Psychoanalytic Approaches to Shakespeare.* Ed. M. D. Faber. New York: Science House, 1987. 411-28.

Hooker, Richard. *Of the Laws of Ecclesiastical Polity.* Eds. A. S. McGrade and Brian Vickers. New York: St. Martin's, 1975.

Howe, Nicholas. *Migration and Mythmaking in Anglo-Saxon England.* New Haven, Yale UP, 1989.

Howse, Ernest Marshall. *Spiritual Values in Shakespeare.* New York: Abingdon, 1955.

Hubbell, Lindley Williams. "Shakespeare's Histories." *Lectures on Shakespeare.* Tokyo: Nan'un-do, n.d. 181-245.

Huizinga, John. *The Waning of the Middle Ages.* 1924. Garden City, NY: Doubleday, 1954.

Humphreys, Arthur R. "Shakespeare and the Tudor

Perception of History." *Stratford Papers on Shakespeare.*
Ed. B. A. W. Jackson. Toronto: W. J. Gage, 1964. 51-70.

—. "The Unity and Background of 'Henry IV, Part One.'"
*Twentieth Century Interpretations of Henry IV, Part
One: A Collection of Critical Essays.* Ed. R. J. Dorius.
Englewood Cliffs, NJ: Prentice-Hall, 1970. 18-40.

Hunter, G. K. "'Henry IV' and the Elizabethan Two-Part
Play." *Review of English Studies* 5 (1954): 235-48.

Hunter, Robert Grams. *Shakespeare and the Comedy of
Forgiveness.* New York: Columbia UP, 1965.

Hurstfield, Joel. "The Elizabethan People in the Age of
Shakespeare." *Shakespeare's World.* Eds. James
Sutherland and Joel Hurstfield. London: Edward Arnold,
1964. 27-47.

Hyde, H. Montgomery. *Oscar Wilde.* New York: Farrar,
Straus and Giroux, 1975.

Hyde, Thomas. "Identity and Acting in Elizabethan Tragedy." *Renaissance Drama* 15 (1984): 93-114.

Jackson, Gabriel Bernhard. "Metaphors, Models, and Para-
digms: The Fictions of Fact." Seventeenth Annual
Conference, The Ohio State University Center for
Medieval and Renaissance Studies, Columbus, 28 Feb.
1986.

Javierre, Antonio. "Notes on the Traditional Teaching on
Apostolic Succession." Trans. Paul Burns. *Apostolic
Succession: Rethinking a Barrier to Unity.* Vol. 34 of
Concilium: Theology in the Age of Renewal. Gen. Ed.
Hans Küng. New York: Paulist P, 1968. 16-27. 40 vols.

Jenkins, Harold. "Shakespeare's History Plays: 1900-1951."
Shakespeare Survey 6 (1953): 1-15.

Johnson, Samuel. "Preface to Shakespeare." *Samuel Johnson:*

Rasselas, Poems, and Selected Prose. 3rd. ed. Ed. Bertrand H. Bronson. New York: Holt, Rinehart and Winston, 1958. 261-307.

—. *Selections from Johnson on Shakespeare.* Eds. Bertrand H. Bronson with Jean M. O'Meara. New Haven: Yale UP, 1986.

Jones, Ernest. *Hamlet and Oedipus.* New York: W. W. Norton, 1949.

Jones, David Gwilymn. *The Dream of Learning.* Oxford: Clarendon P, 1951.

Jonson, Ben. *Sejanus, His Fall.* Eds. Edd Winfield Parks and Richmond Croom Beatty. *The English Drama: 900-1642.* 690-782.

Jorgensen, Paul A. *Redeeming Shakespeare's Words.* Berkeley: U of California P, 1962.

Juneja, Renu. "Widows and Their Mythic Roles in Shakespeare's Histories." The Eighteenth Annual Interdisciplinary CAES (Committee for the Advancement of Early Studies) Conference. Ball State University, Muncie, 16 October 1987.

Kantorowicz, Ernst H. *The King's Two Bodies: A Study in Mediaeval Political Theology.* Princeton: Princeton UP, 1957.

—. *Laudes Regiae: A Study in Liturgical Acclamations and Mediaeval Ruler Worship.* 2nd ed. Berkeley: U of California P, 1958.

Kelly, Henry Ansgar. *Divine Providence in the England of Shakespeare's Histories.* Cambridge: Harvard UP, 1970.

Kern, Fritz. *Kingship and Law in the Middle Ages.* Trans. S. B. Chrimes. Oxford: Basil Blackwell, 1956.

Kernan, Alvin B. "The Henriad: Shakespeare's Major History

Plays." *Yale Review* 59 (Autumn 1969): 3-32.

Kimbrough, R. Alan. "Olivier's Lear and the Limits of Video." *Shakespeare on Television: An Anthology of Essays and Reviews*. Eds. J. C. Bulman and H. R. Coursen. Hanover, N.H.: UP of New England, 1988. 115-21.

King, John N. *English Reformation Literature: The Tudor Origins of the Protestant Tradition*. Princeton: Princeton UP, 1982.

—. *Tudor Royal Iconography: Literature and Art in an Age of Religious Crisis*. Princeton: Princeton UP, 1989.

Kingsley, Charles. "The Limits of Exact Science as Applied to History." *The Roman and the Teuton*. London, 1891. 307-43.

Kipling, Gordon. "Richard II's 'Sumptuous Pageants' and the Idea of the Civic Triumph." *Pageantry in the Shakespearean Theatre*. Ed. David M. Bergeron. Athens, GA: U of Georgia P, 1985. 83-103.

Klaniczay, Tibor. "Die Reformation und die volkssprachlichen Grundlagen der Nationalliteraturen." *Renaissanceliteratur und frühbergerliche Revolution: Studien zu den sozial-und ideologie-geschichtlichen Grundlagen Europäischer National Literaturen*. Ed. Akademie der Wissenschaften der DDR Zentralinstitut für Literaturgeschichte. Berlin: Aufbau-Verlag, 1976. 131-44.

Knight, G. Wilson. *The Imperial Theme: Further Interpretations of Shakespeare's Tragedies, Including the Roman Plays*. London: Methuen, 1951.

—. *The Olive and the Sword: A Study of England's Shakespeare*. London: Oxford UP, 1944.

—. "On the Principles of Shakespearean Interpretation."

Modern Shakespeare Criticism: Essays on Style, Dramaturgy, and the Major Plays. Ed. Alvin B. Kernan. New York: Harcourt, Brace and World, 1970. 3-12.

—. *Principles of Shakespearean Production, With Especial Reference to the Tragedies.* New York: Macmillan, 1936.

—. *Shakespeare and Religion.* New York: Barnes and Noble, 1967.

—. *Shakespearian Production, with Especial Reference to the Tragedies.* Evanston: Northwestern UP, 1964.

—. *The Sovereign Flower: On Shakespeare as the Poet of Royalism, Together With Related Essays and Indexes to Earlier Volumes.* London: Methuen, 1958.

—. *This Sceptered Isle.* Oxford: Basil Blackwell, 1940.

Korshin, Paul J. *Typologies in England. 1650-1820.* Princeton: Princeton UP, 1982.

Krentz, Edgar. *The Historical-Critical Method.* Ed. Eugene M. Tucker. Philadelphia: Fortress, 1975.

Kretmann, Paul Edward. *The Liturgical Elements in the Earliest Forms of Medieval Drama.* Minneapolis: U of Minnesota P, 1916.

Kyd, Thomas. *The Spanish Tragedy.* Eds. Edd Windfield Parks and Richmond Croom Beatty. *The English Drama: 900-1642.* 249-324.

Labarge, Margaret Wade. *Henry V: The Cautious Conqueror.* New York: Stein and Day, 1975.

LaGuardia, Eric. "Ceremony and History: The Problem of Symbol from 'Richard II' to 'Henry V.'" *Pacific Coast Studies in Shakespeare.* Eds. Waldo F. McNeir and Thelma N. Greenfield. Eugene: U of Oregon P, 1966. 68-88.

Leary, William G. *Shakespeare Plain: The Making and*

Performing of Shakespeare's Plays. New York: McGraw-Hill, 1977.

Leavis, F. R. *The Great Tradition.* Garden City, NY: Doubleday, 1948.

—. "The Logic of Christian Discrimination." *The Common Pursuit.* London: Chatto and Windus, 1958. 248-54.

Leech, Clifford. "Catholic and Protestant Drama." *The Durham University Journal* 33 (1941): 171-87.

Leggatt, Alexander. *Shakespeare's Political Drama: The History Plays and the Roman Plays.* London: Routledge, 1988.

Legge, Thomas. *Richardus Tertius.* Ed. W. C. Hazlitt. *Shakespeare's Library.* 2nd ed. London, 1875. 135-220.

Leverett, James. "Worth the Trip: The Guthrie Presents Shakespeare's Henry Tetralogy." *The Village Voice* 31 (July 1990): 96, 98.

Lewis, C. S. *The Discarded Image: An Introduction to Medieval and Renaissance Literature.* Cambridge: Cambridge UP, 1964.

Lings, Martin. *Shakespeare in the Light of Sacred Art.* New York: Humanities, 1966.

Lockyer, Roger. *Tudor and Stuart Britain: 1471-1714.* New York: St. Martin's, 1964.

Looten, Chanoine Camille. *Shakespeare et la Religion.* Paris: Perrin, 1924.

L'Orange, Hans P. *Studies in the Iconography of Cosmic Kingship in the Ancient World.* Instituttet for sammenlignende Kulturforskning. Oslo: H. Aschelhovig, 1953.

Luther, Martin. *The Bondage of the Will.* Ed. and trans. Ernst F. Winter. *Erasmus-Luther: Discourse on Free Will.* New

York: Frederick Ungar, 1961. 97-138.

Luxton, Imogene. "The Reformation and Popular Culture." *Church and Society in England: Henry VIII to James I.* Eds. Felicity Heal and Rosemary O'Day. Hamden, CT: Shoe String, 1977. 57-77.

Mack, Maynard, Jr. *Killing the King.* New Haven: Yale UP, 1973.

Malory, Thomas. *Le Morte D'Arthur.* Trans. Keith Baines. New York: Bramhall House, 1962.

Manheim, Michael. "The Weak King History Plays in the Early 1590s." *Renaissance Drama* 2 (1969): 71-80.

Manvell, Roger. *Shakespeare and the Film.* Cranbury, NJ: A. S. Barnes, 1979.

Marker, Lisa-Lone. "Nature and Decorum in the Theory of Elizabethan Acting." *The Elizabethan Theatre II.* Ed. David C. Galloway. Toronto: Macmillan, 1970. 87-107.

Marlowe, Christopher. *Edward the Second.* Ed. W. Moelwyn Merchant. London: Ernest Beun, 1967.

—. *Doctor Faustus.* Ed. Irving Ribner. *Christopher Marlowe's Doctor Faustus: Text and Major Criticism.* Indianapolis: Odyssey P, 1966. 3-57.

Marriott, John Arthur Ransome. *English History in Shakespeare.* 1918. Folcroft, PA: Folcroft P, 1969.

Marshall, Mary H. "The Dramatic Tradition Established by the Liturgical Plays." *PMLA* 56 (1941): 962-91.

Martos, Joseph. *Doors to the Sacred: A Historical Introduction to the Sacraments of the Catholic Church.* Garden City, NY: Doubleday, 1981.

Masefield, John. *Shakespeare and the Spiritual Life.* New York: Oxford UP, 1924.

Matthews, Honor. *Character and Symbol in Shakespeare's*

Plays: A Study of Certain Christian and Pre-Christian Elements in Their Structure and Imagery. Cambridge: Cambridge UP, 1962.

Maxwell, William O. *An Outline of Christian Worship: Its Development and Forms.* London: Oxford UP, 1936.

McAlindon, T. *Shakespeare and Decorum.* New York: Macmillan, 1973.

McClure, Judith. "Bede's Old Testament Kings." *Ideal and Reality in Frankist and Anglo-Saxon Society: Studies Presented to J.M. Wallace-Hadrill.* Oxford: Oxford UP, 1983. 76-98.

McCollum, William G. "Formalism and Illusion in Shakespearean Drama." *Quarterly Journal of Speech* 31 (1945): 446-53.

McFarland, Thomas. *Tragic Meanings in Shakespeare.* New York: Random House, 1966.

Mehl, Dieter. "Emblems in English Renaissance Drama." *Renaissance Drama* 2 (1969): 36-57.

Mendl, R.W.S. *Revelation in Shakespeare.* London: John Calder, 1964.

Merchant, W. Moelwyn. [Introduction to *Edward II*] *Edward the Second.* By Christopher Marlowe. Ed. W. Moelwyn Merchant. London: Ernest Benn, 1967. ix-xii.

—. "Shakespeare's Theology." *Review of English Literature* 5 (1964): 72-88.

Meyer, Arnold O. *England and the Catholic Church Under Queen Elizabeth.* Trans. Rev. J. R. McKee. New York: Barnes and Noble, 1967.

Milton, John. *Paradise Lost.* Ed. Merritt Y. Hughes. *John Milton: Complete Poems and Major Prose.* Indianapolis: Bobbs-Merrill, 1957. 211-469.

Milward, Peter. *Shakespeare's Religious Background*. Bloomington: Indiana UP, 1973.

Mitchell, W. J. T. *Iconology: Image, Text, Ideology*. Chicago: U of Chicago P, 1986.

Morgan, Arthur E. *Some Problems of Shakespeare's Henry the Fourth*. 1924. Folcroft, PA: Folcroft Library, 1974.

Morris, Christopher. *Political Thought in England: Tyndale to Hooker*. Oxford: Oxford UP, 1953.

Morris, Harry. *Last Things in Shakespeare*. Tallahassee: U of Florida P, 1985.

Morris, Ivor. *Shakespeare's God*. London: George Allen and Unwin, 1972.

Muir, Kenneth, and Sean O'Laughlin. *The Voyage to Illyria*. Freeport, NY: Books for Libraries, 1937.

Mutschmann, Heinrich, and K. Wentersdorf. *Shakespeare and Catholicism*. New York: Sheed and Ward, 1952.

Neill, Stephen. *Anglicanism*. 4th ed. New York: Oxford UP, 1958.

Noble, Richmond. *Shakespeare's Biblical Knowledge and Use of the Book of Common Prayer, as Exemplified in the Plays of the First Folio*. London: SPCK, 1935.

O'Day, Rosemary. *The Debate on the English Reformation*. London: Methuen, 1986.

Ogburn, Charlton. *The Mysterious William Shakespeare: The Myth and the Reality*. New York: Dodd, 1984.

Oliver, L. M. "Sir John Oldcastle: Legend or Literature?" *Library* 1 (1947): 179-83.

Orgel, Stephen. "Shakespeare and the Kinds of Drama." *Critical Inquiry* 6 (Autumn 1979): 107-23.

Ornstein, Robert. *A Kingdom for a Stage: The Achievement of Shakespeare's History Plays*. Cambridge: Harvard UP, 1972.

Owens, Lewis. "'Richard II.'" *Lectures on Four of Shakespeare's History Plays.* Eds. Lester M. Beattie, John A. Hart, and Raymond E. Parshall. Pittsburgh: Carnegie Institute of Technology P, 1953. 3-18.

Owst, G. R. *Literature and Pulpit in Medieval England.* New York: Barnes and Noble, 1961.

Palmer, Alan. *Kings and Queens of England.* N.p.: Octopus, n.d.

Palmer, Barbara D. "'Ciphers to This Great Accompt': Civic Pageantry in the Second Tetralogy." *Pageantry in the Shakespearean Theatre.* Ed. David M. Bergeron. Athens, GA: U of Georgia P, 1985. 114-29.

Panofsky, Erwin. *Studies in Iconology: Humanistic Themes in the Art of the Renaissance.* Oxford: Oxford UP, 1939.

Parrott, Thomas Marc, and Robert Hamilton Ball. *A Short View of Elizabethan Drama.* New York: Scribner's, 1943.

Parsons, Martin. *The Holy Communion: An Exposition of the Prayer Book Service.* London: Hodder and Stoughton, 1961.

Patrides, C. A. *Premises and Motifs in Renaissance Thought and Literature.* Princeton: Princeton UP, 1982.

Paul, John Steven. "The Horror at the Heart of Farce." *The Cresset* 50 (1986): 23-26.

Pechter, Edward. "The New Historicism and Its Discontents: Politicizing Renaissance Drama." *PMLA* 102 (1987): 292-303.

Pelikan, Jaroslav. *Reformation of Church and Dogma (1300-1700).* Vol. 4 of The Christian Tradition: A History of the Development of Doctrine. Chicago: U of Chicago P, 1984. 5 vols.

Pierce, Robert B. *Shakespeare's History Plays: The Family and the State*. Columbus: The Ohio State UP, 1971.

Pineas, Rainer. *Tudor and Early Stuart Anti-Catholic Drama*. Nieuwkoop: B. de Graaf, 1972.

Pope, Alexander. "Preface to the Works of Shakespeare." *Literary Criticism of Alexander Pope*. Ed. Bertrand A. Goldgar. Lincoln: U of Nebraska P, 1965. 161-75.

Porter, Joseph A. *The Drama of Speech Acts: Shakespeare's Lancastrian Tetralogy*. Berkeley: U of California P, 1979.

Powell, Ken, and Chris Cook. *English Historical Facts, 1485-1603*. Totowa, NJ: Rowman and Littlefield, 1977.

Powys, John Cowper. *Enjoyment of Literature*. New York: Simon and Schuster, 1938.

Prior, Moody Erasmus. *The Drama of Power: Studies in Shakespeare's History Plays*. Evanston: Northwestern UP, 1973.

Purdon, Noel. *The Words of Mercury: Shakespeare and English Mythography of the Renaissance*. Salzburg: Institut für Englische Sprache und Literature, 1974.

Puttenham, George. *The Arte of English Poesie*. Eds. Gladys Daidge Willcock and Alice Walker, Cambridge: Cambridge UP, 1936.

Quinn, Michael. "Providence in Shakespeare's Yorkist Plays." *Shakespeare Quarterly* 10 (1959): 45-52.

Quintillian. *Institutio Oratoria: Quintillian on the Teaching of Speaking and Writing*. Ed. and trans. James J. Murphy. Carbondale: Southern Illinois UP, 1987.

Rackin, Phyllis. "Androgyny, Mimesis, and the Marriage of the Boy Heroine on the English Renaissance Stage." *PMLA* 102 (1987): 29-41.

—. "Shakespeare's Use of Anachronisms." Seventeenth Annual Conference, The Ohio State University Center for Medieval and Renaissance Studies, Columbus, 28 Feb. 1986.

Ralegh, Walter. *The History of the World.* Ed. C. A. Patrides. Philadelphia: Temple UP, 1971.

Ralli, Augustus, ed. Vol. 2 of *A History of Shakespeare Criticism.* London: Oxford UP, 1932. 2 vols.

Ransom, John Crowe. *The New Criticism.* Norfolk, CT: New Directions, 1941.

Ray, Rogert D. "Bede, The Exegete as Historian." *Famulus Christi: Essays in Commemoration of the Thirteenth Centenary of the Birth of the Venerable Bede.* London: Chatto and Windus, 1976. 125-40.

Reed, Robert Rantoul, Jr. "Richard II: From Mask to Prophet." *The Pennsylvania State University Studies* 25. University Park: Pennsylvania State UP, 1968. n. p.

Reese, H. M. *The Cease of Majesty: A Study of Shakespeare's History Plays.* New York: St. Martin's, 1961.

—. "Origins of the History Play." *Shakespeare: The Histories: A Collection of Critical Essays.* Ed. Eugene M. Waith. Englewood Cliffs, NJ: Prentice-Hall, 1965. 42-54.

Ribner, Irving. "Elizabethan Action." *Studies in Philology* 63 (1966): 151-62.

—. *The English History Play in the Age of Shakespeare.* 1957. New York: Octagon, 1979.

—. "The Historical Richard." *Twentieth-Century Interpretations of Richard II: A Collection of Critical Essays.* Ed. Paul M. Cubeta. Englewood Cliffs, NJ: Prentice-Hall, 1971. 13-14.

—, and Clifford Hoffman. *Tudor and Stuart Drama.* 2nd

ed. Arlington Heights, IL: AHM Publishing, 1978.

Richmond, H. M. *Shakespeare's Political Plays*. New York: Random House, 1967.

Riggs, David. *Shakespeare's Heroical Histories: "Henry VI" and Its Literary Tradition*. Cambridge: Harvard UP, 1971.

Rivers, Isabel. *Classical and Christian Ideas in English Renaissance Poetry*. London: George Allen and Unwin, 1979.

Ross, Charles. *Richard III*. Berkeley: U of California P, 1981.

Rossiter, A. P. "Ambivalence: the Dialectic of the Histories." Ed. R. J. Dorius. *Discussions of Shakespeare's Histories*. Boston: D. C. Heath, 1964. 1-15.

—. *"Angel With Horns" and Other Shakespeare Lectures*. Ed. Graham Storey. London: Longmans, Green, 1961. 23-39.

—. *English Drama from Early Times to the Elizabethans*. New York: Barnes and Noble, 1950.

—. *Woodstock: A Moral History*. London: Chatto and Windus, 1946.

Rous, John. *Historia regum Angliae*. Oxford, 1716.

Rowse, A. L. *What Shakespeare Read—and Thought*. New York: Coward, McCann and Geoghegon, 1981.

Saccio, Peter. *Shakespeare's English Kings: History, Chronicle, and Drama*. New York: Oxford UP, 1977.

Sammartino, Peter. *The Man Who Was William Shakespeare*. London: Cornwall, 1990.

Sanders, Norman. "Prince Hal and the Shift of Identity." *Shakespeare Survey* 30 (1977): 29-34.

Sanders, Wilbur. *The Dramatist and the Received Idea:*

Studies in the Plays of Marlowe and Shakespeare. Cambridge: Cambridge UP, 1968.

Santayana, George. *Interpretations of Poetry and Religion.* New York: Scribner's, 1900.

Sauer, Thomas G. *A. W. Schlegel's Shakespearean Criticism in England, 1811-1846.* Bonn: Bouvier Verlag Herbert Grundmann, 1981.

Saussure, Ferdinand de. *Course in General Linguistics.* 1959. Eds. Charles Bally and Robert Reidlinger. Trans. Wade Baskin. New York: Philosophical Library, 1966.

Scarisbrick, J. J. *The Reformation and the English People.* Oxford: Basil Blackwell, 1984.

Schell, Edgar T. "Prince Hal's Second 'Reformation.'" *Shakespeare Quarterly* 21 (1970) 11-16.

Schiller, Gertrud. *Iconography of Christian Art.* Trans. Janet Seligman. Greenwich, CT: New York Graphic Society, 1971-72. 2 vols.

Scholes, Robert. *Structuralism in Literature.* New Haven: Yale UP, 1974.

Schramm, Percy E. *A History of English Coronation.* Trans. Leopold G. Wickham Legg. Oxford: Clarendon, 1937.

Scoufos, Alice-Lyle. *Shakespeare's Typological Satire.* Athens, OH: Ohio UP, 1979.

Selden, Robert. *A Reader's Guide to Contemporary Literary Theory.* Lexington: U of Kentucky P, 1985.

Sen Gupta, S. C. *Shakespeare's Historical Plays.* London: Oxford UP, 1964.

Seward, Desmond. *The Hundred Years War: The English in France. 1337-1453.* New York: Atheneum, 1978.

Seznec, Jean. *The Survival of the Pagan Gods: The Mythological Tradition and Its Place in Renaissance Humanist*

Art. Trans. Barbara F. Sessions. New York: Pantheon, 1953.

Shaheen, Naseeb. *Biblical References in Shakespeare's History Plays*. New York: U of Delaware P, 1989.

Shanker, Sidney. "Shakespeare and the Uses of Ideology." *Studies in English Literature* 105 (1975): 64-75.

Shaw, John. "The Staging of Parody and Parallels in 'I Henry IV.'" *Shakespeare Survey* 20 (1967): 61.

Siegel, Paul N. "Change and Continuity in Shakespearean Criticism." *His Infinite Variety: Major Shakespearean Criticism Since Johnson*. Ed. Paul N. Siegel. Philadelphia: J. B. Lippincott, 1964. 1-5.

—. *Shakespeare in His Times and Ours*. Notre Dame: U of Notre Dame P, 1968.

—. *Shakespearean Tragedy and the Elizabethan Compromise*. New York: New York UP, 1957.

—. *Shakespeare's English and Roman History Plays: A Marxist Approach*. Rutherford: Fairleigh Dickinson UP, 1986.

Siemon, James R. *Shakespearean Iconoclasm*. Berkeley: U of California P, 1985.

Smith, Bruce. "Perspectives on Shakespeare's Pageants-within-the-Play." *Renaissance Papers* (1982): 51-63.

Smith, Hallett. [Introduction to *Cymbeline*]. Ed. G. Blakemore Evans, et al. *The Riverside Shakespeare*. Boston: Houghton Mifflin, 1974. 1517-20.

Sommers, Ronald. English 210 classroom lecture. Valparaiso University, 8 September 1982.

Sprague, Arthur Colby. *Shakespeare's Histories: Plays for the Stage*. London: Robert MacLehose, 1964.

Spurgeon, Caroline F. E. *Shakespeare's Imagery and What It Tells Us*. Cambridge: Cambridge UP, 1935.

Stapfer, Paul. *Shakespeare et les Tragiques Grecs.* Paris, 1888.

States, Bert O. "The Persistence of the Archetype." *Critical Inquiry* 7 (1980): 333-44.

Stauffer, Donald A. *Shakespeare's World of Images.* New York: W. W. Norton, 1949.

Stavisky, Aron. *Shakespeare and the Victorians: Roots of Modern Criticism.* Norman: U of Oklahoma P, 1969.

Steadman, John M. "Iconography and Methodology in Renaissance Dramatic Study: Some Caveats." *Shakespearean Research Opportunities* 7-8 (1972-74): 39-52.

Stevenson, Robert H. *Shakespeare's Religious Frontier.* The Hague: Martinus Nijhoff, 1958.

Stewart, J. I. M. *Character and Motive in Shakespeare.* London: Longmans, Greene and Co., 1949.

Stiring, Brents. *Unity in Shakespearean Tragedy: The Interplay of Theme and Character.* New York: Gordian, 1966.

Stoll, E. E. "'Henry V.'" *Discussions of Shakespeare's Histories.* Ed. R. J. Dorius. Englewood Cliffs, NJ: Prentice-Hall, 1971. 123-34.

Stone, Lawrence. *The Crisis of the Aristocracy: 1558-1641.* Oxford: Clarendon, 1965.

Strong, Roy. *The English Icon: Elizabethan and Jacobean Portraiture.* New Haven: Yale UP, 1969.

Stuart, Otis. "One Tough Dick: Whose Hump Is It Anyway?" *The Village Voice* 7 (August 1990): 97.

Styan, J. L. *The Shakespeare Revolution: Criticism and Performance in the Twentieth Century.* Cambridge: Cambridge UP, 1977.

—. *Shakespeare's Stagecraft.* Cambridge: Cambridge UP, 1967.

Sundelson, David. *Shakespeare's Restoration of the Fathers.* New Brunswick, NJ: Rutgers UP, 1983.

Sykes, Norman. *The English Religious Tradition.* London: SCH, 1953.

Tarleton, Richard. *The Famous Victories of Henry the Fifth.* Ed. Geoffrey Bullough. Vol. 4 of *Narrative and Dramatic Sources of Shakespeare.* London: Routledge and Kegan Paul, 1962. 299-341. 8 vols.

Taylor, John. "Richard II's Views on Kingship." *Literary and Historical Proceedings of the Leeds Philosophical and Literary Society* (January 1971): 189-205.

Thayer, C. G. *Shakespearean Politics: Government and Misgovernment in the Great Histories.* Athens, OH: Ohio UP, 1983.

—. "Shakespeare's Second Tetralogy: An Underground Report." *Ohio University Review* 9 (1967): 5-15.

Thisselton-Dyer, T. F. *Folk-Lore of Shakespeare.* 1883. New York: Dover, 1966.

Thomas, W. H. Griffith. *The Principles of Theology: An Introduction to the Thirty-nine Articles.* Grand Rapids: Baker, 1979.

Thompson, Karl F. "Richard II, Martyr." *Shakespeare Quarterly* 8 (1957): 159-66.

Tillyard, E. M. W. "The Elizabethan World Order." *Shakespeare: The Histories: A Collection of Critical Essays.* Ed. Eugene M. Waith. Englewood Cliffs, NJ: Prentice-Hall, 1965. 32-47.

—. *The Elizabethan World Picture.* New York: Vintage, 1961.

—. *Shakespeare's History Plays.* London: Chatto and Windus, 1344.

Toliver, Harold E. "Falstaff, the Prince, and the History Play." *Shakespeare Quarterly* 16 (1965): 63-80.

—. "Shakespeare's Kingship: Institution and Dramatic Form." *Essays in Shakespearean Criticism*. Eds. Harold E. Toliver and James L. Calderwood. Englewood Cliffs, NJ: Prentice-Hall, 1970. 58-82.

Traversi, Derek. "Henry the Fifth." *Twentieth Century Interpretations of Henry V: A Collection of Critical Essays*. Ed. Ronald Berman. Englewood Cliffs, NJ: Prentice-Hall, 1968. 60-73.

—. "The Historical Pattern from *Richard the Second* to *Henry the Fifth*." *Shakespeare: The Histories: A Collection of Critical Essays*. Ed. Eugene M. Waith. Englewood Cliffs, NJ: Prentice-Hall, 1965. 102-12.

—. *Shakespeare: 'From Richard II' to 'Henry V.'* Stanford: Stanford UP, 1957.

Trinterud, Leonard J. "A. D. 1689: The End of the Clerical World." *Theology in Sixteenth- and Seventeenth-Century England: Papers Read at a Clark Library Seminar, February 6, 1971*. Eds. Winthrop S. Hudson and Leonard J. Trinterud. Los Angeles: U of California P, 1971. 27-50.

Trousdale, Marion. *Shakespeare and the Rhetoricians*. Chapel Hill: U of North Carolina P, 1982.

Tucker, Eugene M. Foreword. *The Historical-Critical Method*. By Edgar Krentz. Ed. Eugene M. Tucker. Philadelphia: Fortress, 1975. v-vi.

van der Spek, Cornelius. *The Church and the Churchman in English Dramatic Literature Before 1642*. Amsterdam: H. J. Paris, 1930.

Varagine, Jacobus de. Vol. 3 of *The Golden Legend*. Trans. William Caxton. Ed. F. S. Ellis. London: J. M. Dent, 1900. 3 vols.

Velie, Alan R. *Shakespeare's Repentance Plays: The Search for an Adequate Form*. Rutherford: Fairleigh Dickinson UP, 1972.

Venezky, Alice S. *Pageantry on the Shakespearean Stage*. New York: Twayne, 1951.

Vergil, Polydore. *Three Books of Polydore Vergil's English History: Comprising the Reigns of Henry VI, Edward IV, and Richard III*. Ed. Sir Henry Ellis. London, 1844.

Villain, Maurice. "Can There Be Apostolic Succession Outside the Chain of Imposition of Hands?" Trans. Theodore Westow. *Apostolic Succession: Rethinking a Barrier to Unity*. Vol. 34 of Concilium: Theology in the Age of Renewal. Gen. Ed. Hans Küng. New York: Paulist P, 1968. 87-104. 40 vols.

Waith, Eugene M. Introduction. *Shakespeare: The Histories: A Collection of Critical Essays*. Ed. Eugene M. Waith. Englewood Cliffs, NJ: Prentice-Hall, 1965. 1-12.

Walter, J. H. "Introduction to Henry V." *Shakespeare: The Histories: A Collection of Critical Essays*. Ed. Eugene M. Waith. Englewood Cliffs, NJ: Prentice-Hall, 1965. 152-67.

Warner, Beverly E. *English History in Shakespeare's Plays*. 1894. Freeport, NY: Books for Libraries P, 1972.

Webb, Timothy. "The Romantic Poet and the Stage: A Short, Sad History." *The Romantic Theatre: An International Symposium*. Ed. Richard Allen Cave. Gerards Cross: Colin Smyth, 1986. 9-46.

Webber, Joan. "The Renewal of the King's Symbolic Role: From Richard II to Henry IV." *Texas Studies in Language and Literature* 4 (1963): 530-38.

Weimann, Robert. *Shakespeare and the Popular Tradition in*

the Theatre: Studies in the Social Dimension of Dramatic Form and Function. Ed. Robert Schwartz. Baltimore: Johns Hopkins UP, 1978.

Wells, Henry W. and H. H. Anniah Gouda. *Style and Structure in Shakespeare*. New Delhi: Vikas, 1979.

Wheeldon, M. J. "'True Stories': The Reception of Historiography in Antiquity." *History as Text: The Writing of Ancient History*. Ed. Averil Cameron. Chapel Hill: The U of North Carolina P, 1989. 33-63.

Whitaker, Virgil K. *The Mirror up to Nature: The Technique of Shakespeare's Tragedies*. San Marino, CA: The Huntington Library, 1965.

—. *Shakespeare's Use of Learning*. San Marino, CA: The Huntington Library, 1953.

Wikander, Matthew H. *The Play of Truth and State: Historical Drama from Shakespeare to Brecht*. Baltimore: Johns Hopkins UP, 1986.

Wilde, Oscar. "The Critic as Artist." *Essays By Oscar Wilde*. Ed. Hesketh Pearson. Freeport, NY: Books for Libraries, 1950. 100-88.

—. "The Decay of Lying." *Essays by Oscar Wilde*. Ed. Hesketh Pearson. Freeport, NY: Books for Libraries, 1950. 33-72.

—. "The Soul of Man Under Socialism." *Oscar Wilde: De Profundis and Other Writings*. New York: Penguin, 1979. 19-53.

—. "To the Editor of the St. James Gazette." Vol. 15 of *The Works of Oscar Wilde*. 1909. New York: AMS, 1980. 219-23. 15 vols.

—. "The Truth of Masks." Vol. 9 of *The Works of Oscar Wilde*. 1909. New York: AMS, 1980. 193-238. 15 vols.

Wilders, John. *The Lost Garden: A View of Shakespeare's English and Roman History Plays.* Totowa, NJ: Rowman and Littlefield, 1978.

Wilson, Edward M. "Shakespeare and Christian Doctrine: Some Qualifications." *Shakespeare Survey* 23 (1970): 79-89.

Wilson, F. P. *Shakespearian and Other Studies.* Ed. Helen

Wilson, Harold S. *On the Design of Shakespearean Tragedy.* Toronto: U of Toronto P, 1957.

Wilson, J. Dover. *The Fortunes of Falstaff.* Cambridge: Cambridge UP, 1944.

—. [Introduction to *Richard II*]. *Richard II.* By William Shakespeare. Cambridge: Cambridge UP, 1966. vii-lxxvi.

—. *Shakespearian Dimensions.* Brighton, Sussex: Harvester, 1984.

Wimsatt, W. K., Jr., ed. *Samuel Johnson on Shakespeare.* New York: Hill and Wang, 1960.

Winney, James. *The Player King: A Theme of Shakespeare's Histories.* London: Chatto and Windus, 1968.

Woodhouse, H. F. "Sixteenth-Century Anglican Theology." *A History of Christian Doctrine.* Eds. Herbert Cunliffe-Jones and Benjamin Drewery. Edinburgh: T&T Clark, 1978. 411-24.

Woolf, D. R. "Erudition and the Idea of History in Renaissance England." *Renaissance Quarterly* 40 (Spring 1987): 11-48.

Wrede, William. *The Messianic Secret.* Trans. J. C. G. Greig. The Library of Theological Translations. Ed. William Barclay. London: James Clarke, 1971.

Wright, Daniel L. "'Lord of His Love': The 'Master Mistress' of Shakespeare's Passion." *James White Review* 6 (Fall 1988): 10.

—. "The Rhetoric of Kingly Grief: Bathos in the Depositions of Edward II and Richard II." Unpublished essay.

Wright, Louis. *Middle-Class Culture in Elizabethan England*.
Ithaca: Cornell UP, 1958.

Wunderli, Richard and Gerald Broce. "The Final Moment
before Death in Early Modern England." *The Sixteenth
Century Journal* 20 (Summer 1989): 259-75.

Yeats, William Butler. "At Stratford-on-Avon." *Essays*. New
York: Macmillan, 1924. 117-35.

Zimbardo, Rose A. "The Formalism of 'Henry V.'" *Shakespeare Econium* (1964): 16-24.